Microcomputer Applications

Using Shareware

Second Edition

Microcomputer Applications

Using Shareware

Fritz H. Grupe
University of Nevada—Reno

Wm. C. Brown Publishers

Book Team

Editor *Kathy Shields*
Production Coordinator *Carla D. Arnold*

Wm. C. Brown Publishers

President *G. Franklin Lewis*
Vice President, Publisher *George Wm. Bergquist*
Vice President, Publisher *Thomas E. Doran*
Vice President, Operations and Production *Beverly Kolz*
National Sales Manager *Virginia S. Moffat*
Advertising Manager *Ann M. Knepper*
Marketing Manager *Craig S. Marty*
Executive Editor *Edward G. Jaffe*
Production Editorial Manager *Colleen A. Yonda*
Production Editorial Manager *Julie A. Kennedy*
Publishing Services Manager *Karen J. Slaght*
Manager of Visuals and Design *Faye M. Schilling*

Cover design by *Mary Sailer*

Library of Congress Catalog Card Number: 89–61283

ISBN 0–697–07738–1

Printed in the United States of America by Wm. C. Brown Publishers, 2460 Kerper Boulevard, Dubuque, IA 52001

10 9 8 7 6 5 4 3 2 1

Contents

Preface

This book has been written to teach its readers how to use word processing, spreadsheet, and database management software effectively. If offers practical "hands-on" instruction in the use of three software packages: PC-WRITE™, As-Easy-As™, and PC-FILE+™. These software packages were selected because they are high quality products that are readily available and economical to acquire. Although inexpensive, this software is fully-functioned and capable of illustrating usages that are possible in much more expensive, commercial software.

Intended to meet several needs, *Microcomputer Applications* can be useful in many settings. It can be used as a supplemental laboratory manual for courses that introduce students to computers and their applications, such as introductions to computing in business, computer literacy, and introduction to microcomputer software courses.

This book can also be used as a stand-alone text for courses that focus on educating students in three main uses of microcomputers. The tutorial orientation of this book also allows it to be used by a learner who wishes to work independently. The instructional approach utilized in this book is almost entirely "hands-on." Exercises are presented with detailed instructions on moving step-by-step from the initiation of a problem's solution to its completion.

One chapter is used to introduce Microsoft's Disk Operating System (MS-DOS). This overview presents students with the basic information they need to do the exercises and to understand how an operating system functions. Five chapters on word processing with PC-WRITE take students through the production of elementary documents, such as memorandums, letters, personal résumés, and term papers—all topics of high student interest. Six chapters on the use of spreadsheets show how As-Easy-As can be used to make projections, analyze budgets, and do project costing. Four chapters acquaint the student with the use of a database manager, PC-FILE+. This software is used to produce several databases, to produce a variety of reports and to print sublists of records meeting particular criteria. A chapter employs PC-WRITE to integrate data from all three programs. Files created by print-to-disk procedures within As-Easy-As and PC-FILE+ are brought into letters that refer to the data they contain. Two closing chapters introduce hard disk usage and communications concepts.

Each chapter concludes with a group of exercises that reinforce the techniques learned in that chapter. To a large degree, the exercises closely parallel the design of the worksheet presented in the chapter. In many cases, exercises are reused in subsequent chapters to enhance the student's product and to enable students to practice new techniques without unnecessary data entry.

Instructors adopting this book will receive a diskette containing all of the files utilized as exercises. A supplemental manual provides some comments about possible problem areas students may encounter, as well as sample questions that might be used to assess student proficiency and understanding.

I would like to thank the people who reviewed the manuscript for the helpful suggestions that contributed so much to its development: Carol Aspulund, College of Lake County; Jacob Gerlach, University of Wisconsin—Whitewater; Mike Wackerly, Delta College; Jim Aulick, Walla Walla College; Norman C. Licht, SUNY College at Potsdam; A. C. "Buddy" Krizan, Murray State University; Bret R. Ellis, Brigham Young University—Hawaii Campus; Thomas Ahlborn, West Chester University; Bruce Elliot, TC Junior College; and Robert G. Goodwin, Husson College.

I am indebted to the students who tested each of the exercises presented in the text and who made many helpful suggestions for changes. I also appreciate the assistance of Victoria Vaughn. As always, my wife Evelyn and my daughters Joelle and Karen deserve thanks for their encouragement, support, and help in this project.

Fritz H. Grupe

Chapter 1

Introduction to Microcomputing

CHAPTER OUTLINE

COMPUTERS IN SOCIETY

The Mirrors of Man

Computers have become the mirrors of mankind. We describe their functions in human terms. They are depicted as "thinking," "expecting," "breaking down," and "solving problems." Humans are portrayed as "crashing," "computing," and "programmed." A sentence like, "The word processor isn't working," is ambiguous as to whether the word processor is a person or a machine. In the cinema we are fascinated by the degree to which we see computers and computerized robots that act as though they were people. In *Star Wars,* R2D2 and 3CPO endear themselves to us in much the same way that a puppy might. They are equal to us in intelligence but lack the emotion we expect from people. In the film *Short Circuit,* Number 5 becomes a robot with emotions: a robot who has become indistinguishable from a human. Computers like these are believable because we see computers at work every day that are maintaining our health, enabling our businesses to operate, creating new music and art, and expanding our scientific horizons. Computers make a positive contribution to society.

In *War Games,* however, the computer is clearly out of control. This computer is symbolic of our ambivalence to computers. The science fiction writer Isaac Assimov once wrote that the first rule for robots was that they should do no harm to mankind. Situations we have heard about and experienced support our distrust of computers. We assume that they are capable of getting out of control and taking on a life of their own. It is of little comfort to say that computers and robots are created and programmed by people; that they are simply doing what they have been instructed to do. If they can issue checks for $1 million when the amount was supposed to have been $1.25, we are not surprised when they call the armed forces to strategic alert when the moon rises, or when the "fail-safe" mechanisms of nuclear power plants seem to compound, rather than simplify, the operation of the plant at times of crisis.

HAL, the advanced computer system in the film *2001,* is not only out of control, but is affected by a seemingly psychological disorder. Its intent is to control its own destiny. Even HAL's malevolent behavior is clearly within the realm of technological feasibility. HAL sets its own objectives and takes on a life that is scarcely distinguishable from our own.

The computers with which we come in contact, the computers we see on the screen, and the computers we read about in magazines and literature give us contradictory messages. We read about people with "computer phobia"—the fear of computers. An estimated 9 million microcomputers are being sold annually, but one study estimated that half of the computers purchased for home usage were unused. How many computers sit idle in business or are greatly under-utilized?

Our society's ambivalence is due in large measure to a lack of understanding about how computers work, about their limitations and about their potential contributions toward the resolution of problems that have beset mankind for centuries. Improving your knowledge of computer systems can make you a more intelligent consumer of computerized goods, a more informed user of computer systems, and a more concerned citizen whose private and public life is ever more affected by computers.

Computer Proficiency

This book has been written to assist its user in becoming proficient in the use of computers. The so-called computer revolution has just begun. The computers of today's cinema will, in fifty years, seem as primitive to us as Gutenberg's printing press does now. The computer revolution will change the workplace, the home, and our recreational pursuits. Sophisticated knowledge of computer applications will be as important to the doctor as to the computer scientist, as valuable to the artist as to the president of a company, as critical to a politician as to a computer manufacturer, and as necessary to a student as to the treasurer of a large corporation.

Computers are and will remain an integral part of your life. They will not only not go away, they will affect you more and more every day. You will have to make decisions about their purchase and about how to use them. You will have to interpret their conclusions. There will always be a great demand for people to operate and program them. Yes, you will probably have to continue to fight with them every now and again. Beyond simply being familiar with computers you must be computer proficient. Computer proficiency requires you to be:

1. Psychologically comfortable with computers. This comfort comes from working with computers at a level where you begin to understand how they work and what they can do.
2. Competent to work effectively with a computer. For some people, computer proficiency will entail computer programming—a skill not taught in this book. For many others, computer proficiency will require technical knowledge of how to use computers effectively in work and other situations. The specific requirements for computer proficiency for any specific vocation will vary, but some knowledge of using

computers advantageously is common to most modern professions and to many semi-professional vocations.

3. Knowledgeable of how computers work. They are not "black boxes" that operate in mysterious ways. They operate within known constraints and limits. Knowledge of what they can do and what they cannot do is essential for the citizen and the worker, for the employer and the employee, for the family member and the consumer.
4. Aware of the impact of the computer on society. Computers can and will change the ways in which we live. For good or ill, computers will have an impact on our lives. You have a role to play in defining what computers should be allowed to do and what they should not be allowed to do. An informed awareness of the social implications computers have for the future is part of computer proficiency.
5. Competent to apply computers to problems that affect you. Perceiving which problems are susceptible to solution with the use of computers, and actually using computers to solve those problems is critical. No person can master all of the potential uses of computers. This does not excuse anyone from mastering some of its capabilities. Skills learned in this book—operating system usage, word processing, spreadsheet development, database management and communications—are the most commonly needed skills. They are not, however, the universe of applications. Be prepared for others.

TYPES OF COMPUTERS

The pervasive influence of computers on our society is partially due to the variety of computers that are produced by uncounted numbers of vendors that sell such systems. Not only do computers come in a spectrum of sizes, but so too do printers, graphics plotters, magnetic storage devices, and other computer-related equipment. Some computers are designed to optimize the handling of specialized problems, while others are general purpose machines. Categorizing computers has become increasingly difficult as the capacities of the computers overlap with one another.

Super computers are the largest computers available. These machines carry purchase costs that are measured in the tens of millions of dollars. They can carry out hundreds of computer instructions every second, serve hundreds of users simultaneously, support a wide range of types of software, generally of a scientific nature, and are very expensive to maintain and operate. They operate in a highly controlled environment in which air conditioning, electrical power stabilization, fire control, and other securities are taken to insure that the computer can function even though external problems arise. Because of their expense, most companies and universities cannot buy their own super computers. Therefore, most super computers are shared by users from around the country who must use software that is "compute intensive," involving many computations before programs are finished.

Main frame computers are large computer systems that cost between 1 and 5 million dollars to purchase. Their computational speeds are rated at from 5 to 20 million computer instructions per second. These systems also operate in a carefully controlled environment. Professionally trained computer support staff are needed to keep the computer running. Most main frame computers are used to support entire companies or large divisions of a company. Some main frames are dedicated to a function like computer-assisted design or transaction processing, but most main frames are general purpose computers that support many aspects of a business.

Mini and super minicomputers, once thought of as a distinct class of machines, now rival mainframes in speed and accuracy. Their cost, though, is considerably lower, often between 100 thousand and 1 million dollars. These machines, as a rule, require less professional support and less environmental control than would a mainframe. Many of these computers function well in an office environment that has air conditioning adequate for people. Super minicomputers may be the primary computer system for a small to medium size company, or for a single department within a company. Many super minicomputers are dedicated to carrying out a small number of related tasks for the organization. They are generally supported by a system administrator and a small support staff of programmers.

Micro and super microcomputers are generally thought of as single-user systems and are operated by persons who have no formal training in computer programming or computer operations. Costing from several hundred to 50 thousand dollars, these systems will fit into an office easily. Most such systems will carry out from 100 thousand to 4 million computer instructions per second. The computers will function well without professional support staff, although users may need assistance from time to time. Super microcomputers acting as multi-user systems are typically capable of supporting up to fifty users.

Microcomputers come in a variety of sizes. Portable and lap top computers are especially light to make them easy to transport. Desktop computers are larger and generally have larger screens. Recreational computers are inexpensive computers that are limited to running games, instructional programs, and some limited capability business software.

The classification of a particular computer into one of these categories is often difficult because the capabilities of machines in each range often overlap. Even single vendors may sell computers that appear to provide competing levels of computing services.

FIVE COMPONENTS OF A MICROCOMPUTER SYSTEM

A microcomputer can be viewed as a system of five interacting components: hardware, software, data, procedures, and users. Figure 1–1 illustrates some examples of these components.

Figure 1–2 illustrates some examples of these components in a typical setting. Although the power of a microcomputer is often attributed to the technical capabilities of its hardware and software, it is more often a function of how well these components work together as a system.

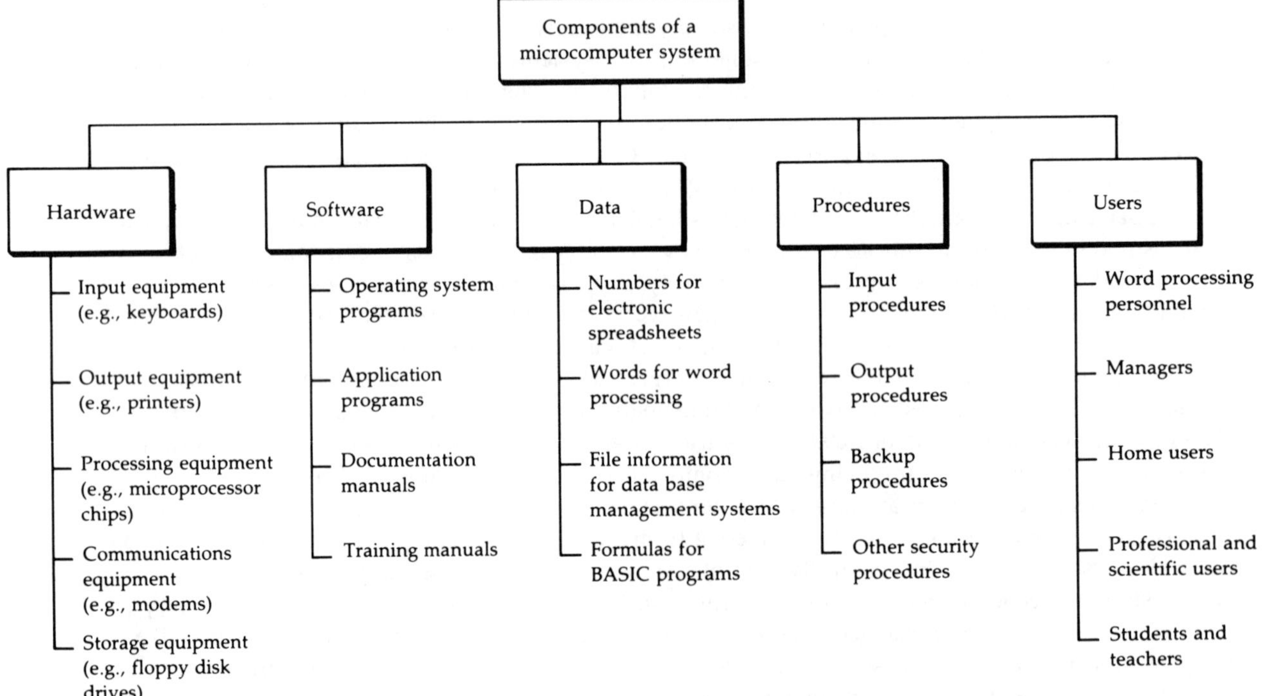

Figure 1–1*

*From M. Simkin and R. Dependahl, Jr. *Microcomputer Principles and Applications.* Copyright 1988 Wm. C. Brown Publishers, Dubuque, Iowa. All Rights Reserved. Reprinted by permission.

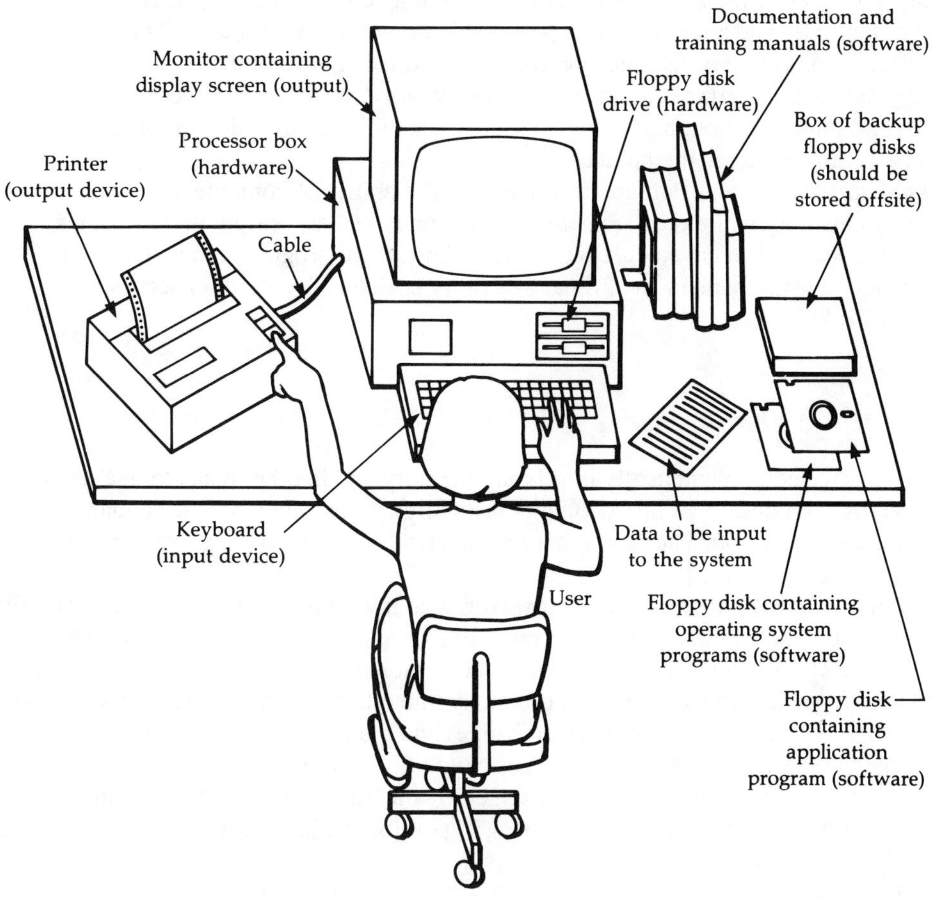

Figure 1–2*

Microcomputer hardware is the physical equipment of the system. The most obvious hardware is the equipment that is visible, such as the floppy disk drive. Some of this equipment, for example, the keyboard, is primarily used to provide data to the microcomputer and is therefore called input equipment. Other equipment, for example, the monitor screen, is primarily designed for preparing outputs from the microcomputer and is therefore called output equipment. Hardware components that are located outside of the processor box are referred to as peripheral equipment.

Software consists of data and programs. Data consists of the information that is to be stored in the computer and operated on by programs. Programs are the instructions stored in the computer that can be executed by the computer to manipulate the data in some way.

The user is the person using the system. Procedures are the methods by which the user and the user's organization collect, input, arrange, output, analyze, save, backup, and utilize the data and software in the computer. Procedures coordinate the usage of data to convert it to useful information.

MICROCOMPUTER HARDWARE

Central Processing Unit

The processing ''heart'' of a microcomputer is its central processing unit, or CPU. The CPU is a microprocessor chip that consists of several integrated components: 1) a control unit; 2) an arithmetic/logic unit; and 3) primary memory. The functions of a microprocessor are:

*From M. Simkin and R. Dependahl, Jr. *Microcomputer Principles and Applications.* Copyright 1988 Wm. C. Brown Publishers, Dubuque, Iowa. All Rights Reserved. Reprinted by permission.

1. To control the processing and movement of data among components of the system, and to control the order and speed at which program instructions are executed. This control is exercised by a portion of the microprocessor called the control unit.
2. To manipulate data in arithmetic operations, for example, addition, subtraction, division, and multiplication; and in logical operations, for example, determining whether a given number is the number 10 or not.
3. To store data and programs that are in active use. The ability of computers to store programs in memory while they are being worked on is the key feature that separates computers from mechanical calculating devices. The stored program concept is implemented in primary memory. Primary memory is also called random access memory, or RAM.

REPRESENTING DATA

Information is stored electromagnetically in primary memory and in other data storage devices in either of two states: zeros and ones. Most microcomputers are digital computers whose fundamental unit storage is the binary digit or bit. The term binary means two, and a binary digit is therefore a digit with only two settings, 0 and 1.

By itself, a bit conveys little meaning. However, a computer is able to represent our familiar letters, numbers, and punctuation symbols by combining individual bits into a binary code. This is a code composed of a specific number of bits, with each combination of bits representing a different character. The most common binary codes in use today, though there are others, are the ASCII (American Standard Code for Information Interchange) and the EBCDIC (Extended Binary Coded Decimal Interchange Code) code, both of which use eight bits to represent characters and symbols. In ASCII, for example, the character "A" is represented by the bit settings, 10000001, and "Z" is represented by 11011010. Eight-bit patterns allow 256 possible combinations and, therefore, the representation of 256 different characters and symbols.

Eight bits, one character or symbol, constitute 1 byte. The memory capacities of computers are generally described by the number of bytes of memory available. Most microcomputers have their memories measured in the number of kilobytes, abbreviated to "K" or "Kb," although newer microcomputers offer RAM sizes measured in megabytes, abbreviated to "M" or "Mb." A kilobyte is 1,024 bytes of data (2^{10}), roughly 1,000, hence the prefix "kilo," while a megabyte is 1,048,576 bytes of data (2^{20}), roughly 1 million, hence the prefix "mega." Common RAM sizes of microcomputers are 256 Kb (Kilobytes), 512 Kb, and 640 Kb. Disk drives are also described by the amount of data that they can store on a single diskette. Commonly, disk drives store 360 Kb, 720 Kb, and 1.2 Mb of data on the diskette.

Bits can be combined into other combinations. These combinations are named based on the number of bits that they contain (see Figure 1–3).

No. Bytes	No. Bits	Name
1	4	nibble
1	8	byte
2	16	half word
4	32	word
8	64	double word

Figure 1–3. Bit Pattern Naming Conventions.

The prefixes "giga" and "tera" are also used to denote billions and trillions of elements. Each of the four prefixes can be combined with bits, as in "kilobits," with bytes, as in "gigabytes," and with words, as in "megawords."

MORE ABOUT MEMORY

Primary Storage: RAM

It has been mentioned that primary memory is also called RAM, random access memory. The computer has the ability to locate necessary data in RAM randomly (by address and not by exhaustive search), and change it. RAM holds the operating system that controls the computer's hardware and supplies the user with commands that can be carried out. RAM is free of programs and data when the computer is first turned on. When the system is turned on, part of the operating system is loaded into memory. When a program like a word processor is started, it is loaded into RAM also. The document that is created with the word processor is also contained in RAM. The size of RAM for your computer may determine what programs can be run, and the size of user-created documents, worksheets, databases, and other files.

RAM stores information only while the computer is turned on. If power is lost the information it contains is lost and cannot be recaptured. For this reason RAM is said to be "volatile."

Secondary Storage

Storage devices like disk drives and tape drives are called secondary storage units. Data that is written into files on diskettes or tape are permanently stored. In order to remove the saved files from secondary storage, the user must either give an explicit command to erase it, or must commit some error, like overwriting the file or damaging the storage medium.

The capacity of floppy disk drives has already been mentioned. Hard disk drive capacities are typically rated at 10 Mb, 20 Mb, and 40 Mb, although they can be considerably larger. Drives larger than 32 Mb operated under MS-DOS must be subdivided into partitions. Each partition will be treated as a separate disk drive even though all of these "logical" drives reside on the same physical disk.

Tape drives are frequently used for backing up data on hard drives. They are rated in the number of Mb per minute that they can transfer, as well as on the number of bytes that they can store on one tape.

Read Only Memory: ROM

Read only memory, or ROM, is found in a ROM chip. This memory stores instructions that the computer uses to begin to operate, and to load the operating system. The instructions are permanently stored in the chip by the manufacturer and cannot be over-written. Nor will they be lost when the system is turned off. For this reason ROM is said to be static.

ROM is also found on some additional cards that may be added to some microcomputers. This ROM may store a complete program like Lotus 1–2–3, a language like BASIC, or a game. If ROM instructions are not available, software of this type has to be provided on a diskette from which the instructions can be read.

ADDITIONAL INFORMATION ABOUT HARDWARE

Microprocessors

The central control unit of a microcomputer is called the microprocessor. Some computers are described in terms of the bit size of the microprocessor's registers—special, very high-speed, storage locations where data is being actively manipulated. 8-bit computers are less accurate than 16-bit computers. 32- and 64-bit computers are still more accurate.

There are many microprocessors that have been installed in microcomputers. They differ in the speed at which they operate and in the number of bits they can operate on for arithmetic operations and for transmission onto the data bus. The characteristics of four of the more popular microprocessor chips that are produced by the Intel Corporation and that are used by manufacturers of MS-DOS compatible microcomputers are summarized in Figure 1–4. The figure also shows which model of IBM computer introduced this chip. The same chips are used by many other companies, some of which have adapted the chip to run at a higher clock speed.

Intel Chip	Processor Clock Speed	Processor Type	Data Bus	Introduced With IBM Model
8088	4.77 Megahertz	16 bit	8 bit	PC
8086	8 Megahertz	16 bit	16 bit	PC XT
80286	12 Megahertz	16 bit	16 bit	PC AT
80386	16 Megahertz	32 bit	32 bit	PS/2 Model 80

Figure 1–4. Selected Microprocessors.

As a rule, the faster the clock speed of a processor, and the greater the number of bits that can be handled, the more powerful is the processor.

The Data Bus

The data bus of a microcomputer is the pathway of circuits that connects the CPU with the major hardware components: the CPU, the disks, primary memory, and the add-in cards that are inserted into expansion slots within the central processor cabinet. A data bus is like a street with 8, 16, or 32 lanes in each direction. The 8 bits that constitute a character are transported along the data busto major components. An 8-bit bus can transport one character's bits simultaneously. A 16-bit bus can transport two characters simultaneously. And a 32-bit bus can transport 4 characters simultaneously.

Expansion Slots

Microcomputers are built with expansion slots into which the add-in cards can be placed. The add-in cards, also informally called boards, extend the microcomputer's functions. Some add-in cards can expand the primary memory into the multi-megabyte range, while others enable the user to connect joy sticks and mouses to the system. Other cards can enable the computer to receive and output sound, connect to real-time data gathering devices like thermometers and geiger counters, and hold a clock with a battery so the computer can keep its own calendar and clock for system usage.

Ports

Externally connected devices like a mouse or a data communications modem communicate with the bus through a port. There are ports through which data is sent or received sequentially, one bit at a time. Such ports are called serial ports and RS-232-C ports. Other ports send and receive data along pathways which carry 8, 16, or 32 bits simultaneously. These ports are called parallel ports since the bits move along in parallel with one another. Printers typically use parallel ports to receive data, while a mouse, a modem, and a joy stick typically use serial ports to send and receive data.

MICROCOMPUTER SOFTWARE

Operating Systems

Operating systems software is the software that controls the hardware components of the computer. It also provides the user with interface commands that permit the creation and manipulation of files that contain programs, documents, worksheets, and databases. Different computer systems use different operating systems. This book focuses on the operating system produced by Microsoft called **MS-DOS,** for Microsoft Disk Operating System. Originally developed for the first IBM personal computers, this operating system has been used by numerous other manufacturers of computers who wished to maintain compatibility of software with the IBM line of computers. Compatibility is a measure of the ability of a computer to run programs and to share files that run on another computer. The large number of MS-DOS compatible machines has greatly enhanced the ability of software developers to create software for computers produced by many manufacturing companies, while facilitating the ability of users within companies to share files.

OS/2 is a relatively new operating system that is designed to run on microcomputers that in the past would have run MS-DOS. It is being produced to allow microcomputers to serve as multi-user systems and to support the concurrent running and displaying of several programs simultaneously. OS/2 is being developed by Microsoft.

The **UNIX** operating system is produced by AT&T and is used on computers of all types: microcomputer through super computer. Originally designed to support multi-user, interactive computer systems, UNIX has only recently become popular on larger micro and super microcomputers. Although there are several versions of UNIX available, users making a transition from one system running UNIX to another system will not encounter major problems in switching environments. Also, companies that use UNIX will find it easier to incrementally add new computers without multiplying the number of operating systems that must be supported by computer staff.

There are many microcomputer manufacturers that produce their own, **proprietary,** operating systems along with their own hardware. Apple computers and Atari, for instance, produce their own operating systems. Due to the central role operating systems play in determining how computers will function, the operating system often constrains the level of compatibility one computer will have with another.

Some microcomputers can support multiple operating systems. These computers allow the user to select from among these systems and to choose which system will control the computer at any point in time.

Programming Languages

People who need to develop programs that are unique to their situations have to prepare their own software to use. These programs are frequently written in programming languages that allow them to have great flexibility and control over how the application program will function and how it will look to the users. There are hundreds of programming languages. The most popular languages are:

1. **COBOL,** an abbreviation for "*Co*mmon *B*usiness *O*riented *L*anguage," a language that is heavily used in business and industry.
2. **FORTRAN,** an abbreviation for "*FOR*mula *TRAN*slator," a language that is designed to support scientific and engineering applications.
3. **BASIC,** a relatively easy to learn language that is especially used in education for instruction and the production of computer-assisted-instruction, and in business for small projects.
4. **Pascal,** a language that is used in instruction.
5. **C,** a language that is increasingly popular for writing operating systems and for instructional purposes.
6. **LISP,** for "*Lis*t *P*rocessing," and **Prolog**, for "*Pro*gramming in *Log*ic," that are being employed in the area of artificial intelligence.

7. **ADA,** a new, multipurpose language introduced to standardize the language for defense and other governmental programming projects.

Essential Applications Development Software

Most users of microcomputers do not write completely original programs using the languages listed above. There was a time when programming was the only avenue by which a company or an individual could produce a usable product. But programming takes a considerable amount of time even when the programmer is well trained. Most novices found it considerably beyond their skill and their interest to produce a satisfactory program that was adequate to a real world task. Fortunately, one does not have to write one's own word processor in order to use one. The same is true for other types of programs. Software can be purchased that addresses, users' needs without users having to become involved in the intricacies of programming, though comprehension of the fundamentals of programming will certainly reinforce one's ability to use some software at the most productive levels possible. The majority of computers purchased for home or for business use are acquired to make use of software that is written in a language like assembler or Pascal, but which functions in such a way as to eliminate any need to have any knowledge of this language.

Word Processing software is used to make the production of documents more efficient. Common tasks carried out by word processors are preparing mailing labels, creating form letters for ''personalized'' communications, supporting the movement of information between documents and between the word processor and some other type of program, and the development of documents with demanding technical requirements such as multiple columns, the formatting of equations, and the use of special type styles. Word processors encourage the use of laser printers, graphic images, and spell checkers that lead to higher quality documents than would be possible if typewriters were the only technology present. This book focuses on the use of WordPerfect, one of the most widely used word processors.

Work Sheet Programs are programs that ease the preparation of financial and other quantitative reports and analyses. Such programs are used to analyze complex business problems, to keep checkbooks balanced, to study the financial desirability of pursuing alternative courses of action, to project future expenses, and to test the impact of options for action. Lotus 1–2–3, the standard work sheet processor for industry, is used in this book to illustrate how this type of software can be applied.

Data base software is used to record, track, modify, and organize information about people, events, activities, and objects that are of interest to the computer user. Inventories of cars on a car lot, personnel files, lists of Supreme Court jurists votes, and parts listings are examples of data bases. Records (a record is all of the information about one entity in the data base) can be edited when information changes, sorted into an order that is appropriate for some function, deleted when the information is no longer needed, or printed in a report format that is of use to decision makers. The most popular database software, dBASE III Plus, is used in this book to illustrate how databases function. Although this text does not cover programming, dBASE III Plus provides a command language that offers the same types of programming statements that are contained in traditional languages like FORTRAN and Pascal.

Communications software is software that can be employed in appropriately configured microcomputers to communicate with larger computers. Communications capabilities are needed to make the transfer of documents between users possible and to use programs and data that are found on the larger computer but not on the microcomputer. Access to electronic mail and electronic bulletin boards is also important. Software called Kermit is used to illustrate how communications software operates.

Increasingly Important Software Packages

Use of the four types of applications development software noted above is the most frequent reason given for the purchase of computers. These four are, in fact, the most commonly purchased types of software. They do not constitute the universe of software available, however. As the microcomputer industry has matured, other types of software are being acquired and are having their own impact. These types of software are not covered in this book.

Graphics software comes in various types. Business presentation graphics, bar charts, and pie charts can be produced by Lotus 1–2–3, and higher caliber graphics can be created with packages intended to serve this purpose. Free form art software allows you to "paint" objects and pictures in much the same way that you would if you were using a paint brush and an easel. Computer-assisted-design (CAD) software enables architects, engineers, and designers to plot out complex pieces of machinery, houses, circuit boards, and computers.

Project Management software is used to plan definable projects more effectively. A project manager displays when the various phases of a project should begin and end, what resources will be needed, and what the costs for the project should be. Project managers help to organize the activities that go into a major project and will help to identify ways by which economies can be realized.

Desktop publishing software improves on word processing software by enabling users to produce documents at levels that are indistinguishable from documents typeset by a professional printer. Going beyond the traditional capabilities of word processors, desktop publishing software enables users to integrate high quality graphics into text, to draw on ornate type styles, to obtain expensive looking output from laser printers, and to format complex documents that use serpentine columns and elaborate tables and charts.

Decision support software strengthens the ability of managers to reach decisions with a multitude of factors to consider. This software goes beyond worksheet programs by supplying complex statistical and financial functions to analyze, forecast, and interpret data.

Expert system shells are software packages that expedite the process of programming a computer to evaluate problems in the same way that a human expert would evaluate the same problem. Expert systems are used for trouble shooting technical problems, diagnosing diseases, prescribing remedies to problems, recommending configurations for computers sufficient to meet a customer's needs, and to evaluate battlefield maneuvers in a specific war-time situation.

Computer-based instructional software can be used to teach students basic concepts, to provide drill and practice experiences, and to augment other educational practices with instructional techniques that reinforce, extend, and strengthen a learner's capacity to deal with new concepts and relationships.

Integrated software packages are programs that combine the capabilities of several, single purpose software packages. For instance, many integrated software packages assemble a word processor, a database manager, a worksheet, business presentation graphics, and a communications package into one program. The advantage of integrated software is that the user can carry out many functions that have a familiar, unified set of commands and operations.

Turn-Key Applications

The production of computer programs to solve problems is an essential activity for many companies and organizations. Writing and then maintaining the programs is often an expensive undertaking, even when the user is employing applications development software and not a programming language. Many companies do not have the staff or budget to do this. To address problems that they have in common with other organizations, they may choose to buy or lease software that is capable of being used immediately. This software is called "turn-key" or "ready-to-go" software since it can be used with minimal company involvement. They simply supply the data that is to be processed.

Turn-key applications are readily purchased for microcomputers to deal with problems such as billing, mailing list production, accounts payable and accounts receivable, and customer records maintenance. Some of these applications are specifically developed for a particular industry or profession, while others are more generic and can be used by companies with very different objectives.

BUYING A MICROCOMPUTER

Taking a course on computing? Read a book about computers? Know anyone who has a computer? You are already on the road to becoming a recognized computer consultant. Before you know it people will be asking you what kind of a computer they should buy. There is no doubt that as your knowledge of how to use a computer grows, you will want to acquire your own computer. What will you recommend or choose? What do you need to think about before buying a computer?

Determine Which Software Will Be Used

This chapter has listed four basic and seven increasingly popular categories of microcomputer software. Before buying a computer, the purchaser must make as accurate an assessment of the software that will be used as possible. To utilize many packages you will have to have specific types of hardware to use, or to make full use of, the software. Without adequate consideration, a user may find that a newly purchased computer cannot satisfy the objectives for which the computer was acquired.

For instance, if you plan to use computer assisted design software you will need a computer with high processor speed, a color monitor, and probably a math co-processor that increases the speed by which certain types of calculations can be completed. If you plan to generate large spreadsheets your computer might need more memory than is typically found on microcomputers. The use of desktop publishing implies the need for a high-resolution graphics monitor, a hard disk drive, and a mouse for cursor movements. Even this superficial list of examples illustrates how the software you use should determine how a microcomputer should be configured before it is purchased. Don't let the hardware determine which software you can run. The more specific you can be in identifying software you want to use, the more clearly you can define what computer you want and what add-ons will be needed.

How will you know what software you will want to use? What software fits your courses and the business or industry you work or intend to work in? Do you know, or do you have friends who know, which software products are the leaders for their types of applications? Do you have access to free software libraries that can augment your commercial software purchases to give your computer more functionality? In many cases you will need to go beyond, "I think that I'll be doing word processing and programming." Figure out which products you will purchase. Check with knowledgeable people to find out what kind of hardware is required by the software, and which additional hardware purchases will optimize your use of the system.

Identify Which Operating System Will Be Used

Just as hardware can constrain which programs you can run, so too will the operating system limit which software will be available to you. There are significant differences between Apple and MS-DOS computers. UNIX systems are notably different from both of these. Not only do the commands change from system to system, but the software available to each type of system is quite different. Generally, you can find the same types of products in each environment, but the brand names and their capabilities will be quite different. Very few products manage to run in more than one operating environment. Try out computers by different manufacturers to get a feel for how they work. Ask users of the computers you are interested in how they feel about their system after they have grown accustomed to it. Find out whether you need to buy a computer that can run the same software you use at school or at work. These factors will help you screen out the computers you can't use as much as others.

Determine The Hardware Needed

Although there are many opportunities for making an incorrect purchase, most beginning users of computers who have made an effort to define their software needs will not make decisions that cannot be corrected easily if they find that they under-bought their hardware. The primary decisions you will have to make about hardware are the following:

1. **How much RAM is needed?** Many manufacturers do not provide the maximum amount of RAM that your software may need to run or to build adequate sized files. Read the manuals of the software you plan to run and see what size RAM, and other hardware, is required. Main memory has become sufficiently inexpensive to make it

desirable to acquire as much as you can afford so that you need not worry about whether you have enough.

2. **Which processor is needed?** How much speed and power do you need? The various models increase in cost in direct relation to the processor they use. If you plan to use statistical, computer-assisted design, or expert systems software that are computer-intensive packages, you will need a faster processor than you would use for word processing or spreadsheet development.
3. **Do I need a hard disk?** Many persons can save money and be quite satisfied using floppy disk systems. A hard disk adds several hundred dollars to a computer purchase and is more expensive to repair and replace if it fails. To some extent a hard disk requires you to know more about organizing your files. It also permits you to run some programs that are delivered on multiple diskettes. It reads and writes files faster than a floppy diskette and it enables you to switch between programs rapidly and conveniently. There are some programs, programs like desk managers, that can be loaded from the hard disk automatically when the system is booted.
4. **Do I need a color monitor?** Again, several hundred dollars can be saved by using a monochrome monitor. Will you be dissatisfied when you are unable to use color for games, computer art and drawing, or even for enhancing the appearance of your word processor? For many programs color is not essential, but it can improve the appearance of the screen none-the-less.
5. **Do I need a co-processor?** Programs which must carry out numerous floating point calculations, programs like statistical and computer assisted design programs, will be speeded up by the addition of a co-processor chip. Co-processor chips augment and speed up the basic microprocessor, but may not have any effect on some types of computer operations.
6. **Do I need expanded memory?** Persons who expect to build large spreadsheets or expert systems, or who expect to run multiple programs simultaneously will need more primary memory than is normally provided. Additional memory can be added with an add-in board.
7. **What level of graphics support is required?** Most microcomputers provide a low level of graphics. Will the programs you expect to run require very clear graphics output? Enhanced graphics may require the addition of an add-in board and the acquisition of a monitor that is consistent with the level of graphics provided.
8. **What peripherals are needed?** You will have to think about what quality printer you will need. Do you want a plotter? A mouse? Any of hundreds of other peripherals? These needs may not become evident until you have worked with a computer for some time.

Part I

Microcomputer Hardware and Software

Chapter 2

Meet Your Microcomputer System

CHAPTER OUTLINE

System Hardware Components
    The System Unit
    The Monitor
    The Keyboard
    Other Peripherals
Floppy Diskettes
    The Structure of a Floppy Diskette
    Nine Rules for Handling and Storing Diskettes
Software Versus Hardware
Using the Disk Operating System (MS-DOS)
    Booting the Microcomputer
    Files, Filenames, and Filename Extensions
    Prompts and Default Drives
    Basic DOS Commands
    Common Error Messages
Backing Up Files
Copyright Versus Copy Protection

The microcomputer you use to complete the exercises in this book is small in size, but large in power. It is capable of many operations that were unheard of a decade ago. You will find that its primary limitation is what you, the user, don't know about the system and its software. The more you know, the more the microcomputer can do. The less you know, the more difficult it will be to make it produce what you want to create.

In this chapter you will obtain a general understanding of microcomputer hardware. You will learn

1. What the primary components of the system are;
2. How the keyboard is designed and how the keys are used;
3. What floppy disks are and how they should be handled;
4. How to name files that store programs and data;
5. What DOS is;
6. Which disk operating systems are present to help you manage files and disks;
7. How to deal with some common DOS problems.

SYSTEM HARDWARE COMPONENTS

There are many types of microcomputers. This book will use an IBM Personal Computer (PC) with two disk drives to illustrate the primary components of a microcomputer system. Other brands and models of

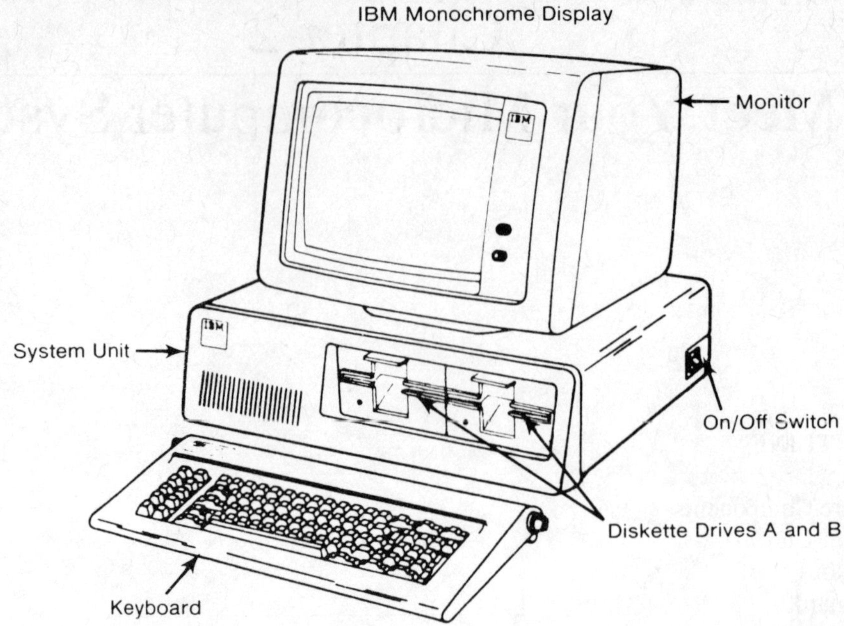

Figure 2–1. IBM Personal Computer—A Standard Microcomputer System.

computers exhibit differences in appearance and operation. An illustration of the type of computer discussed is shown in Figure 2–1.

The primary hardware components of a microcomputer are the system unit, the monitor, the keyboard, and any peripherals (disk drives, printers, plotters, etc.) that are attached to the processing unit.

The System Unit

The **system unit** is the heart of the microcomputer system. This box contains the **processor,** a computer chip that controls the major operations of the computer. The processor chip controls the input of data from the keyboard, output of data to the monitor, manipulation of mathematical data, and the reading and writing of data to disk. The processor is physically located on a board that is known either as the processor board or as the mother board.

Inside the system unit are located **random access memory** (RAM) chips, the computer's "main" memory. The amount of RAM determines the maximum size of programs and files that the microcomputer can accept. Common RAM sizes of microcomputers are 128 Kb (kilobytes, or 1,024 characters), 256 Kb, and 640 Kb.

An **on/off switch,** generally located to the right rear of the system unit, must be switched on to operate the microcomputer. This switch may or may not also turn on the monitor. If the monitor does not come on automatically, look for an on/off switch on the front of the monitor with which to turn on the monitor.

The Monitor

The monitor will display what the user is typing, what the system is prompting the user to enter next, or what the output of a computer program is. Monitors, also called video displays or cathode-ray tubes (CRTs), may display characters, or, if a computer has a graphics board, graphic presentations. The display may be in color or in monochrome (one color against a black background).

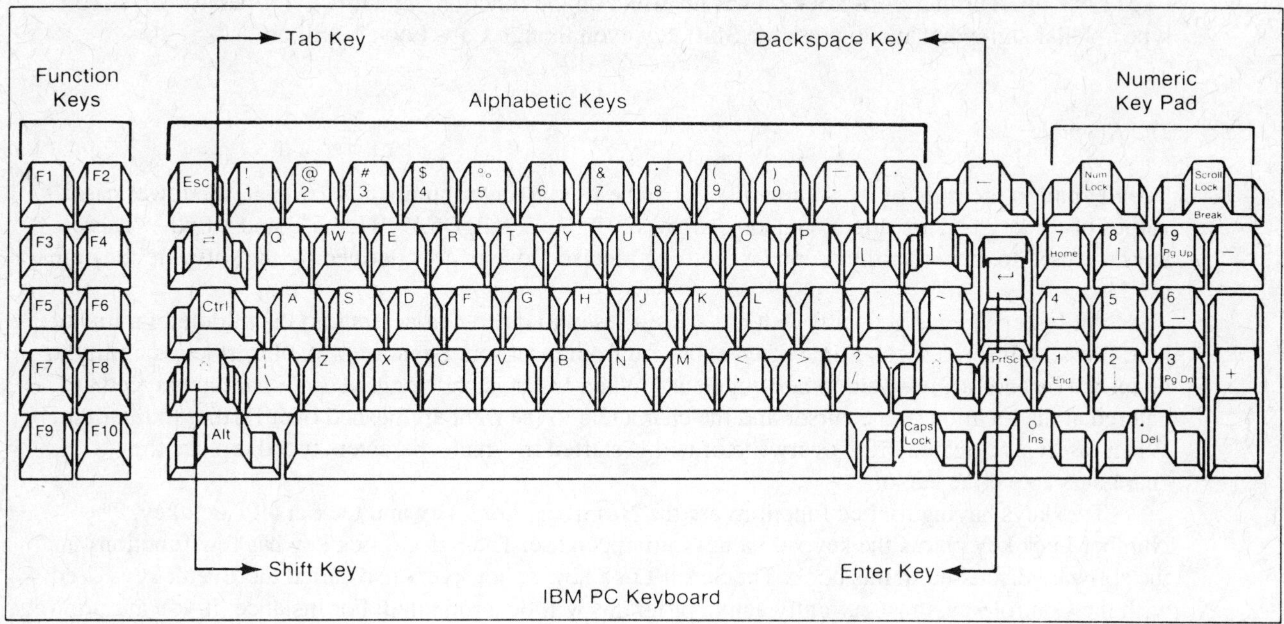

Figure 2–2. A Typical Microcomputer Keyboard.

The Keyboard

The detachable keyboard is similar to, but not identical with, a typewriter keyboard. A typical keyboard is displayed in Figure 2–2. The **standard keys** are found in the center of the keyboard. Several additional keys and groups of keys are also present.

To the left of the standard keys are the **function keys,** labeled F1 through F10. Function keys are typically assigned to carry out complex operations. The exact nature of each function key varies from one software program to another.

There are five keys located in a vertical line between the function keys and the standard keys. The **Escape** key, marked "Esc," normally is used to escape from commands and menus that have not yet been completed, allowing the user to avoid taking actions that would be undesirable.

The **Tab** key, which on IBM computers is marked only with left and right arrows pointing to vertical lines, will move the cursor in steps larger than one character at a time. The cursor is a flashing underscore character that shows where the user is to enter data or commands. The movement caused by the Tab key depends on the program in which the tab is issued. Pressing the Tab key moves the cursor to the right. Simultaneously pressing the Shift (uppercase) key and the Tab key will move the cursor to the left. Movements of five spaces are common, but this can be changed by the user.

The **Shift** keys are simply marked with a broad, upward pointing arrow (they may have "Shift" printed on them). The Shift keys put alphabetic, operator (e.g. comma, period, etc.), and numerical character keys into their uppercase value. The Shift keys may, in some programs, give alternative meanings to function keys also.

The **Ctrl** (Control) key and the **Alt**(ternate) key are used in conjunction with other keys. As with the Shift keys, these keys are held down and another key is pressed simultaneously. Pressing these keys alone has no effect. Pressing these keys along with another standard or function key gives the second key a new or alternate meaning. The alternate meaning assigned depends almost entirely on the software in use.

The **Backspace** key, marked only with a left-pointing arrow and located to the right of the equal sign key, is used to erase characters to the left of the cursor. The **Del**(ete) key erases characters immediately above the cursor.

The **Return** key, also called the **Enter** key, is used like a carriage return on a typewriter. The Return key is marked with a broken left-pointing arrow.

Caps Lock is pressed to place the **alphabetic** characters into uppercase. The Caps Lock key is said to be "toggled" on and off. Pressing it once turns the Caps Lock on. Pressing it again turns the

Caps Lock off. Turning Caps Lock on has no effect on the function, numerical, or operator keys. To type a dollar sign you have to press the Shift key even though Caps Lock is still on.

The Keypad

The **keypad** to the right of the standard keys can be used to enter numbers. However, the lower case values of the key pad are directional keys:arrows, "PgUp," "PgDn," "Home," and "End." These keys are used to move rapidly around a file. The precise movement is defined by the software they are used in.

An **Ins**(ert) key is generally, but not always, used to insert characters into the middle of a line of text. Pressing Insert a second time often exits you from insertion. Because of the Insert key's ability to be turned on and off, it is said to be "toggled." When Insert is on "toggled on" characters typed are entered at the location of the cursor and the characters to the right are pushed over further to the right. When insert is "toggled off," overwrite of text is started in which characters typed replace the characters above the cursor.

Two keys having limited functions are the **Num**(ber) **Lock** key and the **Scroll Lock** key. The Number Lock key places the keypad values into uppercase. The Scroll Lock key has few functions in the software discussed in this book. The Scroll Lock key is, however, also called the **Break** key. Used with the Control key, most currently active programs will be terminated. For instance, if you are printing a file and discover an error, you can often stop printing by simultaneously pressing the Control and Break keys.

The key marked with an asterisk and "PrtSc" is the **Print Screen** key. The asterisk is used in programming as the symbol for multiplication. This is identical with the uppercase "8" character. Shift and PrtSc will print the image of the monitor screen.

On the far right are the **grey plus** and **grey minus** signs. Usually these keys are used to enter the mathematical operators. In WordPerfect they are used to move the cursor.

Other Peripherals

The term "**peripheral**" refers to devices that are outside of the processing portion of the system unit. The monitor is one peripheral. The disk drives are peripherals even though they are inside of the cabinet containing the microprocessor. Other peripherals include external hard disks, printers and plotters, mouse devices, and sound generation devices.

Disk Drives

Two **disk drives,** drive A on the left, drive B on the right, accept floppy diskettes. Some computers have the drive doors placed in a vertical position with drive A continuing to be placed to the left of drive B. Other computers may stack the drives on top of one another. In this case, drive A is usually in the top position. Floppy diskettes that are inserted in the two drives are used as secondary memory. Secondary memory is, by comparison to RAM, relatively stable. If data is saved on a disk, the data will remain there until it is explicitly erased by the user. On the other hand, the contents of RAM memory will be lost if the machine is turned off and the data were not stored on disk. Diskettes are placed in the disk drives with the labels at the front of the disk drive, facing up.

Some computers use fully self-contained "hard" drives that store much more data than does a floppy drive. The hard drives are normally referred to as drive C.

Printers and Plotters

To use the software discussed in this book, the only peripherals required are the disk drives, the monitor, and a printer. A **dot matrix printer** is a printer that produces its letters with a column of wires in the print head. The wires produce blocks of dots and spaces that can be identified as letters. Although dot matrix printers are usually quite fast and can create reasonably good type, they are often considered to be draft quality printers.

Letter quality printers create a letter from the impact of a printer ball or daisy wheel which has completely formed letters on them. Letter quality printers are generally slower than dot matrix printers, but they create sharper letters.

Plotters are devices that draw images, including the images of characters on paper.

FLOPPY DISKETTES

Computer users, even computer users whose machines have hard disk drives, must use floppy diskettes. Software is delivered on "floppies" and backup copies of files are usually stored on this medium. Although diskettes have a lengthy life when they are treated well, they can be rendered useless by an act of carelessness.

The Structure of a Floppy Diskette

Floppy diskettes get their name from their flexibility. Diskettes are generally sold in protective boxes and removable **sleeves** or **envelopes**. Both of these forms of protection should be used as much as possible.

Most microcomputers use floppy diskettes that are 5 1/4 inches in diameter. A diskette is shown in

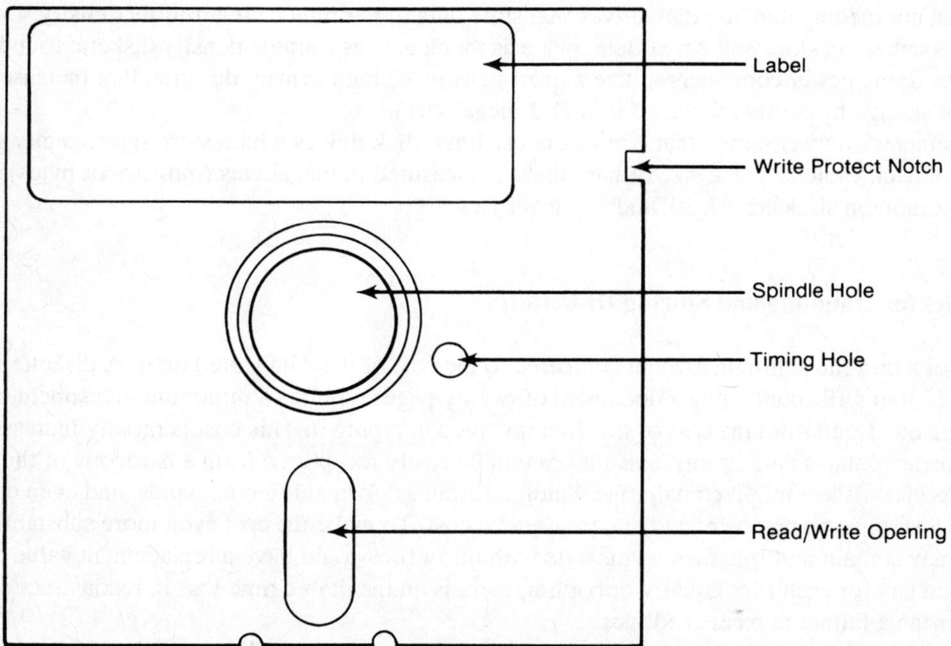

Figure 2–3. A Standard 5 1/4 Floppy Diskette.

Figure 2–3.

The circular diskette is covered by another protective device, the surrounding nonremovable **jacket.** The envelope has a **manufacturer's label** and space on the same side for a **user's label** which can be used to identify the files that are stored on the diskette. When handling the diskette place your fingers on the label edge of the diskette and carefully avoid contact with the shiny recording surface of the diskette.

A write-protect notch in one side of the envelope is used by the microcomputer to determine whether the user wishes to allow files on that diskette to be modified. When diskettes are purchased, the manufacturer provides adhesive tabs that will cover the write-protect notch. If a tab is present, the machine will detect this and prevent the user from adding a file or from changing a file on the diskette. If no tab is present the machine will write to the diskette as the user instructs it to do so. The tab can be removed and replaced as is necessary.

Oval openings on opposite sides of the diskette are used by the computer for reading and writing operations. Access to the recording surface is made through these **read/write openings.** A device in the computer called a read/write head electronically places data on the diskette by moving back and forth over the diskette.

Timing holes on opposite sides of the envelope allow light to pass through whenever a hole in the diskette passes between them. The microcomputer uses the timing hole to determine the starting location for addresses of files stored on the diskette.

The broad circular opening in the center of the diskette is the **spindle hole.** When the diskette is placed in the drive and the drive door is closed, the spindle of the disk drive is placed in the hole and is tightened. The spindle rotates the diskette under the read/write head of the disk drive.

The diskette that is largely hidden from view is circular in appearance. When a diskette is formatted (prepared to receive data), the diskette is written to by the computer in a pattern that allows the computer to identify, read from, and write to specific sets of sectors and tracks. It has a top and bottom **recording surface,** hence it is said to be double-sided. Each surface has forty concentric **tracks** on which data can be written. Each diskette is divided into nine pie-wedge-shaped **sectors.** Directories stored on diskettes provide information about where the contents of files are found on the diskette. The user of the computer is generally unaware of the precise locations of the files.

Most microcomputers use disk drives that store data in a format called **double density.** Double density diskettes can store 360 Kb of data, twice as much data as a single density diskette found in older computers. Some newer computers utilize a quad-density, or high density diskette, that increases the amount of storage by another factor of four (1.2 megabytes).

It is increasingly common that computers use **hard disk drives** which store significantly greater amounts of data. Generally, the size of hard disks is measured in megabytes (millions of bytes) storage capacity. Common sizes are 10, 20, and 30 megabytes.

Nine Rules for Handling and Storing Diskettes

The cost of a diskette is minimal when compared to the cost of the data stored on it. A diskette's value is less than $3, but a file containing a document of twenty pages requires a minimum investment of around $100 when one figures out the cost of the time involved in typing it. This cost is rapidly increased when the document contains data or formulas that cannot be easily recaptured from a hardcopy of the file. For instance, a spreadsheet might contain one hundred formulas, formatting commands, and even data that, if it were lost, must be reconstructed at considerable cost. To make the cost even more substantial, each diskette may contain multiple files. A diskette with thirty files could have a replacement value of several hundred dollars for each file. Equally important, there is an inevitable time loss in reconstructing a file that can mean a failure to meet deadlines.

The point is clear and unarguable: Be careful in your use and handling of diskettes. Follow these rules:

1. *Only touch the envelope or jacket of the diskette—never the recording surfaces.* Dirt and oil on your fingers will destroy the recording surface. Severe dirt on the diskette can damage the read/write head of the disk drive.
2. *Don't subject the diskette to other contaminating factors.* Soda, food, tabletop dirt, dust, and a host of other contaminants may scratch, mar, or coat the recording surface, making the diskette useless.
3. *Avoid bringing the diskette in contact or even in close proximity with any magnetically charged objects.* Many electronic devices produce as much magnetism as magnetized objects. Some copy holders which are placed next to computers to hold pages of text being entered use magnets. The information stored on diskettes is stored in a magnetic

pattern that is easily destroyed by an external magnetic field, rendering the contents of the diskette undecipherable.

4. *Write on the diskette label with a felt tip pen, not with a ballpoint pen or pencil.* The label for filenames, if it is not already on the diskette, is placed on the same side and edge of the diskette as the manufacturer's label. The recording surface of the diskette is sensitive to pressure. Hard-pointed writing implements can produce such pressure. Used lightly, a felt tip pen can be used to retitle the label without harming the data. If you can, write on the label before it is attached to the diskette's envelope.
5. *Store diskettes vertically in hard boxes.* A hard box will protect the diskettes from pressure when being transported. Storage in a vertical position will keep them from warping.
6. *Store diskettes in the jacket.* Don't rely on the diskette's envelope to protect the exposed portions of the recording surface. Place the diskette in the removable jacket whenever the diskette is not in use.
7. *Don't bend or crease the diskettes.* Even though the diskettes are somewhat flexible, they are not indestructible. Distortions of the surfaces will destroy the diskette's usefulness.
8. *Don't remove the diskette from the disk drive when the red light is on.* Many programs, and the operating system itself, will display a message on the monitor noting that operations requiring writing to the diskette have been completed before the drive is actually finished. The write is completed when the red light on the front of the disk drive goes out, not before. Premature removal of the diskette will cause the file and the directory of the diskette to be incomplete. This almost always means that the corrupted file cannot be recovered.
9. *Make backup copies of your diskettes.* If you work extensively with microcomputers, you will occasionally lose some of the files that you have created. The discipline of making backup files will save you hours of work in recreating these files if a diskette is lost or damaged.

SOFTWARE VERSUS HARDWARE

The hardware components alone are incapable of carrying out many useful operations. To provide word processing or database capabilities, for example, the hardware needs programs and data. The instructions and data contained in programs that are stored on diskettes are called software.You can see the diskette, but you cannot directly see the programs and data stored on it. Software may be stored in a text form that can easily be read by the computer to produce screens understandable by humans, or it can be stored in a binary form composed of machine-readable zeros and ones, which are less easily translated into a form that can be read by humans.

USING THE DISK OPERATING SYSTEM (MS-DOS)

IBM and IBM-compatible computers, as well as some noncompatible microcomputers, use the Microsoft Disk Operating System (MS-DOS[1]). An operating system is an important type of software that carries out a variety of tasks. Among these are:

1. Providing the structure with which to create, store, and retrieve files you have constructed;
2. Providing the means by which diskettes are formatted;
3. Providing communications among the several hardware components. For example, letters typed at the keyboard must be associated with specific commands, entered into files being modified, etc. Directories of files must be kept up to date on the diskettes being used so the integrity of data and programs is protected;
4. Providing the coordination between different processing tasks—printing, keyboard entry, program processing—so that coherence among these activities is preserved.

---

[1]MS-DOS is a registered trademark of Microsoft Inc.

These and many other functions are carried out by the software known as the Disk Operating System (DOS).

Booting the Microcomputer

Beyond simply turning on the microcomputer, parts of the Disk Operating System must be loaded into RAM. In a two-disk drive system, this is accomplished by putting the DOS diskette into drive A.

Hold the disk with the label up and slide the diskette into the drive with the recording oval entering first. Close the disk drive door and turn the machine on. After the computer completes its procedures for checking its circuits and memory, it seeks to load DOS from drive A. Part of DOS is loaded and this part helps to load more of DOS. This process of loading more and more of the operating system until the system is up and running is called ''booting.'' The term ''booting'' is an abbreviated form of ''pulling oneself up by one's bootstraps.''

The final stage of the booting procedure is the appearance of DOS prompts for the date and time. The prompts and examples of the responses that you might type appear in Figure 2–4.

```
A>date
Current date is Tue 1-01-80
Enter new date: 6-15-89

A>time
Current time is 0:00:15:87
Enter new time: 10:30
```

Figure 2–4. Time and Date Prompts.

It is not required that you type in either the date or time, but it is generally a good idea to enter this information. If you hit the Enter key without entering the date and time, DOS will use the date and time originally displayed. DOS uses this information to date the last change that was made to a file.

Booting the system by turning the system on is called a ''cold boot.'' ''Cold'' is used because the system is booted from a completely powered-down state.

At times, when a program ''freezes'' or when you simply want to return to DOS from a program that permits ''ungraceful'' exits, you will want to reboot the system without turning off the computer, or powering down. Total powering down causes the system to go through all of its internal rechecking before the date and time prompts appear. This is unnecessarily time-consuming. By simultaneously holding down the **Ctrl, Alt,** and **Del** keys, the system will return to the initial date and time prompts quickly. This is called a ''warm boot.''

Files, Filenames, and Filename Extensions

As you create programs, documents, data bases, and worksheets with a computer you need to store these groups of data on hard disks or on diskettes. When a letter is created, for instance, with WordPerfect, it is initially created in the RAM, or ''main,'' memory of the computer. You must save the letter on the diskette. When the letter is written to the diskette, DOS reserves portions of the diskette specifically for that document in a space called a file. The directory that DOS maintains on the diskette is a listing of the names of files that are currently accessible and information about those files. Some of this information is visible to you, but some of it is not. The starting location of the file on the diskette is not available to you. Neither is a listing of the tracks and sectors where the file is found. Usually, the absence of this data is unimportant.

Rules for Filenames

Just as you need to have a correctly spelled word to look up a word in the dictionary, you must use correctly formed filenames to have DOS save, manipulate, and retrieve files on the diskette. Filenames are normally assigned by the user of the computer, not by the computer. Sometimes filenames are modified or created by a particular software package. When you are asked by the computer to name a file you are saving, these are the rules you must follow:

1. The filename can have no more than eight characters;
2. An extension to the filename (discussed below) can have no more than three characters. An extension is used by typing the filename, a period, and the extension characters (e.g., MYFILE.DOC);
3. The characters in a filename are limited to:
    a. The upper and lower case alphabetic characters,
    b. The numbers **0** through **9,**
    c. The special characters: **/ ! @ # $ % & ( ) - _ [ ] ' ‘.**

   Although you can use these characters, you should avoid doing so since they make filenames unreadable;
4. Periods (except to separate the filename from the extension), commas, and spaces are among the characters which cannot be part of a filename.

   Here are five examples of valid filenames you could assign to a file:

D	Single letter filenames are alright.
MEMORAND	Extensions are not required.
MYFILE	
86LEDGER	Numbers can be in a filename.
XY56JTZ	
FEB13.LTR	Extensions can be added.
ACCOUNTS.D86	Numbers can be used in an extension.

   Here are five examples of invalid or incorrectly constructed filenames:

	At least one valid character must be in a filename.
CHAPTER12	Not illegal, but the 2 will be dropped by DOS since only eight characters are permitted. This means that a file named CHAPTER1, if it exists, will be replaced by the CHAPTER12 since DOS can only use CHAPTER1 and drops the 2.
.BAS	An extension must also have a preceding filename.
SALE ACCT.FIN	Spaces are not allowed in the filename.
1,385BUD.FIN	Commas are not allowed in the filename.
PROJ.BUD.BAS	Period is allowed only for the extension.

By looking at filenames and their extensions you can frequently tell what their contents are and which programs use them. You can tell this if the filenames which have been assigned to files are meaningful and if you know which programs assign particular extensions. You will come to recognize that the filename CHAP1 is a user-created file, while files having extensions of .COM or .EXE are DOS files, and files with extensions of .DBF and .PRG belong to dBASE III Plus.

Prompts and Default Drives

After you have typed in the date and time, DOS responds by placing

A>

on a new line. This is called the DOS prompt. A prompt from DOS or from a software package requires you to type a valid command or to enter information of the type the program expects to receive. In this instance the prompt tells you that you are expected to type a valid DOS command and that the computer is using disk drive A as its **default drive.** A default value is a value that the computer will use if you do not explicitly tell it to use some other comparable value. In this instance, if you ask it to print a file, DOS will look to drive A for the file first and usually no further. WordPerfect, to cite another default value, will give you automatic margins at columns 10 and 74, but you can change these if that is desirable. If you wish, you can change the default drive by typing[2]

```
b:
```

which changes the default drive to B. The letter designating the drive (or any DOS command) can be typed in either upper or lower case. After execution of this change you will receive the prompt

```
B>
```

meaning that the default drive is now drive B and commands will be interpreted based on the contents of that drive and not on those of drive A.

Basic DOS Commands

To use DOS effectively you must learn some of its commands. There are many options that can be used with these commands that will not be described here, but that are described in the DOS manual. The following commands are fundamental to using your microcomputer to achieve productive results. Failure to use these commands appropriately can lead to confusion at minimum and to a loss of your files at the extreme.

The use of upper or lower case in the typing of commands and filenames is of no consequence to DOS. DOS automatically translates lower case characters to upper case.

The DIR Command

Entering the command

```
dir
```

produces a directory listing of the default drive, a columnar listing of filenames, and other information about the files on a disk. Sample output for the **dir** command is shown in Figure 2–5.

```
DOCUMENT TXT     10440    10-20-86  12:00p
PAPER            10070     1-01-80  12:26a
MEMORAND BAK     87876    10-29-86   3:44a
APPENDIX         10115    11-05-86   1:13a

         4 FILE(S) 242688 bytes free
```

Figure 2–5. Response to the DOS Command.

---

[2]Each command shown must be followed by the pressing of the Enter key or the computer will not begin to execute the command.

This listing shows the filename, the extension (no period, only a space is displayed), the number of characters in the file, the date the file was created, and the time the file was created. If the DOS diskette is in drive A and the ''A>'' prompt is showing, you would see a listing of files that compose the operating system.

Since a diskette can have many more files stored on it than can appear on one screen, the **dir** command has two useful options. Typing and entering

```
dir/w
```

will produce a **wide** listing that only shows the filenames and their extensions. The extensions are shown in separate columns. The period separating the filename from the extension does not appear. The command

```
dir/p
```

will produce the complete information provided by **dir** but the listing will **pause** with every screen of data to allow you to find files you are looking for.

If you wish to display the directory for drive B even though the default drive is drive A, you must have a diskette in drive B and then you must type

```
dir  b:
```

Any drive reference can be typed after the dir command.

*The **FORMAT** Command*

Before you can use a diskette for saving files, the diskette must be formatted; that is, made ready to receive the files. If you wish to format a disk, and assuming that the DOS disk is in drive A, place your DOS diskette in drive A, an unformatted diskette in drive B, and type the command

```
format  b:
```

You will then receive a prompt

```
Insert new diskette in drive B:
Strike any key when ready
```

If you have not already done so, place the diskette to be formatted in drive B and press Return. If the diskette was already in the drive, just press Return and the formatting of the diskette begins. A diskette need only be formatted once in order to store many files on it. You must be very careful in issuing the format command since it *destroys all data that was already on the disk.* DOS allows you to format a diskette that has already been formatted and used. No warning is given that data may be lost. When in doubt, use the **dir** command to make sure that there are no files on the diskette that are still useful to you.

When the formatting is completed, you will receive a message

```
Format another? (Y/N)_
```

to which you can respond ''y'' if you wish to format additional diskettes, or ''n'' if you do not.

Make sure that you always have several formatted diskettes before you begin to create files. The format command is an external command that must be retrieved from the DOS disk. DOS should be in drive A. If you do not have a formatted diskette at hand many programs will force you to exit the program to format a diskette. This means that the files you are working on will be lost since they cannot be saved. Some programs will allow you to format diskettes from within the program, but it is foolish to rely on this option.

The COPY Command

The copy command is used to make a duplicate or a backup of a file. The backup copy is needed in case the original file, or the diskette it is found on, is erased, lost, or damaged. One common method of making backup files is to use the **copy** command. The command

```
copy  memo3.txt  b:
```

copies the file named MEMO3.TXT on drive A (if your prompt is "A>"), the default drive, to the diskette in drive B. Notice that the file is assumed by DOS to be on drive A because A is the default drive, and that the copy of the file being placed on drive B will have the same name on drive B as it did on drive A. If you wish to change the name you could type

```
copy  memo3.txt  b:memo3.bak
```

which keeps the old filename, but changes the extension. The original file on drive A is still there. In either command, the file being copied will replace any existing files with the same name without giving a warning. The command

```
copy  a:memo3.txt  b:
```

will copy the file on drive A to drive B even if the default drive is drive B.

In these and in other examples in this section, the inclusion of the extension to the filename is required. If you had three files with the names MEMO3, MEMO3.TXT and MEMO3.BAK on the same diskette, the extension would distinguish among them. If your diskette only had the file MEMO3.TXT on it, DOS would not assume that the command

```
copy  memo3  b:
```

referred to that file since the extension was missing.

The ERASE Command

You can selectively remove files from your diskette with the erase command. Again, for this command to be properly executed, complete identification of the file is required. The command

```
erase  memo3.txt
```

will remove the file MEMO3.TXT from the diskette on drive A. If a file with the same filename existed on drive B, the file on drive B would not be removed. DOS removed the file on drive A because the prompt showed drive A to be the default drive. If you wished to remove the file on drive B you would type either

```
b:
erase  memo3.txt
```

or

```
erase  b:memo3.txt
```

The TYPE and PRINT Commands

The **type** command allows you to view the contents of some files and to print those files at the printer. The command

```
type   b:memo3.txt
```

will list the file MEMO3.TXT on your screen, if it exists and if the file only contains normal text characters. Neither the type, nor the print command, will list files that contain embedded characters or that consist of non-printable characters. They will not print WordPerfect, Lotus, or dBASE III files, for instance. To print the file on the printer, make sure the printer is turned on and paper is available, and that the "A>" prompt is displaying. Then type

```
print   b:memo3.txt
```

Like the format command, both of these commands, type and print, are external commands that only function correctly if DOS can retrieve the commands from the DOS diskette. Thus, the DOS diskette must be in drive A when the command is issued.

The MORE Command

A command like type can rapidly help you to see what the contents of a file are. However, if you wish to view the contents of a lengthy file more closely, the rate at which the file scrolls off the screen is so fast that this is impossible. The more command modifies the output of type and other commands so that you see only one screen full of information at a time. To use the more command the diskette must not be write protected (an adhesive tab should not be covering the write protect notch). To see the contents of the hypothetical file MEMO3.TXT one screen at a time, you would type (don't since you don't have such a file)

```
type   b:memo3.txt    |   more
```

The more command is an external file found on the DOS diskette. It can only be accessed if the DOS diskette is in drive A.

The RENAME Command

The **rename** command changes the name of a file. Rename does not produce a second copy of the file. This command is often used to alter a filename to make it more useful. For instance

```
rename   23xyz.txt   chap1.txt
```

which will give the file 23XYZ.TXT the new name, CHAP1.TXT.

*The Diskcopy versus Copy *.* Command*

Files can be copied from one diskette to another with the copy command. Periodically, there is a need to copy all files from one diskette to another. One variation of the copy command involves the use of the asterisk wild card character. An asterisk matches any string of characters in a filename. The filename *.TXT will match all files that have the extension .TXT, and the filename XYZ.* will match all the files that have the name XYZ regardless of the extension. To copy files from one diskette to another type

```
copy   *.*   b:
```

which copies all files from drive A to drive B. This procedure will replace any files on drive B which have the same name as those on drive A with the version on drive A. Files on drive B that are not duplicated by name on drive A will be left alone.

The diskcopy command causes DOS to create the diskette on the destination drive an exact copy of the diskette on the source drive. To execute the diskcopy command, the DOS disk must be in the default drive. The command

```
diskcopy  a:  b:
```

will cause DOS to prompt you to place the disk you wish to duplicate, the source disk, in drive A (therefore, the DOS diskette must be removed) and then place a diskette in drive B to receive the contents of the disk in drive A. DOS will format the diskette in drive B destroying its previous contents and will duplicate the contents of the A drive diskette on the B drive diskette. You can leave the DOS disk in drive A and DOS will duplicate itself on the diskette in drive B.

Common Error Messages

*The **BAD COMMAND OR FILE NAME** Error Message*

In executing the commands cited, you may receive the error message, **"Bad command or file name."** There are several possible causes for this message to appear. One reason is that you may have misspelled a command. The command

```
dri
```

will not be recognized as the directory command. A second possible cause for this error message is the misspelling of the filename. The command

```
type  emmo13.txt
```

illustrates the misspelling of MEMO3.TXT. A third possibility is that the extension is omitted. The command

```
type  memo3
```

will not send the file MEMO3.TXT to the screen. Another possibility is that the file does not exist on the default drive. Perhaps the command should be altered to address a different drive. The command

```
type  memo3.txt
```

may fail because MEMO3.TXT is on drive B. The correct command is

```
type  b:memo3.txt
```

If you receive the bad command or filename error message you can determine what files are actually on the disk with the dir command.

*The **ABORT, RETRY, IGNORE** Error Message*

A second common error message is **"Abort, Retry, Ignore."** This error message generally appears because a disk drive is not ready for reading or writing because the printer is not ready for printing or because a diskette has been damaged or is unformatted. When you receive this message check to see that

1. There is a diskette in the drive involved;
2. The diskette is properly inserted in the drive;
3. The drive door is closed properly;

4. The diskette is not write protected;
5. The diskette is not damaged or unformatted;
6. The printer is plugged in and turned on;
7. The printer has the Select (or on-line) button turned on;
8. The printer has paper in it and that the paper is not jammed;
9. The printer's cables are tightly connected.

Once the error condition is corrected, press ''r'' for retry and printing will proceed. If you cannot correct the condition, press ''a'' for abort. Aborting an operation may exit you from a program and return you to DOS. Only press ''a'' if you cannot correct the condition causing the error. Do not press ''i'' for ignore since this may cause the machine to attempt operations that will cause a loss of data.

BACKING UP FILES

One point cannot be stressed often enough: Back up your files! Backup files can be created in several ways:

1. Use the diskcopy or copy command to duplicate files from an original to a backup disk;
2. From within a program such as WordPerfect which has a file saving procedure, first save your file on the original files diskette. Then use the WordPerfect command to save the file again on another diskette, the backup diskette;
3. Save or copy the file a second time to the same diskette, but save it under a different filename. This procedure protects against inadvertent erasure of one of the files. It does not protect against diskette damage, formatting errors, or diskette loss.

Valuable files should be stored on diskettes that are in physically separated locations. Originals and backups may both be lost if the diskettes are in the same box.

COPYRIGHT VERSUS COPY PROTECTION

Many commercially available software packages are copyrighted programs. They have been protected by federal law as the intellectual properties of the companies that possess software copyrights. Generally, it is illegal to make unauthorized copies of this software. Up to $50,000 in fines can be levied against persons who violate the copyrights applied to these software packages for each violation. The copyright protection extended to these packages is the same as it is for textbooks, sheet music, and other printed materials.

Some programs are copy protected. These programs require either that you have the ''key,'' or system disk in drive A in order to load the program properly, or the software must be installed on drive C. When copy protected software is installed on a hard drive, the key disk cannot be used on another computer, nor can copies of the key disks be made and have the software load and run properly. The programs are restricted to one user at a time. Modification of these diskettes to behave differently is, again, a violation of copyright law.

Unlike many commercial packages of equivalent quality, PC-Write, As-Easy-As, and PC-File+ are not copy protected but they are copyrighted. The diskettes are capable of being copied and installed on multiple machines and of being shared with other persons. This is encouraged by the corporations that produced the software, though they ask that users who find the software valuable contribute money toward further development of the package. These companies did not copy protect their software so that purchasers of the software would be able to try out the software before spending money on it, and would be able to make backup copies easily. In no way does the philosophical decision not to copy protect the diskettes signify that the copyright laws do not apply to these software packages. Alteration of the program and/or copying of the diskette for use on multiple machines is still illegal.

On the assumption that you will find the software to be beneficial to you, instructions on registering your software are appended at the end of the book. Registration of the software makes available to you telephone support services, printed manuals and updates on the latest version of the software.

EXERCISES

A. Write out the DOS commands you would use to:
   1. Change the name of a file BOOK.001 to CHAPT.01.
   2. Delete all of the files on disk drive A with the prompt displaying "B."
   3. Copy a file named FIRST.DOC on drive B to drive A, giving it the name FIRST.BAK.
   4. Display only the names of the files on a disk without displaying any other information about the files.
   5. Display the files on a disk that end with the extension .BAK.
   6. See the contents of a file named GOODSTUF.
   7. Send the contents of the file named GOODSTUF to the printer.
   8. See the names of all of the files on an unlabeled disk.

B. Indicate whether the following filenames are acceptable or unacceptable to DOS as they are shown.
   1. @E
   2. WRONG.!#-
   3. RIGHTRIGHT.RIG
   4. 1,200.SYS
   5. ().
   6. A3.PART.NME
   7. .PAS
   8. 123.456
   9. goodone.txt
   10. *.*
   11. -----.---

C. With the MS-DOS diskette in drive A and a blank diskette in drive B, execute the following commands. Use the **dir** command to confirm that the commands you issue are executed correctly.
   1. Format the disk in drive B.
   2. Format the disk in drive B as a bootable diskette. Try booting the system with this diskette. What file names are on this disk?
   3. Copy all files on drive A that begin with the letter C to drive B.
   4. Change the default from drive A to drive B.
   5. Delete the file COMMAND.COM from the disk in drive B.
   6. Copy all files in drive A with the extension .COM to drive B.
   7. Remove all files on drive B that begin with C and end with .COM.
   8. Remove all files from drive B.
   9. Carry out a diskcopy reproducing the DOS disk on the disk in drive B.

D. If you have access to the shareware diskette *Computer Tutorial* (PC-SIG disk 403) from Computer Knowledge, place it in drive A and enter "tutor" to start the program. Work your way through the following modules:
   1. Description of the IBM-PC computer keyboard and special keys.
   2. A short history of computers.

Part II

Word Processing with PC-Write

Chapter 3

An Easy Entry into Word Processing with PC-Write

CHAPTER OUTLINE

- Introduction to PC-Write
    - Terminology
    - PC-Write Operations
- Creating a PC-Write Working Diskette
    - Diskette Preparation
    - The Workdisk Command
    - Using Multiple Printers
- A Business Memorandum
- Loading PC-Write
    - The Text Entry Screen
    - The Status Line
    - The Reminder Lines
- Exiting PC-Write
- Entering Text
- Moving the Cursor
    - Arrow Keys
    - Home and End Keys
    - Shift and Arrow Keys
    - Control and PgUp/PgDn Keys
    - Tab
- Editing
    - Deleting Characters
    - Deleting Words
    - Undoing a Deletion
    - Push
    - Reformatting
    - Over(type)
    - Character Transposition
    - Removing Blank Lines
    - Breaking Lines
- Using Help Screens
- More on the System/Help Menu
- Printing Your File
- Backing Up Your File and Exiting the Editor
- Invoking the Editor Without Naming a File
- Exercises

PC-Write is a word processor that can be used to create documents as simple as a one-page letter or as complex as a textbook. It is easy to begin using PC-Write and, as your requirements grow more complex, you will find that PC-Write has capabilities to meet all but the most complicated formatting requirements. In this chapter, you will create a brief business memorandum with few special formatting requirements. By doing so, you will have the opportunity to

1. Understand how word processors function,
2. Create a PC-Write working disk,
3. Enter text into a document,
4. Examine the command structure of PC-Write,
5. Move the cursor in small and large steps,
6. Edit and correct text with operations such as *insert* and *delete,*
7. View the help screens available,
8. Print, save, and back up your file.

INTRODUCTION TO PC-Write

Once you have used it, word processing is something you'll never want to do without. How many times have you had to make do with a poorly typed document because you didn't have the energy to retype it? Or, have you wanted to redo a term paper because you found typographical errors, strikeovers, misspellings, or missing sentences, yet there wasn't time for another draft? Have you had to retype an entire page of a term paper to leave room for footnotes? Or have you wished that you had the luxury of moving some of the paragraphs and sentences to different places in your paper to give it better flow?

These and a hundred other "wishes" are answered with a word processor like PC-Write. Word processors enable you to create documents that are stored as files on diskettes. Once created, these documents can be recalled, edited, and printed any number of times. To make changes and to review your revised documents without having to retype them is one of the most useful capabilities of your microcomputer.

PC-Write is powerful. It is among the fastest word processors available, and it provides features that are only found in much more expensive packages. Among the features that you will appreciate having are:

1. Extensive **help screens** that are quickly called up to help you if you forget how to complete a procedure.
2. **WYSIWYG.** (*W*hat *y*ou *s*ee *i*s *w*hat *y*ou *g*et.) The screen in front of you will print almost exactly as you see it. Only small changes will be made from the screen appearance in some circumstances. These changes will be apparent before printing.
3. Extensive **cursor and screen movement capabilities** that allow you to move around documents you create with speed and accuracy.
4. **Function key commands** that are efficient to use.
5. **Editor commands** that allow you to alter and revise text material with ease. These include moving and duplicating blocks of text, reformatting files and recalling blocks of text that are deleted in error.
6. **Page formatting commands** that help you to design the appearance of printed output with control over the placement of such features as footnotes, page numbers, headers, and footers.
7. Other **special features** include global search and replace, the combining of files, the use of alternate font styles such as italics and boldface, and the merging of files.
8. Control over **rulers and ruler files** to enable you to shape text in correct, aesthetically pleasing patterns.

Not all of the diverse features of PC-Write can be covered in this workbook. By working through the exercises and by reading the explanations of how PC-Write functions, you will become proficient in its use. If you wish to go on to more advanced features, you will have no difficulty in doing so. The on-disk Quick Guide will explain PC-Write's advanced capabilities.

Terminology

Word processing is different from typing in the nicest ways. Although most new words and concepts will be introduced to you as they are needed, perhaps a few terms introduced now will be helpful in obtaining a feeling for what word processing software can do that typewriters cannot.

Word wrap allows you to type the words of a paragraph without hitting the Enter key. On a typewriter, you would have to press the carriage return at the end of every line. In word processing, you continue typing, and the software determines how many words will fit on a line. When the number of words exceeds the line length, the next word is automatically "wrapped around" to the next line. If you are a good typist, you can continue keying without looking at the screen to see where the margins are.

PC-Write places a **soft return** at the end of a line when it is using word wrap. A soft return will permit easy reformatting to adjust words when different margins are desired. Pressing the Enter key, however, enters a **hard return** that cannot be reformatted by the word processor.

The **cursor** is the flashing underline that appears in the work area on your screen. The cursor identifies where text will be placed if you start typing or where commands for actions such as deleting or inserting will take effect.

Keys **automatically repeat** when held down for more than a fraction of a second. PC-Write is sufficiently fast that you will rarely experience "type ahead," in which the remembered keystrokes exceed the typical limit of nineteen used by MS-DOS.

If you exceed nineteen remembered strokes, as when you hold down an Arrow key too long, PC-Write will **beep** at you. The beep makes no changes to your file. It is a gentle reminder that you are attempting to type something that PC-Write cannot execute whether this is a twentieth keystroke or an inappropriate command.

If you reformat a paragraph or an entire document to new margins, PC-Write will automatically **fill** the lines with the greatest number of words that it can. If the margins are widened, the number of words is increased. The number is decreased if the margins are narrowed. You do not need to pattern the words on the line to fit properly.

Keys are not restricted to typing only one character or carrying out one function. **Alternate meanings** can be assigned to alphabetic and function keys. These alternate meanings are brought out when the keys are pressed at the same time as either the Ctrl, Alt, or Shift keys.

When text **justification** is turned on, PC-Write will automatically insert blank spaces, represented by dark circles on the screen, in front of words to place the last printable character next to the right margin. When justification is turned off, you have a "ragged" margin because no blanks are inserted in the line before printing.

PC-Write does not do **automatic hyphenation** of words by breaking them into syllables. You may wish to hyphenate a word manually to structure the appearance of a sentence.

PC-Write Operations

There are five kinds of operations that you can conduct with PC-Write.

1. **File movements** allow you to load, save, or read files on the disk.
2. **Data entry** allows you to enter text, visible page control commands, and alternate fonts (type styles) into your document.
3. **Editing** commands change the text on the screen.
4. **Cursor and screen movement** commands change the location of the cursor or alter your view of the text but do not change the text in any way.
5. **Ruler definition** changes affect margins and tab stops.

When you must work on large blocks of text, for instance, when you wish to move a paragraph from one location to another, a process called **marking.** By pressing a function key used for marking, you "mark" the beginning of the block. You move the cursor to a new location and press the same function key. This causes the block to be **marked.** Marked text has a different appearance from the surrounding text: reverse video on monochrome monitors and red background on color monitors. After the text has been marked, the block operation can be undertaken. Block operations include movement of a block from one location to another, copying (duplicating) the block in another location, writing part of a document into its own file, and deletion of a block of text.

CREATING A PC-Write WORKING DISKETTE

When using PC-Write, you must have a working copy of PC-Write as well as formatted diskettes on which to save the files that you create. If you already have a working copy of PC-Write, you can skip this section.Otherwise follow these steps to create your own copy of PC-Write. The PC-Write procedure for making a working disk takes time to carry out successfully so do not start the process unless you have at least 20 minutes to commit to the task.

Start (boot) your microcomputer with the MS-DOS diskette in drive A. Enter the date and time. You should have the prompt ''A>'' on your screen before proceeding. Leave this diskette in until you are told to remove it.

Diskette Preparation

Read this section in its entirety before proceeding. You will need to format 7 diskettes which will be used for: making backup copies of the PC-Write program, utility and reference diskettes (3), making a working copy of PC-Write (2), and storing files (2) to receive enough of the MS-DOS operating system to be able to make the diskette self-booting and to receive the PC-Write files by placing a blank diskette in drive B. You may wish to review the section on formatting in chapter 1. Check first to make sure that there are no files of value on the diskette by typing the command

```
dir b:
```

If the diskette has already been used, examine the file names to see if there are any that will be destroyed by the format command. If there are any files that you wish to save, use another diskette. If you execute the DIR command and receive the message

```
Not ready error reading drive B
Abort, Retry, Ignore?
```

type ''A'' for abort to return to the ''A>'' prompt because the disk has not been formatted. If the diskette has no valuable files, or if it has not yet been formatted, type,

```
format  b:/v
```

This command formats the diskette in drive B and asks you to give the diskette a volume label or name. A volume label is a name that identifies the diskette and is stored internally on the diskette. It appears when filenames are listed with dir command. The format command will prompt you to put a diskette in drive B to be formatted. When prompted to enter a volume label, enter the volume name (label) and press the Enter key. If the disk is already in, press the Enter key, otherwise put the disk in and then press Enter. When the diskette is formatted, the prompt,

```
Format another (Y/N)?_
```

appears. Respond either with ''Y'' if you have another blank diskette that must be formatted or with ''N'' if you do not need to format another diskette. Give a volume name of up to 11 characters to each diskette as shown below. Label each of the diskettes with an adhesive label properly marked with your name and with the external label shown below. You should have the following diskettes:

Volume Label (Internal)	External Label
PCW-Program	PC-Write Program (Backup)
PCW-Utility	PC-Write Utility (Backup)
PCW-Refrnce	PC-Write Reference (Backup)
PCW-<Your initials>-1	PC-Write Program (Working Copy)
PCW-<Your initials>-2	PC-Write Word List (Working Copy)
Files	Files
Backup-Files	Files (Backup)

Figure 3–1. Volume and Disk Labels.

The Workdisk Command

It is desirable to go through the process of creating backup and working copies of PC-Write with someone who is familiar with your computer system and with PC-Write. Remove the MS-DOS diskette from drive A and replace it with the diskette holding PC-Write. To transfer the files you need from the original PC-Write disk in drive A to the working disk for PC-Write in drive B type,

```
workdisk  b:
```

The command WORKDISK is a PC-Write command that will prompt you for a number of pieces of information and will periodically request that you change the diskettes in both drives. The Yes/No (y/n) questions you will be asked should all be responded to in the manner suggested by PC-Write unless you are sure you know why the alternative is preferable. If you enter the responses that PC-Write suggests, you will not need to know much about your system. There are several questions that require something other than a simple "Y" or "N" response or which you should have a ready response.

- You will be asked if you wish to display the registration number. Respond "N." Student copies of PC-Write are not registered copies, therefore you do not have a registration number to display. When you purchase a registered copy of PC-Write, you will want to re-install the system to display the registration number.
- You will be asked if you wish to have your own special message on the front screen. You will probably wish to respond with a "Y" to this question and enter your name, address, and telephone number. Then if you lose your diskettes someone could return them to you.
- You will be asked whether you wish to have one inch margins by default. Respond "Y" otherwise portions of this text will differ from what you see on the screen.
- Do not print either the Tutorial or the Quick Guide if you are working in a group since the printing of these documents is lengthy. You should print these on your own computer at another time.
- You will be asked to identify the printer you are using so that a file PR.DEF will be created. The interaction of PC-Write with the printer connected to your system is guided by the file PR.DEF. If the wrong printer is selected, printing cannot be carried out successfully. Be sure that you identify your printer correctly. You should know precisely which company manufactured your printer and which model printer you have.

If at any point, you wish to restart the process of backing up and creating working disks, enter

Ctrl-C

which will "kill" the program. You will receive the prompt, *"Terminate Batch Process (Y/N)"* Respond "Y." The MS-DOS prompt will appear. Reissue the WORKDISK command to start over.

Using Multiple Printers

If you do not use one printer, but several different printers at different times, type

```
erase  b:pr.def
```

then, if you will use a dot matrix or daisy wheel printer

```
menuprt  b:filename
```

or, if you are using a laser printer,

```
menulaz  b:filename
```

to create a file for one printer. For instance, for an Okidata 93 printer you would type

```
menuprt  b:oki
```

and choose Okidata as choice "T" among the manufacturers and then choose another letter as the specific model printer you are working with. Repeat the MENUPRT command for each printer you plan to use.

The ERASE command erases a default ruler that prevents you from selecting different printers. You replace the word "filename" in the MENUPRT command with the name of your printer, for instance, EPSON or OKI. When you print a document, PC-Write will ask you to choose the printer ruler that you wish to use.

If you find that when you print documents and special features such as underlining and bolding do not appear, the printer has not been identified correctly, or the file PR.DEF has not been deleted. Also, some printers, especially many letter quality printers, cannot boldface text.

This completes the creation of the PC-Write working diskette.

A BUSINESS MEMORANDUM

It may come as a surprise, but many important applications for computer usage do not involve the user in mathematical manipulations. Word processing is, perhaps, the most readily identifiable use for a computer. Increasingly, businesses and organizations of all types are using word processing to improve their communications. Word processing is not solely the domain of secretaries. Many professionals spend considerable amounts of time writing. The first application for which PC-Write will be used is to create a business memorandum. A memorandum is a useful document to start with because it is not difficult to format. The memorandum that you will see in Figure 3–4, for instance, uses block paragraphs (the first line is not indented), and it does not have any underlining, bolding, or special columnar information. Learning to create this memorandum will provide you with enough information about word processing to enable you to create many other documents that do not require special features, documents like letters, class notes, and simple term papers.

LOADING PC-Write

If PC-Write has been properly installed, the following procedure will enable you to get started.

1. Boot your computer with the MS-DOS diskette in drive A. See that your printer and monitor are turned on. Sometimes these are activated at the time the computer is turned on, but often they must be switched on separately. You should have the MS-DOS "A>"prompt.
2. Place the PC-Write Program Working Disk in drive A and the Files diskette in drive B.

Generally, when you are creating a new file you should have mentally selected a filename before you enter PC-Write. When you edit an existing file you should know the full filename of that file. Use a command in the format,

ed diskdrive:filename.ext.

The disk drive and the extension are optional. However, if you omit the disk drive, PC-Write will look for the file on drive A and will save the file on drive A. Since the PC-Write Working Disk is already full, using drive B as the default drive is essential. If you omit the extension, PC-Write may not find the file you want. Create a file called MEMO by typing,

memo

The "b:" forces PC-Write to use drive B as the default drive for reading and writing the file.

You will then see the Copyright/Registration screen with the request to cancel with retype (the filename and/or drive) or to continue with F9. You will see a screen that looks like Figure 3–2. Press Esc to retype, or F9 to create "b:memo"

```
File not found; Esc to retype, or F9 to create "b:memo"
```

```
Fritz H. Grupe, Univ. of Nevada-Reno, Reno NV 89557, 702-784-1110
---------------------------------------------------------------------------
PC-Write (R). Version 3.02. Released on: 12-Dec-88. Registration #9375.
(C) Copyright 1983-1988 by Bob Wallace, Quicksoft. All Rights Reserved.
---------------------------------------------------------------------------
PC-Write is shareware in the U.S. and Canada. Please help us distribute it,
by sharing unmodified copies of the disk set. Please don't copy the manual. PC-Write
is not shareware outside the U.S. and Canada; don't copy it there.
===========================================================================
If you use PC-Write often, please buy a registered copy, or a manual.
===========================================================================

  Buying a registered copy provides you all of these benefits, for only $89:
  Hardbound copy of the 480 page PC-Write User Guide and Quick Guide.
  Current PC-Write diskette set, and your unique registration number.
  PC-Write support service for one year: includes telephone support,
  quarterly newsletter and two coupons for free updates or utilities.
  Discounts on writing and printing add-on products from our catalog.
  A $25 commission when someone registers and gives your reg. number.
  Sincere thanks; your support helps us continue to improve PC-Write!
  When you register, include registration number above to credit its owner.

Quicksoft. 800/888-8088, 206/282-0452. 219 First Ave N.  #224, Seattle WA 98109
Please call to order, or for more information. Prices subject to change.
```

Figure 3–2. The Copyright/Registration Screen. Note the Options at the Top.

F9 Function key F9, to create the document

When the Copyright/Registration screen is showing you can press the Escape key to retype, or rename, the file. Pressing the Escape key a second time allows you to cancel entry into the editor.

The Text Entry Screen

When the PC-Write text entry screen appears (see Figure 3–3), the area for text will take up almost all of the screen. Immediately above the screen appears: 1) the **status line,** the top line; and the reminder lines which consist of; 2) the main menu, the second and third lines; and 3) the default ruler, the fourth line. Inside of the text entry screen, the cursor is blinking on the next line.

```
Esc:Menu Push Wrap+Se- R:F 99%    1/0, 1  Edit "b:xx"
 F1:System/help F3.Copy/mark      F5.Un-mark     F7.Paragraph     F9:Find-text
 F2:Window/ruler F4.Delete/mark  F6.Move/mark  F8.Lower/upper  F10.Replace
L0--+---T1----+-T--2----T----3--T-+----4T---+---T5----+-T--6----T----7--T-+--R
```

Figure 3–3. The PC-Write Text Entry Screen.

The Status Line

The status line, line one, offers visual insight into some aspects of how PC-Write will format the text you are about to enter. The status line changes as you create the document. Most of the meanings of the entries on the line will be explained as it becomes appropriate.

The word "Push" indicates that characters typed in the middle of the line will push other characters over to the right. If you see "PUSH" instead of "Push" on the status line, Caps Lock is on. Press the Caps Lock key once to return to lowercase.

The word "Wrap+" tells you that as you type words on a line, the words will be automatically wrapped to the next line when they exceed the right margin.

The "99%"portion of the status line represents the extent to which the text you are creating has occupied the RAM memory available for your document. If this percentage approaches 0%, the file cannot get any larger. With a small amount of RAM, you will have to create small files.

The "1/0, 1"segment of the line represents the current line number that the cursor is on (the first "1;" the total number of lines currently contained in the file, the "0;" and the page number that the cursor is currently located on, the second "1").

The Reminder Lines

The three lines beneath the status line are reminder lines. These will not appear if, during installation, you indicated that you did not want them to appear. Reminder lines one and two highlight the uses of the function keys in the editor. The default ruler is shown on line three. The default ruler shows an "L" which identifies the left margin is located in column 10. The numbers 1 through 6 denote increments of 10 print column positions. Since these numbers are added to the left margin, the 1 actually represents the 20th column position (the default margin of 10 plus 10 additional print columns). Other, uses of these lines will be discussed below. The reminder lines can be toggled on and off as desired. Press,

`Shift-F1`	The Shift and F1 keys pressed simultaneously, to toggle the reminder lines off, thereby exposing three additional lines in the editor
`Shift-F1`	The Shift and F1 keys pressed simultaneously, to toggle the reminder lines on

EXITING PC-Write

If you have to exit PC-Write before you finish with the exercise, **press F1,** then **press F3** to save that portion of the file you have been able to create. Then **press F1 and F2** to exit. Retrieve your file by loading PC-Write with the command **"ed b:memo"** described above.

ENTERING TEXT

When entering text, the cursor is placed at the start of the document. If you are revising a document that existed already, the cursor would appear at the same location. The first portion of this exercise is to help you become familiar with text entry. A memorandum that you are to type is shown in Figure 3–4. When creating this memorandum, do not press the Enter at the end of most lines. As you type, you will notice how PC-Write wraps the words from one line to the next. You do not have to hit the Enter key after each line. To create a blank line, press the Enter key

1. Twice after the lines that begin with "Date:," "To:," "Fr:" and "Re:"
2. Twice after the last character of the first paragraph.

There are several words deliberately misspelled. These errors should be typed as they appear. They will be corrected later. If you make mistakes of your own, don't worry. If you catch a mistake right away, use the Backspace key to erase the character that is to the left and start typing again. If you miss mistakes, correct them later.

If you chose, as recommended, that PC-Write conduct automatic backups every 5 minutes, you will experience occasional delays as the file is written to the disk.

Type the memorandum now.

```
Date: February 15, 1989

To: Vice President T. L. White

Fr: Mr. F. Y. Black, Director, Marketing & Sales

Re: Departmental Computer Equipment

It has become increasingly clear that our department can save the
company money in a number of areas if it had immediate access to
a microprocessor. I will cite three instances in which we could
have doe a better job and have been more productive. J. Grey
produced a fifty page report for the XYZ Company that had to be
retyped 3 times as it was revised and improved. We needed to
produce three graphic displacys for a presentation to the ABC
Corporation and were told by the Graphics Department that they
could not be made abailable until two weaks after they were
needed. Finally, I had to produce a projection of our
expenditures for the next three year planning period. Without
access to a spreadsheet accounting program, this three hour task
took a full day.
```

```
I believe that the Makreting and Sales Department should be
allowed to acquire a microcomputer with approopriate spreadsheet,
graphics and word processing software. M.Brown in our
department has taken several computer courses and workshops. She
feels that she can provide the training required for our staff.
With your approval and budgetary support, we can help to maintain
corporate profitability.
```

Figure 3–4. Mr. Black's Memo.

MOVING THE CURSOR

Excellent typists make typographical mistakes. Great writers rewrite their work. No matter how careful you are, documents you create will need to be reworked. Before you can begin to edit your document, you must be able to move from one location to another. You cannot use the Backspace key because this key will erase all letters to the left of the cursor, not just move over them. You do not wish to have to retype large portions of your text simply to correct spelling errors.

PC-Write provides a variety of commands to move the cursor to different locations without destroying any of the text that has been created. Following are five groups of cursor movement commands. Practice them as they are described.

Arrow Keys

The Arrow keys on the keypad move the cursor one character at a time in the direction that the arrow is pointing.

Home and End Keys

Pressing the Home key moves the cursor to the left margin. If there is any text on a line, the first visible character in the word is also in the first position. The first printable character need not necessarily be in the first character position, however, since there may be spaces in front of this character. The End key will move you to the last character on a line. This character also may be a blank.

Shift and Arrow Keys

You can move the cursor to the top, bottom, left, and right edges of the screen by pressing the Shift key simultaneously with any of the arrow keys. The cursor moves in the expected direction.

Control and PgUp/PgDn Keys

Pressing the Control key simultaneously with either the PgUp or PgDn key moves the cursor to the beginning of the next paragraph towards the top or bottom of a file. A paragraph is recognized by the hard return at the end of the paragraph, not by the paragraph's contents.

Tab

The Tab key or the Shift and Tab keys struck simultaneously will move the cursor according to tab settings contained in a ruler. The default ruler (line 4) at the top of your screen, the ruler for the version of PC-Write provided with this book, is used if you don't create your own. Tabs are marked with "T." This ruler has tabs set at the ninth character position and at every eight positions thereafter. Unlike some word processors, the PC-Write Tab key does not insert tabs, it only places the cursor at that tab location. The Tab key will move the cursor, marked on the ruler with the symbol o, from tab setting to tab setting. The Shift and Tab keys pressed simultaneously will move the cursor backward from one tab setting to the next tab setting. From the last tab setting on a line, the cursor will move to the next line.

Experiment with these movement keys. A summary of the cursor movement commands discussed so far is shown in Figure 3–5. When you are moving the cursor, try to make moves as quickly as possible. Much time is wasted by moving one character at a time with the arrow keys when another keystroke combination will get you to your destination faster. You will be surprised at how quickly you will memorize the keystrokes as you practice them.

The memorandum is short enough that you can see most of it on one screen. Many documents, of course, are not this short. Many of the cursor movement keys will move you into those portions of the document that are out of view, but which are nonetheless, part of the document.

KEY	ACTION
Up Arrow	Up One Character
Down Arrow	Down One Character
Right Arrow	Right One Character
Left Arrow	Left One Character
Home	First Visible Character, Current Line
End	Last Visible Character, Current Line
Shift-Up Arrow	Top Line Of Screen, Current Column
Shift-Down Arrow	Bottom Line Of Screen, Current Column
Shift-Right Arrow	Right Side Of Screen, Current Line
Shift-Left Arrow	Left Side Of Screen, Current Line
Control-PgUp	Up One Paragraph
Control-PgDn	Down One Paragraph
Tab	Right To Next Tab Setting
Shift-Tab	Left To Next Tab Setting

Figure 3–5. Selected Cursor Movement Commands.

EDITING

The rewriting of a document involves many kinds of changes. The most obvious change is the correction of typographical errors. The changes may be more significant including the movement of large blocks of text from one place to another. Several editing commands will be utilized here and others will be introduced later. Assume that you had printed out the memorandum, that you had corrected it by hand, and that the changes you wished to make are those that appear in Figure 3–6. What commands will help you to make those corrections?

The following instructions will guide you through some of the changes outlined in the edited copy. Others you can make on your own after you have been shown the correct technique.

Deleting Characters

The Delete key deletes the character immediately above the cursor. Place your cursor under the first "o" in the misspelled word, "approopriate." Press

`Del`	Delete key. Notice that the "o" was removed and that the rest of the line was pulled left

The Backspace key deletes the character to the left of the cursor. There is an unneeded "c" in the word "displacys." Place your cursor under the "y" and press

`Backspace`	The Backspace key. The letter "c" is erased and the line to the right is pulled over. This is only true when the status line shows "Push." If "Push" is replaced by "Over," as explained later, the Backspace erases the character to the left and leaves a blank space in its place

Deleting Words

The words "help to" at the end of the second paragraph are superfluous and should be removed. With the cursor underneath the first letter in a word, the simultaneous pressing of the Control and Escape keys will delete the entire word. Move your cursor under the "h" in "help" and press

`Ctrl-Esc`	Control and Escape pressed simultaneously, to delete "help." The space following a word is deleted along with the word
`Ctrl-Esc`	Control and Escape again, to delete "to"

Undoing a Deletion

Sometimes you can delete a word, or even a larger block of text, only to find that it really should not have been deleted. When PC-Write deletes any block of characters, it places a copy of those characters in a portion of RAM called a Hold Area. You can "undo" the deletion. Press

`Ctrl-F4`	Control and F4 pressed simultaneously. The deleted text "help to" is inserted at the location of the cursor. The inserted text is highlighted because PC-Write has marked this word. Notice the word "Marking" on the status line
`F5`	Function key F5, to unmark the text and to restore the text to the document

Practice the deletion process by deleting "help to" again with Control and Escape. Do not restore the two words.

Date: February 15, 1989

To: ~~Vice President~~ T. L. White

Fr: M~~r.~~F. Y. Black, Director, Marketing & Sales

Re: Departmental Computer Equipment

could

It ~~has~~ become increasingly clear that our department can save the

^

company money in a number of areas if it had immediate access to a

computer 3

micro~~processor~~. I will cite ~~three~~ instances in which we could

n could ^

have doe a better job and have been more productive. J. Grey

^ 50 ^

produced a ~~fifty~~ page report for the XYZ Company that had to be

^

retyped 3 times as it was revised and improved. We needed to

3

produce ~~three~~ graphic displacys for a presentation to the ABC

^

Corporation and were told by the Graphics Department that they

v 2 e

could not be made abailable until two we~~a~~ks after they were

^ ^ ^

needed. Finally, I had to produce a projection of our

3

expenditures for the next three year planning period. Without

^ 3

access to a spreadsheet accounting program, this ~~three-~~hour task

^

took a full day.

rk

I believe that the Ma~~kr~~eting and Sales Department should be

allowed to acquire a microcomputer with approopriate spreadsheet,

^

graphics and word processing software. M. Brown in our

department has taken several computer courses and workshops. She

by

feels that she can provide the training required ~~for~~ our staff.

With your approval and budgetary support, we can help to maintain

corporate profitability.

Figure 3–6. Mr. Black's Memo Marked for Changes.

Push

On the status line you will observe the word "Push." PC-Write has two methods of accepting characters typed at the keyboard. "Push" signifies that when you type characters they are inserted in the text. Characters to the right of the characters being inserted will be "pushed" further to the right. Place your cursor under the "e" in the word "doe." To insert "n," press

n The letter "n." It is inserted into the word

Place the cursor under the space between "and" and "have been." Insert a space and the word "could" by typing it. Remember to type in the space to separate the words.

Reformatting

With this insertion, the characters on the line exceed the line length. If enough characters are entered, some of the characters to the right may disappear from view. They are not lost from the file. As the characters disappear from view the last visible character is highlighted on a color screen to warn you of extra characters to the right. A monochrome screen may not show the highlighting well. Regardless of how the last character is displayed, the paragraph must be reformatted. Place the cursor anywhere to the left and/or above the location where reformatting is needed and press

F7 Function key F7, to reformat the paragraph. Reformatting realigns the paragraph from the location of the cursor within the current margins

You may need to reformat paragraphs when text is deleted as well as when text is added. There are three options for the way in which PC-Write reformats lines of text in a paragraph. By default, the status line displays "Wrap+," to show that: 1) words will be wrapped from one line to the next, and 2) paragraphs that are changed will have to be reformatted with the F7 key. Press

Shft-F7 Shift and Function key F7 pressed simultaneously, to change "Wrap+" to "Para+." This option will have PC-Write automatically conduct word wrap and paragraph reformatting. The addition of the latter feature means that you do not have to use the F7 key to reformat paragraphs that are modified. This is desirable if you are using standard paragraphs, however, it can be disruptive when you are working with tables or lists which do not conform to the standard paragraphing structure

Shft-F7 Shift and Function key F7 pressed simultaneously, to change "Para+" to "Wrap-." This option will have PC-Write toggle off both word wrap and paragraph reformatting.

Shft-F7 Shift and Function key F7 pressed simultaneously, returns the status line to "Wrap+."

Replace the spelled out numbers with the Arabic numerals. This requires you to delete the words with Control and Escape.Then, insert the numbers by typing them in.

An entire document may be reformatted by pressing Control-F5 to highlight, or mark, the entire file. The pressing of F7 will then reformat all lines in the document that begin at the left margin and the lines immediately above those that begin at the left margin.

Over(type)

In addition to allowing you to insert text, PC-Write will also allow you to type text that replaces or "overwrites" existing text. The word "microprocessor" is to be replaced by the word "microcomputer." You do not have to delete an entire word, only to have to retype part of it. There are many ways to approach this change. You can delete part of the word letter by letter with the Delete key, or you can delete the entire word by placing the cursor under the first letter and pressing Control and Escape. You could also place the cursor under the "p" and press Control and Escape to delete the "processor" portion of the word. Instead, place your cursor under the "p." Now press

`Scroll Lck`	The Scroll Lock key. Observe that the word "Push" in the status line changes to "Over." "Over" is short for "Overwrite," the mode of typing in which the letters you type replace the letters previously on the line
`computer`	The replacement text which leaves you with the word "microcomputerr"
`Del`	The Delete key, to delete the extra "r"
`Scroll Lck`	Scroll Lock again. The mode of character entry "toggles" between insertion (Push) and replacement (Overwrite) each time Scroll Lock is pressed. The mode in which you leave PC-Write is a matter of choice, although most people prefer push mode

Character Transposition

Typists often reverse two letters in a word. For example the "kr" characters in the word, "Makreting" should be reversed, or transposed. Place your cursor under the "k" and press

`Shft-Esc`	Shift and Escape keys pressed simultaneously. This key stroke combination transposes the characters

On microcomputers with extended keyboards the transposition of characters is made with the Control and Insert keys instead of the Shift and Escape keys.

Removing Blank Lines

If you have extra blank lines in your text, they can be removed in two ways. One way is to place your cursor behind the last letter of the previous line and to press the Delete key, bringing up the following line. You can also put the cursor on the blank line and use the Backspace key, which also joins the two lines.

Breaking Lines

Lines of text can be broken by placing your cursor at the point where a break is to occur and pressing the Enter key.

The editing commands introduced thus far are summarized in Figure 3–7. Finish editing the memorandum with these commands. Remember to reformat the paragraphs by placing your cursor on the first word of each paragraph and pressing F7. Some paragraphs may not need to be reformatted even though changes have been made to it.

KEY	ACTION
`Del(ete)`	Delete Character Above Cursor
`Backspace`	Delete Character To Left Of Cursor
`Control-Esc(ape)`	Delete Word Above Cursor
`Control-F4, F5`	Undelete, Retrieve Hold Area
`Scroll Lock`	Toggle Between Push And Overwrite Mode
`Shift-Esc(ape)`	Transpose Character Above Cursor With Character To Right
`F7`	Reformat Paragraph

Figure 3–7. Selected Editing Commands and Their Action.

USING HELP SCREENS

If you need assistance with some of the commands you may choose to use while creating, editing, and printing documents, eight menus and forty useful help screens are available to remind you of the commands you can access. Call up the System/Help Menu by pressing,

F1 Function key F1, to replace the Status Line with the System/Help menu shown below. *Do not press these keys unless instructed to do so*

```
Esc F1:Help F2.Exit F3.Save F4.Command F5:Name F6:File F7:Print F8:Dir F9:Unsave
Esc:Cancel   Arrows: Select a menu option Shf F1: Switch these lines on/off.
```

Figure 3–8. System/Help Menu.

F1 Function key F1. There is a brief delay, but when pressed again, the key that called up the System/Help screen displays forty titles of help screens that can be made to appear at the lower half of the screen. "Basic editing" is highlighted. Some of the help screens, like this one, show the phrase, "More:PgDn," to indicate that by pressing the PgDn key you can view additional text about the topic highlighted. By moving the highlighted block over the titles by pressing the arrow keys, the lower half of the Help screen changes

```
Esc: Help off, cancel. F1: Help off, to last menu. Arrows: Select Help topic:
Basic editing     Deleting text      Formatting          Page layout        Shortcuts
Auto-numbering    DOS commands       Headers/Footers     Paragraph style    Shorthand
Box operations    Dot lines          Index/contents      Printer setup      Spell checker
Change margins    Enhancing text     Margins/tabs        Printing           Status line
Characters        Entering text      Marking text        Problem solving    Switching files
Columns           File conversion    Measuring           Recording keys     Typewriter mode
Control files     File management    Merging             Repaging           Window
Copy/move text    Find/replace       Misc.operations     Ruler lines        Support service
Cursor moves      Footnotes          Page elements       Shell to DOS       Shareware
B A S I C   E D I T I N G

Using Help Screens
Use the four arrow keys, Home, End, and Tab key to select a topic.
Use the PgUp and PgDn keys to scroll a long help screen, like this one.
Shifted PgUp and PgDn keys scroll a screenful at once.

File Operations

1. Create or load a file      A>ED filename
2. Enter text                 type on keyboard
3. Save the text to disk      Press F1 F3
4. Edit the text              Bksp, Del, Ins
5. Print the file             Press F1 then F7
6. Save the file, exit        Press F1 then F2
```

Figure 3–9. Help Menu.

Esc Cancels help and returns you to the editor

MORE ON THE SYSTEM/HELP MENU

The System/Help Menu obtained with the F1 key provides you with a variety of useful options. These include:

F1 Calls up the Help Menu.

F2 Exits the editor and, after saving your file, returns control to MS-DOS. If the document was revised, the changes will be saved. If you are revising a file that existed before you started PC-Write and, if you pressed the F9 key at the Copyright/Registration Screen, the version of the document that existed before you called up the file will be present on the diskette with an "&" in the beginning of the extension to the filename.

F3 Saves the current version of the document that was in view before you pressed F1 and then will return you to the PC-Write editor. This will allow you to save your file periodically always a good idea to avoid the loss of work due to a power failure or to turning off the machine before a file was properly saved. Even if PC-Write is automatically saving the file, it is still a good idea to save your file whenever the document has reached a new stage of completion.

F4 Saves the current, edited version of the document that was in view before you pressed F1 and then allows you to access MS-DOS commands such as those for changing the default drive and viewing the directory of a drive. In order to execute this command, you will need to place the MS-DOS disk in drive A.

F5 Allows you to change the name of the file you are editing. For instance, suppose you had a letter of application for a position with one company. You wish to retain a copy of the file so you can reuse it when you apply to other companies. For each new application, you want to modify the document and save it in the final form under a new filename. F5 allows you to change the name of the current file. When you save it, it will be saved with the new name and the original file will be preserved. That way you can have copies of all correspondence, but you can avoid having to retype letters that are largely identical.

F6 Saves the document you are currently working with and allows you to switch to a new file. F6, if pressed (but don't), would show the prompt:

```
File to load or create (Esc:cancel F8:dir):"b:memo"
```

The cursor is placed under the "b" expecting you to type in a new filename. If you type in a new name, B:MEMO2 for example, and that file does not exist already, after you press the Enter key, you would see a prompt,

```
File not found; Esc to retype, or F9 to create "b:memo2"
```

If the new filename typed is present on the diskette, it will be retrieved. If the file is not present, a blank screen will be presented to allow you to create it.

F7 Saves the file and then sends the file to the printer.

F8 Enables you to display the filenames in a directory. Pressing F8 will display the prompt,

```
Search name for directory (Esc:cancel):"*.*"
```

The "*.*" will list all of the files in the current directory. You could press Enter or type in such entries as:

a:*.* To list the files on drive A

b:*.doc To list all files on drive B with the extension of DOC

b:memo.* To list all memo files, regardless of their extension

F9 Prevents the writing of a file to disk. This is sometimes necessary when you find that extensive changes have been made to a file and you do not wish to use these changes. It is easier to return to the old file than to edit the current version.

It is important to recognize that the actions taken by the function keys described above are taken only after the F1 key has been pressed first. Function keys change their mode of operation when the F1 key has not been pressed.

PRINTING YOUR FILE

Now that the editing of the memorandum is finished, consider this file complete. Print out the document in draft form so you can edit the hardcopy.In the next chapter you will revise and add text to the memorandum. To print out the file, press

F1 Function key F1
F7 Function key F7, to save the document and to print out the document. You will see the prompt,

```
File to print (Esc:cancel F8:dir): "b:memo"
```

↵ Enter key. If you elected to have several print rulers on the PC-Write diskette, you see the prompt screen,

```
Print control filename (Esc:exit Enter:none): " "
```

to which you enter the filename for the printer you are currently using; for instance, OKI or EPSON.

↵ Enter key.

If you have only the default printer file, you will not see this prompt. The next prompt will be,

```
Esc:Exit F9:Print to a disk F10:Printer is ready
```

Check to see that the printer is turned on, that the on-line (or select) light is on, that the printer is connected to your computer and that there is paper in the printer.

F10 Function key F10. You will see a menu of choices that you can make while the printing is in process. The screen shows:

```
Waiting. Print from "b:memo" to "PRN." Ready to begin.
F1.Help-screen F3.Back-to-Edit F5:Input-end F7:Repeat-pages F9.Page-stop
F2.Exit-to-DOS F4.DOS-command F6:User-input F8:Skip-pages F10.Continuous
Show help screen, giving dot commands and other information
```

```
PC-Write (R). Version 3.02, Print Program. Released on: 12-Dec-88.
These keys are active when printing has been stopped for a command:

F1: Show Help screen with Dot lines and font characters.
F2: Exit to DOS, even if printing started from the edit program.
F3: Go to Edit program, even if printing started from DOS.
F4: Stay resident, but do a DOS command shell until DOS "exit" command.
F5: Force end of current input file (if last input file, end printing).
F6: Enter input text or Guide Lines (like .U, enter lines typed by user).
F7: Repeat a page then stop, or repeat each page to print multiple copies.
F8: Skip pages then stop, or skip pages each time to print every Nth page.
F9: Print one page, then stop for another one of these commands.
F10: Start continuous printing of pages (but stop if Esc key pressed).

© Copyright 1983-1988 by Bob Wallace, Quicksoft. All Rights Reserved.
```

Figure 3–10. Print Control Menu.

F10 Function key F10, if your printer is using continuous paper, or press F9 if your printer uses a single sheet feeder. Pressing F9 will cause the first page of a document to be printed. PC-Write will pause at the end of every page and reproduce the same menu for you to respond to until the document has been printed in its entirety

BACKING UP YOUR FILE AND EXITING THE EDITOR

When the printing has been completed, you will be returned to the last view of your document, and you will be back in the editor. The printing procedure automatically saved your document. Save your file again to your backup diskette by removing the diskette from drive B and replacing it with your backup diskette. Save the file on the backup diskette by pressing F1, followed by the pressing of F3.

Stop working on your document by pressing F1, then F2 to exit to DOS. When you receive the error message,

```
Insert disk with \COMMAND.COM in drive A
and strike any key when ready
```

place the MS-DOS disk in drive A and press any key. The MS-DOS prompt will be the next line placed on your screen. You can confirm that the file was saved by entering,

```
dir b:
```

to see the response such as,

```
Volume in drive B is FILES
Directory of B:\]
MEMO 1343 2-15-87 1:07a
1 File(s) 360448 bytes free
```

You can now go on with other computing activities at this point or you can turn the computer off.

INVOKING THE EDITOR WITHOUT NAMING A FILE

This chapter began the editing process with the naming of file, ''ed b:memo.'' Another option for entering the editor is available. Do not execute this option. It is shown for information only and is not recommended as the preferred method of entering the editor. If you do not name a file and simply enter the command, ''ed,'' PC-Write will present you with a menu screen that looks like that shown in Figure 3–11.

(To get these options later when you are editing, press the F1:System/help key)

```
Welcome to PC-Write, Version 3.02, by Quicksoft!

Please press one of the following function keys:

F1 Help.....Give information about PC-Write operations and features.
F2 Exit.....Return back to DOS, saving the file you were working on.
F6 File.....Enter the name of a file to edit.
F7 Print....Enter the name of a file to print.
F8 Dir......Get a directory of disk files, pick one to edit or print.
```

Figure 3–11 . The File Selection Menu Screen.

in which 5 function keys are identified with actions that you can take at this point. From this screen you can press any of the following keys:

F1 Obtain a help screen that will further explain the options.

F2 Exit from PC-Write if you entered it in error.

F6 Select the name of a file to work with. If the file exists already, it will be retrieved. If the filename is not found on the disk PC-Write will create a new file.

F7 Print a document file that is already in existence. The print portion of PC-Write obtained is the same as the print program you will use later in this chapter, but which is called from within the editor.

F8 List the names of the files on the disk. The listing can be used to select a file to be edited or to be printed.

You would proceed by pressing F6 to name a document. PC-Write will suggest the name ''work.doc'' as the file to create in a prompt,

```
File to load or create (Esc:cancel F8:dir): "work.doc"
```

This filename is a default filename that PC-Write will use if you do not change it. It is preferable to choose a filename at the start since you may not remember to look for the file under this uncommon name. It is also possible that you may already have another file by this name and it will be retrieved, rather than a new file being started. Replace WORK.DOC with the filename of your choice.

EXERCISES

A. Create the following letter with the filename, B:PLAINSMN, as it is written:

```
Charles D. May
Editor, Daily Plainsman
Mountsville, IA 97673

Dear Mr. May:

I am a freshman at the state university this yaer. My major is
journalizm. Professor Margaret Scotte who was a teacher of yours
suggested that I contact you about the possibility of obtaing a
summer job with your newspaper.

Thus far, I have taken two English composition courses and Jour.
200, Newspaper Writing. I especially ejnoy preparing human
interest articles. Three of my class assignments have been
published in our school newspaper. Dr. Scotte said that she
would be happy to be a reference for me if you wished to contact
her.

I will retrun to Mountsville for summer vacation on June 2nd.
Iwill contact you then to see if any opening exist.

Sincerely,


Milton Morehoutte
Box 123
Duffy Dormitory
State University
Anytown, IA 97621
```

After you have created the file, make the following changes:

1. Use the Shift and Escape keys to reverse the incorrectly placed letters in ''yaer,'' ''ejnoy,'' and ''retrun.''
2. Insert,
   —a blank between ''I'' and ''will'' on the first line of the third paragraph,
   —''in'' in the word ''obtaing,''
   —the sentence, ''I received an A in all three courses.'' after sentence one of paragraph two,
   —the sentence, ''I will be available from June 2 to Sept. 3.'' between the two sentences in paragraph three,
   —the student's telephone number (3035667899) after his address,
   —an ''s'' after ''opening,'' in the last paragraph,
   —commas before and after the phrase, ''who was a teacher of yours.''
3. Replace,
   —the lowercase ''s'' and ''u'' in ''state university'' with uppercase letters,
   —the ''z'' with an ''s'' in ''journalizm,''
   —the words ''your newspaper'' in the last line of the first paragraph with ''the Daily Plainsman,''
   —the word ''happy'' with ''pleased.''
4. Reformat all paragraphs with the F7 key.
5. Separate the sentence beginning, ''Dr. Scotte said . . .'' into a separate paragraph by inserting a carriage return.

6. Correct any remaining errors in the document.
7. Print the document.

B. Create the following letter with the filename, B:JOHNSON, as it is written:

```
June 19, 1989

Jack Johnson
Acme Campers and Trailers
270 East Market Street
Warbuck, CA 27779

Dear Mr. Johnson:

This letter is to advice you that Ms. Marsha Dean who has been your
acount representative for the last four years hsa been promoted
to the position of Vice President for Design and Production. In
her new position, Ms. Dean will be able to apply her knowledge
about the recreational vehicle retail sales market to the
introduction of a new product line. The phaeton line of camper
tops to be announced shrotly will be trend setters for sure.

Mr. Hugh Falkner will be assigned to service your account as of
June 21, 1989. Mr. Falkner has been with the company for six
years and has a through knowledge of the campout products line of
camper tops and trailers. He has owned his own camping supplies
company, so I am sure that he will be able to solve you problems.
Pleaselet us know if their is any way by which we can sevre you
better.

Sincerely,



Mary Muldowner,
Pressident
Campout Products
```

After you have created the file, make the following changes:

1. Use the Shift and Escape keys to reverse the incorrectly placed letters in "hsa," "shrotly," and "sevre."
2. Insert,
   —a blank between "Please" and "let" in the last sentence,
   —the second "c" in the word "acount,"
   —the sentence, "Mr. Falkner can be reached at 205–566–7672." after the single sentence in paragraph three,
   —the phrase, "I am pleased to announce that Mr. Hugh Falkner . . .," as an introduction to the first sentence in paragraph two,
   —an "o" in the word "through" to make it "thorough,"
   —an "r" after "you" in "you problems,"
   —the word "quickly" before the period, but after the word "problems."
   —an apostrophe after the "s" in "campout products" in paragraph two
3. Replace,
   —the lowercase "c" and "p" in "campout products" with uppercase letters in paragraph two
   —the "c" with an "s" in "advice,"

—the lowercase ''p'' in ''phaeton'' with an uppercase ''P'',
—''their'' with ''there'' in the last paragraph,
—the word ''sure'' at the end of paragraph one with ''certain,''
—Replace the spelling of the name ''Falkner'' with the spelling ''Faulkner'' throughout.

4. Delete,
—the extra ''s'' in Pressident,
—the phrase ''line of'' in the 2nd paragraph.
5. Reformat all paragraphs with the F7 key.
6. Correct all remaining errors in the document.
7. Print the document.

C. Create another memorandum for Mr. Black in which progress in a new sales campaign is reported to the president of XYZ Corporation.

D. Write a letter home carefully explaining to your parents how the costs at college have risen dramatically and asking for money.

E. Begin writing your next term paper with PC-Write.

F. Prepare a one-page, biographical sketch of yourself.

Chapter 4

Some Next Steps in Word Processing: Revisions

CHAPTER OUTLINE

Retrieving a File
Editing Text
- Adding Text
- Tabs and Rulers
- Embedded Rulers
- Inserting Tabs

Additional Cursor and Screen Movements
- Shift and PgUp/PgDn
- Control and PgUp/PgDn
- Shift/Control and PgUp/PgDn
- Alternate and =/-
- Control and Left/Right Arrow

Using Special Fonts
Searching for Character Strings
Searching for Words
Saving Under a New Filename
Printing
Backing Up Your File
Searching and Replacing
- Replacement with Confirmation
- Replacement without Confirmation
- Variations on Searching and Replacing

Printing
Quitting without Saving a File
Exercises

It is a rare document that can be created and printed without revision. The memorandum created in chapter 2 was short and simple; it could have been written in one session by a person familiar with word processing. Often, however, a document is typed by one person and edited by another.Revisions made by the editor might be made in the file by still another person. This chapter will extend your knowledge of PC-Write by showing you how to

1. Retrieve a previously created file,
2. Add text to the file,
3. Use the search and the search and replace commands,

4. Incorporate special fonts for boldfacing and underlining text,
5. Modify the margins and tabs for your document.

RETRIEVING A FILE

To retrieve your memorandum, boot your computer or, if it is already running, obtain the ''A>'' prompt. Place the PC-Write diskette in drive A and your files diskette in drive B. Then type,

ed *b*:memo

This will cause PC-Write to load the editor in RAM along with your document file. You will see the copyright/registration screen and the request to make a backup file. If you should make a major blunder like erasing a large section of your file or replacing all spaces with Xs, you will still have an uncorrupted version of the file. Press F9 to make a backup file and to continue.

PC-Write retrieves your file and places the cursor at the top of the document. The file should be identical to the file that you saved and printed out in chapter 2. You are now ready to alter the document.

EDITING TEXT

Mr. Black has decided to have his document edited to look as it does in Figure 4–1.

```
Date: February 15, 1989

To: T. L. White

Fr: F. Y. Black, Director, Marketing & Sales

Re: Departmental Computer Equipment

It has become increasingly clear that our department could save
the company money in a number of areas if it had immediate access
to a microcomputer. I will cite 3 instances in which we could
have done a better job and could have been more productive. J.
Grey produced a 50-page report for the XYZ Company that had to be
retyped 3 times as it was revised and improved. We needed to
produce 3 graphic displays for a presentation to the ABC
Corporation and were told by the Graphics Department that they
could not be made available until 2 weeks after they were needed.
Finally, I had to produce a projection of our expenditures for
the next 3-year planning period. Without access to a spreadsheet
accounting program, this 3-hour task took a full day.

This is the only department that does not have a microcomputer to
use for word processing and data processing operations.

I believe that the Marketing and Sales Department should be
allowed to acquire a microcomputer with appropriate spreadsheet,
graphics and word processing software. M. Brown in our
department has taken several computer courses and workshops. She
feels that she can provide the training required for our staff.
With your approval and budgetary support, we can maintain
corporate profitability.
```

```
An assessment of the needs of our department completed by M. Brown
has determined that we need a system with these components:

Personal Computer With Hard Drive                        $2,000.00
Letter Quality Printer                                     1,500.00
Dot Matrix Printer                                           750.00
Plotter                                                    2,000.00
Computer Furniture                                           675.00
Supplies, Cables, Power protector                            950.00
TOTAL                                                     $9,375.00

I shall set up an appointment with you for next week to discuss
our request.
```

Figure 4–1. New Version of Mr. Black's Memo with Tabular Material.

Adding Text

The sentence added between paragraphs will be entered now and underlined later. Using the cursor movement keys noted in chapter 2, move the cursor to the blank line currently separating the two paragraphs. Press,

↵ Enter key, to enter another blank line above the cursor. Type the sentence,

This is the only department that does not have a microcomputer touse for word processing and data processing operations.

↵ Enter key after the period

Practice using the cursor movement keys noted in Figure 2–4. After a short while (believe it or not), the commands will begin to come to you with no more thought than it takes to press alphabetic character keys. Move to the last character of the last paragraph. Use Shift and PgDn to move to the last sentence and the End key to place your cursor at the end of the line. Press

↵↵ Enter key twice to end the paragraph and to insert a blank line between it and the paragraph being added

Tab Tab key, to indent the paragraph

An assessment of the needs of our department completed by M.
Brown has determined that we need a system with these components:

The sentence to be inserted

↵ Enter key. Stop here

Tabs and Rulers

Thus far, the Tab key has not been used. Before continuing, press the Tab key several times. PC-Write has a hidden default ruler (a ruler used if you don't deliberately use a different ruler) that it uses to create tab settings and to define the location of the left and right margins. The F2 key, when pressed from within the editor (as opposed to pressing it after the F1 key has been pressed and having the help screen in view), displays the PC-Write ruler currently in use. Press,

F2 Function key F2 to call up the ruler menu and the ruler. The screen with the default ruler can be changed, but it will probably look like this,

```
Esc F1  F2.Un-split  F4.Embed-ruler  F6:Control-file  Grey
Right Margin Letters:  Center  Flush  Justify  Ragged (normal)  Spring

Other Ruler  Letters:  Paragraph  Tab  Decimal  Bell  @10i: set spacing 1/10 in.

L---+---T1---+-T--2----T----3--T-+----4T---+---T5----+-T--6----R----7--T-+--

^     ^
|     |                                                 Right margin at 65th
|     Tab markers                                       character column
Left margin at 10th character column
```

F2 Function key F2, to save the ruler
F2 Function key F2, to retrieve it again

The tab markers, capital T's, are found at every fifth character column position. Capital "L" marks the placement of the left margin. Only one letter "L" is allowed in the ruler since there can be only one left margin. Pressing capital "L" in a new location will cause the previous left margin marker to change to lowercase. The lowercase "l" will be ignored, but it serves as a reminder of where the previous left margin was should you wish to return to that margin in a subsequent ruler.

The letter "T" marks tab stops and can appear as often as you wish. The pressing of the Tab key will move the cursor to the next tab marker.

The capital letter "R" fixes the right-hand margin. There can be only one right margin. Pressing "R" will cause the previous "R" to be replaced by a lowercase "r," which will be ignored.

A capital "P" can also appear in the ruler to indicate the location of a new paragraph tab. If a "P" is present, the cursor will automatically be placed at this position after the Enter key has been pressed. The Enter key creates a "hard return" at the end of the line and is used by PC-Write to represent the end of a paragraph. PC-Write will assume that you wish to begin a new paragraph and moves the cursor to the paragraph marker.

When you press the Tab key, the cursor will move to the next "T" marked tab setting. Characters you type after the Tab key will be typed after the tab marker. Your ruler can include a "D," which is a decimal tab. When you press the Tab key and the next tab marker is a "D," the cursor will move to that marker and the numbers (or other characters) you type will be pushed to the left until a period is typed. You will use a "D" marking to line up numbers such as those in the equipment cost column to be added to your memorandum.

A "B" can be placed in your ruler to signify the point at which a bell will sound to notify you that your cursor is approaching the end of the line. There is no B in the current ruler.

There can be only one B, P, L, and R on each ruler. There can be as many T's and D's as you wish.

Changes can be made in the ruler by typing over the letters that are currently there. A "T," for instance, can be replaced by either a non-Grey Minus sign or a blank space to remove it as a marker. A letter B, P, L, or R entered into the ruler will automatically cause PC-Write to replace the previous B, P, L, or R with a lowercase letter of the same type that will be ignored.

Return the cursor to the beginning of the ruler line. You can move the cursor on the line with the arrow and tab keys. Alternatively delete existing markers and insert the new markers until the old ruler, is changed to look like,

```
1--L---1----+----2---------3----+----4----+---5--+--D6--R--7---+---
^  ^                                                ^   ^
|  5                                                59 65
0
```

Be sure that there are no letters to the right of the ''R'' in column 76. This ruler will continue to indent the left margin by 10 spaces, remove many of the tabs that existed previously, and allow you to use the Tab key to line up the computer component names at column 15 and the prices for each component of the proposed system at column 59. The pluses and numbers have no effect on the ruler, but are useful in marking off the column locations of the old Tab markers in case you wish to modify this ruler. Press

F2 Function key F2, to save and remove the ruler from your screen. The ruler you created will affect the formatting of all subsequently typed text. It has no affect on those portions of the document already typed.

Existing text can be deliberately or accidentally reformatted (but don't) with the new ruler. A combination of cursor movement, Insert, Delete, and F7 keys is used to reformat the existing paragraph. If the cursor is in a paragraph, the pressing of the F7 key will reformat that paragraph according to the new ruler. Do not reformat the existing paragraphs in this exercise. Enter the following,

↵ Enter key. Notice that the cursor moves to a new left margin

Personal Computer With Hard Drive
The name of the first component of the system

Tab Tab key, to bring the cursor to column 59

$2,000.00 The amount of this component. Notice the numbers move to the left and then to the right when the period is pressed

↵ Enter key, to move the cursor to a new line

Enter the remaining components and their prices as they appear in Figure 4–1, pressing the Tab key, between the name and the price. After entering the total, use the F2 key to recall the ruler that is currently in use. Return it to its original appearance with a left margin at column 10 and a tab marker at every 5 places. Save the ruler with the second pressing of the F2 key.

Enter the rest of the memo.

Embedded Rulers

Most of the options for working with rulers are not used in this book. This text only contains exercises that use one ruler per exercise. Often it will be necessary to have two rulers in use. One ruler may, for example, be used to format paragraphs while another ruler is used to format tables or double column text. If you are only working with the default ruler, it is quite easy to reformat one type of text with the ruler for the other. The F4 key enables you to embed a ruler in the document. An embedded ruler will appear on your screen and will be a part of your file, but it will not print. Embedded rulers control the formatting of all text that follows them up to the next ruler. Then that embedded ruler controls the text that follows it.

Inserting Tabs

PC-Write does not normally ''insert'' tabs as you press the Enter key. Rather, it moves the cursor over the spaces on the line. Since a space is a character, the spaces define the indentation. Tabbing while you are entering new text is the fastest way of indenting text. But, as in this memorandum, if the document has already had text entered and you wish to enter tabs, you will find that the cursor simply moves over characters between tab markers in response to pressing the Tab key. Use the following approach to insert the blank spaces for a tab. Place your cursor under the ''I'' in ''It'' on the first line of the first paragraph and enter,

Ctrl-I Control and I simultaneously, to insert 5 spaces

F7 Function key F7, to reformat the paragraph. If the status line reads ''Para+'' the reformatting is not needed since it is carried out automatically

Insert tabs and reformat the other 5 paragraphs. Do not indent or reformat the price list.

ADDITIONAL CURSOR AND SCREEN MOVEMENTS

As your document becomes larger, it no longer can be seen on one screen. It is harder to move to specific locations. Several PC-Write commands are especially helpful in moving between screens and in making bigger jumps from one place to another.

Shift and PgUp/PgDn

Move from one screen to the next with the Shift and PgUp or PgDn keys. Shift PgUp will take you to the screen above the current screen, while Shift PgDn will take you to the next screen below.

Control and PgUp/PgDn

The cursor can be moved from one paragraph to another toward the end of the file by simultaneously pressing the Control key and the PgDn key. The Control and PgUp keys will move the cursor toward the beginning of the file paragraph by paragraph. A paragraph is recognized by the hard return at the end of the paragraph, not by the paragraph's contents.

Shift/Control and PgUp/PgDn

If you press the Shift, Control, and PgUp (or PgDn) keys, the cursor will jump from one page to the next. Since the file is still less than one page long, this command cannot be used yet.

Alternate and =-

Often you will wish to move rapidly to the top or bottom line of a file. The Alt key when pressed simultaneously with the Equal Sign, will return to the beginning of the file. The Alt and the Hyphen key will move to the end of the file.

Control and Left/Right Arrow

Within a line, too, there are faster cursor movements than the Arrow keys alone. Moving one character at a time with the Arrow keys is slow. You can move rapidly by pressing the Control and left or right Arrow keys to jump forward and backward word by word.

Experiment with these movement keys to see their effect. The new commands are summarized in Figure 4–2.

KEY	ACTION
Ctrl-Right Arrow	Right One Word
Ctrl-Left Arrow	Left One Word
Ctrl-PgUp	Up One Paragraph
Ctrl-PgDn	Down One Paragraph
Shift-PgUp	Up One Screen
Shift-PgDn	Down One Screen
Shift-Ctrl-PgUP	Up One Page
Shift-Ctrl-PgDn	Down One Page
Alt-Equal	Top Of File
Alt-Minus (non-grey)	Bottom Of File

Figure 4–2. Additional Cursor-Movement Commands.

USING SPECIAL FONTS

There are two sections of the text in the memorandum that are to be underlined. PC-Write enhances the impact of your writing with the use of differing styles of printer output. A change in typeface is a change in "font." Place your cursor under the "m" in "money" in paragraph one and press,

Alt-U The Alternate and U keys pressed simultaneously. Notice that a special graphics symbol appears in the blank space and the line is pushed to the right. The remainder of the line may change in intensity or may be underlined. The underlining stops at the end of the line. The entire line will be underlined. Now place the cursor in the space after the word "money"

Alt-U The Alternate and U key combination to stop the underlining at this point. The underlining symbols will not be printed in your hard copy. You will now delete this underlining. Place the cursor at the first underline symbol

Del Delete key. Place the cursor underneath the second underline symbol.

Del Delete key

Place your cursor at the beginning of the second paragraph and again type Alt and U. You will have to repeat these key strokes at the beginning of the second line of the paragraph. Now underline the two lines of the fourth paragraph. Special font characters affect the characters to their right, up to the end of the line, or up to the second use of the special font marker if it appears on the same line.

The alternate fonts available are shown in Figure 4–3. All of these fonts are begun and ended by pressing the Alternate key and another key simultaneously.

FONT STYLE	ENTRY	SCREEN SYMBOL	FONT STYLE	ENTRY	SCREEN SYMBOL
Boldface	Alt-B	●	Overstrike	Alt-O	!!
Compressed	Alt C	♠	Pica (10 cpi)	Alt-P	♣
Double Wide	Alt-D	►	Quality	Alt-Q	▬
Elite (12 cpi)	Alt-E	♥	Second Strike	Alt-S	☺
Fast (Draft)	Alt-F	∟	Underline	Alt-U	↨
Higher (Superscript)	Alt-H	↑	Variable (Proportional Type)	Alt-V	♦
Italics	Alt-I	§			
Lower (Subscript)	Alt-L	↓	Double Underline	Alt-W	↕

Figure 4–3. Alternative Fonts.

Be aware that when compressed or double-wide type fonts are used (they are not used in this book), the margins must be adjusted to accommodate the size change.

In the two examples used in the memorandum, underlining was introduced after the text was typed. The underlining was applied from the cursor to the end of the line. Underlining, or any other font change, can be started during the entry of text. As you are typing, press the Alt key along with the alternate font letter, continue typing and press the Alt key along with the alternate font letter to return to normal type. If several lines are to be underlined, the alternate font symbol would have to be placed at the beginning of each line.

If you are editing existing text, you can press the alternate font at the beginning of the text you wish printed, and then press the alternate font combination at the point in the text you wish the font to stop. This will return the text to normal type.

The symbols used to represent the alternative fonts won't appear or take up space in the printed document.

SEARCHING FOR CHARACTER STRINGS

Often, changes to be made in a document are far apart. Visually searching for an incorrectly spelled word or for a phrase can be tedious. You can move directly to a specific location with the PC-Write search command. Press,

Alt-= The Alternate and Equal Sign, a key combination that will move your cursor to the top of the file. Suppose that you wished to search for the word ''clear'' on the first line

F9 Function key F9, to receive the prompt,

```
Esc F9:find "." F10:replace "."
```

The first portion of the search command is asking you to type in the string (one or more) of characters for which you wish to search. You will not use the F10 portion of the command now. Enter

clear The word to be searched for

Grey+ The grey-colored Plus Sign on the right-hand side of the keyboard. The pressing of this key will advance you to the first occurrence of the word being sought. The word ''clear'' is marked (on a color monitor it is highlighted). The cursor stops at the first letter of the word

Grey+ The grey-colored Plus Sign, to search for ''clear'' once more. Since this is the only occurrence of the word ''clear,'' you receive a message,

Did not find ''clear''

Alt-= Alternate and Equal Sign, to return to the top of the file. Searches always begin at the location of the cursor. Therefore, to search through an entire file, you should return the cursor to the top of the document

F9 Function key F9, to search again. Type in the word ''the,'' which replaces ''clear,''

Grey+ The Grey Plus key. You can press it three more times and find the word ''the'' each time. After the next pressing of the grey Plus key, however, you will find the character string ''the,'' but the entire word is actually ''they.'' PC-Write located the character string ''the,'' not the word ''the.'' Because PC-Write finds the precise string of characters you type in, it could find ''the'' in ''other,'' ''either'' or a thousand other words. The shorter or more common the search string is, the more likely it is that PC-Write will not find the occurrence of the word you are actually seeking

Use the Grey Minus key to reverse the direction of the search. Press this key until you are told that there are no more occurrences of ''the'' to be found.

F5 Function key F5, to stop searching for text

SEARCHING FOR WORDS

There are times when you will want to search for a word and not a character string. Words, in one sense, are defined by the presence of blank spaces to either side of the printable characters. Press,

F9 Function key F9, to start another search. This time type a blank space with the space bar before and after the characters "the" so that the prompt line reads,

```
F9:find " the " F10:replace "."
```

This will define the word more accurately. The space in front will prevent PC-Write from finding "the" in such words as "bathe" or "lathe." The space behind will prevent PC-Write from finding the search string in such words as "they," or "these."

Grey+ The grey-colored Plus Sign to confirm that PC-Write only finds "the" as a word. Enter the Grey Plus Sign until the word is not found

F5 Function key F5, to exit the search procedure

Three helpful strategies for searching for a word without having to locate intermediate occurrences of the same search string are:

1. Include the spaces on either side of the word to avoid finding the string inside of other words.
2. Don't search for a common word, but search for an uncommon word in the same line. For instance, if you wished to change "the aliens," to "those aliens" don't search for "the," search for "aliens."
3. Search for more than one word. The find string can be "the XYZ" that will have many fewer instances of occurrence than the word "the" alone.

SAVING UNDER A NEW FILENAME

Normally, when you edit a file you will save the file under the same name that you used when you invoked PC-Write. Periodically you will wish to save the file under a different name. By changing the name, a new file will be created and the file with the filename used originally will be left unchanged. The memorandum that has been edited and improved can, for instance, be saved as MEMO2 leaving the file MEMO unaltered. Do this by pressing,

F1 Function key F1, to call up the main help screen

F5 Function key F5, to obtain the prompt,

```
Name to use for saving (Esc:cancel F8:dir): "b:memo"
```

Retain the "*b*:" directory, but change the filename to MEMO2 by typing "*b*:memo2"

↵ Enter key, to complete the renaming. Notice that the status line above the work area now displays the new name of the file

PRINTING

The memorandum is complete. Print MEMO2 by pressing,

F1 Function key F1, to bring up the help menu

F7 Function key F7, to start the printing process. The choices you will see are the same as those that appeared in chapter 2. You will see the prompt,

```
File to print (Esc:cancel F8:dir): "b:memo2"
```

↵ Enter key. If you elected to have several print rulers on the PC-Write diskette, you see the prompt screen,

```
Print control filename (Esc:exit Enter:none): ""
```

to which you enter the filename for the printer you are currently using; for instance, OKI or EPSON and then pressing the Enter key. If you have only the default printer file, press Enter. The next prompt will be,

```
Esc:Exit F9:Print to disk file F10:Printer is ready
```

F10 Function key F10, to indicate that the printer is ready, if the printer is turned on and if it is connected to your computer. You will see a menu of choices that you can make while the printing is in process

F10 Function key F10, if your printer is using continuous paper, or press F9 if the printer uses a single-sheet feeder

If the underlining is not reproduced by the printer, it is because PC-Write does not have the correctly installed PR.DEF file noted in ''Creating a PC-Write Working Diskette'' in chapter 2. You will have to repeat the creation of the working disk and correctly identify your printer.

BACKING UP YOUR FILE

The printing procedure will have automatically saved your document. Save your file again to your backup diskette by removing the diskette from drive B and replacing it with your backup diskette. Save the file on the backup diskette by pressing F1, followed by the pressing of F3.

SEARCHING AND REPLACING

The search procedure outlined in the ''Searching'' section of this chapter is useful for changing one occurrence of a word. Frequently, there is a need to change many occurrences of a word or phrase. For example, it may not be until after a paper has been completed that it is found that ''key board'' should be ''keyboard'' or that ''back space'' should be ''backspace.'' The search and replace command will go through an entire file and make the desired changes where these corrections are to be made. There are two variations on the search and replace technique, replace with confirmation and replace without confirmation. Both variations begin with the pressing of the F9 key.

You will be making many changes to the memorandum that you have created. The file will not be saved after the changes have been made. Do not worry that the changes you are making for illustrative purposes will damage the properly constructed memorandum saved with the filename MEMO2.

Replacement with Confirmation

There are two occurrences of the phrase ''our department'' in the memorandum. Suppose that Mr.Black decided that this phrase should be changed to read, ''the Marketing and Sales Department.'' In a short memorandum like this, visually locating and changing the two phrases would not be difficult. It would be difficult if the file was twenty pages long and contained fifteen instances of the phrase. Press

Alt-= Alternate and Equal Sign, to move to the top of the file
F9 Function key F9. You will receive the prompt,

```
Esc F9:find "the" F10:replace "."
```

PC-Write remembers the previous search string. Replace the search string '' the '' with,
our department
The replacement string

F10 Function key F10. Pressing the F10 key tells PC-Write that instead of simply finding the occurrences of the search string, you also wish to replace that string with another string.
the Marketing and Sales Department
The replacement string
Grey+ Grey Plus Sign, to find the first occurrence of the string
F10 Function key F10, to effect the replacement. The line of text is extended and will have to be reformatted later
Grey+ Grey Plus Sign key to locate the next occurrence of ''our department''
F10 Function key F10, to make the replacement a second time

Each time the grey Plus Sign is pressed to locate the next occurrence of the search string, the cursor stops to wait for you to press F10 to carry out the replacement operation. If you do not wish the replacement to occur, press the grey Plus Sign key again and the phrase will remain as it was.

Exit the search and replace operation by pressing the F5 key (to cancel the marking operation started by the replacement operation).

The two paragraphs that were changed must be reformatted if your status line says ''Wrap'' but not if it says ''Para+.'' Place your cursor on the first word of each paragraph and press

F7 Function key F7, to reformat the paragraph from the location of the cursor.

Try the search and replace operation again. Press,

Alt-= Alternate and Equal Sign, to move to the top of the file
F9 Function key F9, to start the search and replace operation
produc Search for the string, ''produc'' by typing in the word
F10 Function key F10, to replace the previous search string with the string ''creat.''
creat The replacement string.
The search string will find ''produce,'' ''produced'' and ''productive.'' Now press the greyPlus Sign key to locate the first occurrence of ''produc'' in the word ''productive''
Grey+ Grey Plus Sign, to avoid making the replacement. This causes PC-Write to locate the next occurrence of the search string. You can continue to cancel the change by pressing the grey Plus Sign key each time it finds an instance of the string that is to be left as it was, to locate the search string by pressing the Grey Minus Sign, or you can selectively make the change by pressing F10

Exit the search and replacement operation with the F5 key.

Replacement without Confirmation

The ability to see each location of the search string is useful. You may wish to be able to prevent changes if you do not wish to have a change made. For example, substitute "our department" for "we" in one operation by pressing,

Alt-Equal Alternate and Equal sign keys pressed simultaneously, to move the cursor to the top of the document
F9 Function key F9, to begin the replacement operation
we The word " we " is the search string. Make sure that you enter spaces around the word.
F10 Function key F10, to enter the replacement string
our department
Alt-F10 The Alternate and F10 keys pressed simultaneously to see the prompt,

```
Esc:Cancel F9:Repeat-replace F10:Un-replace
```

F9 Function key F9, to make the substitutions throughout the file
F5 Function key F5, to stop marking. The replacements have been made throughout the file. This process is often referred to as a global replacement. In the fourth paragraph add an "s" to the word "need" after "our department" for grammatical correctness

Remember to reformat paragraphs with the F7 key.

Variations on Searching and Replacing

You may start the global replacement operation at any time after a search and replace with confirmation has begun. If you are cautious and confirm the first several replacements, you may conclude that changes from that point forward will not cause any difficulty. The pressing of the Alt and F10 keys can be initiated any time to make the remaining changes.

The grey Minus Sign key can be used to conduct a search or a search and replace operation in the opposite direction (toward the top line of the file). Text in the opposite direction will not be searched. Both types of search begin at the location of the cursor and stop at the first or last line of the file.

QUITTING WITHOUT SAVING A FILE

You have made several changes to your memorandum. It is not uncommon that global changes create more difficulties than they solve. If that happens, as the case is assumed now, you should not save it as MEMO2 because the altered document will replace the good version that was saved just before the printing operation. Press,

F1 Function key F1, to call up the main help screen. Notice the words, "F9:Unsave" in the top line
F9 Function key F9, to notify PC-Write that you do not wish to save the file. The words "[no-save]" appear
F2 Function key F2, to exit PC-Write returning you to DOS. The DOS prompt will appear quickly and the disk drive light will not go on; two indications that the file was not written to disk

EXERCISES

A. Retrieve the letter, PLAINSMN, and
—underline the name of the newspaper, Daily Plainsman,
—search for every occurrence of the letters "ou,"
—insert tabs at the start of each paragraph

Save the file and then,
—replace every instance of ''ti'' with ''xx,''
—replace every other instance of ''al'' with ''qq,''
—print the corrupted file. If you wish to avoid overwriting the ''good'' version of the file, rename the file with the F1, F5 sequence.

B. Retrieve the letter, JOHNSON, and
—boldface the first appearances of the names, ''Marsha Dean,'' and ''Mr. Hugh Faulkner,''
—underline the phrase, ''solve your problems quickly.''
—insert tabs at the start of each paragraph.

Save the file and then,
—search for all instances of the word ''the,''
—search for all instances of the character string, ''the,''
—change all instances of ''am'' to ''xx,''
—change every other instance of ''ou'' to ''in,''
—print the corrupted file. If you wish to avoid overwriting the ''good'' version of the file, rename the file with the F1, F5 sequence.

C. Reproduce the first page of the first chapter of this book and practice the use of underlining by underlining one complete line, the last half of a line, and six words on different lines.

On the page created, try locating the character string ''is.'' Try changing ''is'' to ''are'' without altering the words ''misspelling'' or ''disk.''

Chapter 5

Creating a Résumé

CHAPTER OUTLINE

The next document you will create is a résumé that requires the use of many advanced features of PC-Write. In this chapter you will

1. Create and save a ruler designed specifically to help you prepare résumés,
2. Save files under different names,
3. Insert font changes as you enter text,
4. Center individual lines and blocks of text between page margins,
5. Move and delete blocks of text,
6. Change uppercase letters to lowercase and vice versa.

Résumés are important documents for individuals since they are often a key component of the applicant screening process employers go through. Résumés are intended to provide up-to-date information about candidates. Consequently, résumés change each time the person's background changes.

The format structure of a résumé is quite different from many other documents. This structure requires the use of a different ruler than you might use for a memorandum or book. The résumé you create now will be modified significantly to illustrate how major changes can be made in a document.

In Figure 5–1 is a résumé that a student believes will be helpful in applying for jobs after graduation.

HARRIET HARTLEY

22 Elm Street
West Washington, NV 89888
707-555-5665

PROFESSIONAL GOAL:

To work within a challenging company and to interact with the public in a problem-solving environment.

EDUCATION:

WEST WASHINGTON HIGH SCHOOL
2100 Parker Drive
West Washington, NV 89888
Academic Diploma, 1985

UNIVERSITY OF THE MOUNTAINS
Lake Hicauma, CA 12880
Bachelor of Science, Business Administration
1989

WORK EXPERIENCE:

SMITH & BAKER RETAILERS
1 Black Oak Lane
West Washington, NV 89888
Assistant Buyer
Summer, 1986–1988

UNIVERSITY OF THE MOUNTAINS
Lake Hicauma, CA 12880
Student Activities Programming Assistant
Academic Year, 1987–1989

FLOWERS ARE FOREVER
Market Square
West Washington, NV 89888
Sales Clerk–Floral Arranger
Academic Year, 1985–1986

AWARDS AND SCHOOL ACTIVITIES:

Varsity Basketball, Omega Phi Beta, Outstanding Student Volunteer, President's Honor Roll, Crisis Call Volunteer.

SPECIAL SKILLS:

Programming in BASIC and Pascal, Spanish (3 Yrs.)

Figure 5–1. Harriet Hartley's Résumé.

In comparison with the memorandum, this document is considerably harder to construct. In developing the first draft of the résumé you will

1. Create and save a new ruler,
2. Use a different ruler than ED.DEF,
3. Enter boldface characters while you type,
4. Center text on a line.

CREATING AND SAVING A RULER

People who work with word processors frequently find that many documents are structured similarly. In a university, a secretary may find that journals in one discipline follow the same stylistic expectations (margins, line spacing, use of footnotes). A budget officer in a corporation may create differing project budgets with tables that use the same tab stops and margins. Students may find that term papers at their college are restricted to a particular style manual.

When there are recurring guidelines for the production of documents, it is often desirable to create a ruler that can be made a part of documents as soon as you begin to create them. The default ruler on the PC-Write diskette comes from the file ED.DEF. You have seen that the F2 key can be used to modify a ruler once you have started a document. Modifying this ruler over and over again takes unnecessary time and your modifications may be inconsistent from one document to the next. You can create and save rulers that are appropriate for the kinds of documents with which you work. You may then use these rulers in two ways.

A New Default Ruler (ED.DEF)

You can create a ruler that is appropriate for the majority of documents you create and give it the name ED.DEF. Thereafter, this ruler will be the default ruler for the creation of any file for which you have not specifically indicated to PC-Write that a different ruler file exists.

The ED.DEF that came with your version of PC-Write may not be the most desirable ruler for typing term papers or other documents you need to create. Place your PC-Write diskette in drive A and type,

```
ed ed.def
```

↲ Enter key
F9 Function key F9, to see a screen that looks like Figure 5–2.

```
Esc:Menu Push Guide. R:F 99% 0/3, 1 Read "A:\ed.def"
F1:System/help F3.Copy/mark F5.Un-mark F7.Paragraph F9:Find-text
F2:Window/ruler F4.Delete/mark F6.Move/mark F8.Lower/upper F10.Replace
ǫ--+--T1--+-T-2--T--3-T-+--4T--+--T5--+-T-6--T--7-T-+-R
|L--+--T1--+-T-2--T--3T-+--4T--+--T5--+-T-6--T-7-7-T-+-R
!pr.def
!ed.*
%M
%R] &R:5
L--+--T1--+-T-2--T--3T-+--4T--+--T5--+-T-6--R---T-+-
.X:10
.XT:6
.XB:6
```

Figure 5–2. The ED.DEF File.

In addition to the status line and the reminder lines, one of which is the default ruler, you now see the contents of ED.DEF, the file which contains the default ruler and other commands. The lines have been numbered to identify the lines.

1. The status line.
2. First function key usage reminder line.
3. Second function key usage reminder line.
4. Reminder line showing the default ruler for editing this file. This is confusing, perhaps, because the ruler appears again on lines 5 and 10.
5. An embedded, default ruler that exists as the first line of the file ED.DEF; the file being edited. This ruler guides the formatting of the text in the file up to line 10.
6. This command tells PC-Write that the default printing control file to use for printing documents is PR.DEF.
7. This command tells PC-Write that the default edit control file to use is any file that begins with ED followed by the filename extension given in the "ed" command.
8. The "%M" is the command for showing the reminder lines as a default.
9. The "%R] &R:5" commands cause PC-Write to automatically save your file every 5 minutes.
10. The third appearance of the ruler. This embedded ruler is modified when alternative rulers to the ED.DEF file are being created.
11. The dot command ".X:10" sets the default left margin (at 10).
12. The dot command ".XT:6" sets the default top margin (at 6).
13. The dot command ".XB:6" sets the default bottom margin (at 6).

Press,

Scroll Lck Scroll Lock key, to change the status line from "Push" to "Over"
Caps Lock Caps Lock is toggled on and "Over" changes to "OVER"

Modify the ruler on line 10, the third ruler, to have tab stops every five places and to look like this,

```
 ↨ L--P--T--T--T--T--T--T--T--T--T--T--R--
   ^  ^  ^
   |  |  |
   |  |  |
   |  5  10
0
```

Figure 5–3. The New ED.DEF File.

Save the file and exit the editor by pressing,

F1 Function key F1, to call up the help/system menu
F2 Function key F2, to save the file ED.DEF and to exit the word processor. You have constructed a new default ruler that will have a left-hand margin (L) of 10, a right-hand margin (R) of 75, an automatic paragraph (P) indent of five spaces, and tab stops every five columns. This ruler will now be used whenever PC-Write cannot find a ruler that matches the extension of the file to be edited. If, for example, you type (but don't),

ed b:paper

the file PAPER will be started using ED.DEF because the filename does not have an extension.

Creating Use-Specific Rulers

Filenames can have an extension of three letters. One function of filename extensions is to identify files that have something in common. For instance, all backup files created by PC-Write have the character "&" as the first letter of the extension. The person using the computer might use numerical extensions such as .001, .002, and .003 to represent different versions of a document.

PC-Write uses extensions to determine whether a ruler file exists that should be used to begin the formatting of the document named. For example, if you type the command (but don't),

```
ed b:resume.res
```

PC-Write will look for a file ED.RES because the file being edited ends with the extension RES. If the file ED.RES exists, it will use it as the ruler for the document called RESUME.RES. If ED.RES does not exist, ED.DEF will be used as the default ruler instead.

Assume that you are working in an office that frequently types résumés of the type illustrated in Figure 5–1. You would want to create a ruler that facilitated the accomplishment of your task. Even though you are only creating one résumé, create a ruler for this task by typing,

```
copy ed.def b:ed.res
```

↵ Enter key, which duplicates the ED.DEF file under the name ED.RES on the diskette in drive B

Now edit the ruler contained in ED.RES using PC-Write by typing,

```
ed b:ed.res
```

↵ Enter key
F9 Function key F9, to continue
Esc Escape key, to keep from creating a backup file. Remember that you are in the editor; hence, the "Push" mode is on. Turn "Push" to "Over" by pressing,
Scroll Lock Scroll Lock key. Edit this ruler by replacing the "P" with a "T" and the next two T's with minuses so that the ruler looks like,

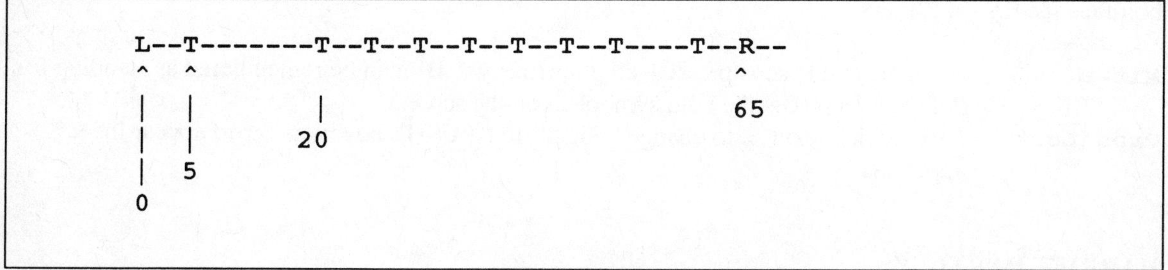

Figure 5–4. Résumé Ruler.

This ruler will reduce the number of tabs that must be pressed to indent the entries for Work experience and education in the résumé to be created.

SAVING THE RULER FILE

Next, save the file B:ED.RES by pressing,

F1 Function key F1, to call up the System/Help menu

`F3`	Function key F3, to save the file, but not to exit. As long as this file is on your diskette, whenever you begin to edit a file with the extension .RES, this ruler will be used instead of ED.DEF.

CHANGING THE FILE NAME

There is no need to exit PC-Write whenever you have finished working on one file and wish to begin another. Exiting and re-entering PC-Write takes time. Begin creating the sample résumé by typing the command,

`F1`	Function key F1. Wait for the status line to appear
`F6`	Function key F6, to change the filename. Upon completion of this command, the contents of the text entry screen will have been cleared.
`b:hartley.res`	The name of the file to be started
↵	Enter key, to begin a new file
`F9`	Do not make a backup copy since this is a new file. A new file cannot be loaded since it is not there to recall. However, the extension RES tells PC-Write that it should use the file ED.RES as the source of the ruler for this file. When the text entry screen appears examine the ruler and see the ruler shown in the reminder line (or retrieve the real ruler in use with the F2 key). You will see that the ruler you created to format text in résumé files is in use

LINE AND BLOCK MANIPULATIONS

Making In-Line Font Changes

When you created documents in the preceding chapters, several lines and phrases were underlined after the text had been entered in the document. In the résumé, the first line, as well as many other lines of text, are boldfaced. There is no point in typing in the text only to have to return to each line that is to be boldfaced to insert the bolding commands. The boldfacing can be inserted as you are typing. To boldface the first line, press,

`Alt-B`	Alternate and B keys pressed simultaneously. ''B'' can be remembered as standing for *B*old, which places the bold symbol ☺ on the screen.
`Caps Lock`	Caps Lock key once, to change ''Push'' to ''PUSH'' so letters typed appear in uppercase

HARRIET HARTLEY

	The student's name
`Alt-B`	Alternate and B key combination again to close the bold text. *Do not press the Enter key*. The second pressing of the Alt and B keys is optional. The boldfacing started by the first Alt and B will remain in effect to the end of the line. The second Alt and B are generally used when additional, unboldfaced text follows the boldfaced text on the same line

On a color screen you can see that the two words appear highlighted indicating that a special font is in use.

Hiding Font Face Symbols

Don't let the appearance of the font symbols bother you. They will not appear when you print the file. If you do not wish the symbols to display on the screen,

Alt-Space	The Alternate key and the Space bar. The font symbols will disappear. A triple line will appear across the screen to tell you that the symbols are hidden
Alt-Space	The Alternate key and the Space bar. The symbols will be toggled on
Caps Lock	Caps lock, to toggle to lowercase character entry

As you type the remainder of the résumé, remember that text on a line displaying font symbols will not appear in the column that it will print in. PC-Write cannot display a font symbol and a letter in the same location. To check for correct alignment, press the Alt-Space Bar key combination to see the line without the symbols.

Centering a Line of Text

PC-Write, because of the ruler file ED.RES, knows the document's margins. It can automatically compute the center point for the current margins. With the cursor behind the name, center the name by pressing,

Shift-F8	Shift and Function key F8 pressed simultaneously. The line is automatically centered
↵↵	Enter key twice,to move to the next line of text to be entered

Marking and Centering a Block of Text

The next three lines of the résumé are not in caps, although individual words do begin with capital letters. You could enter and center these lines individually by typing each line and pressing Shift with F8 in turn. This is perfectly acceptable. Another option, however, is to center a block of text. For illustrative purposes type,

22 Elm Street
West Washington, NV 89888
707-555-5665

The three lines of the address. Press the Enter key at the end of each line. Move the cursor under the first "2" in "22"

There are several operations that PC-Write allows on blocks of text, for instance on these three lines, on two words, or on five characters. Among these operations are moving the block from one place in the file to another, deleting a block from the file, and copying the block in another location. At this point you will center the block of text.

The procedure used to define the block of text involved in a block operation is called "marking." Once a block has been defined, it is said to be marked. Notice that the second function key reminder line shows F6 as the key for moving and marking. Begin the marking procedure by pressing,

F6	Function key F6. Notice that "Wrap+" changes to "Marking"
↓↓	Down Arrow twice, to highlight the first two lines
End	End key, to highlight the third line. The highlighting identifies the marked block of text
Shift-F8	Shift and Function key F8, to center the text. Notice that even though the operation is complete, the status line continues to display "Marking" and that the highlighting of the three lines is still in effect

F5 Function key F5, to unmark the block, otherwise cursor movements will continue to mark text

Function key F6 was used for marking in this exercise. The function key reminder lines show, however, that F3, F4, and F6 all can be used for marking. The marking procedure is the same for all three keys. When used to copy, delete, or move, however, they are not identical.

Entering Text

Enter the remainder of the sample résumé with the following reminders:

1. Press the Alt and B keys to boldface lines. You have to press these keys a second time to close the boldfacing if there is unbolded text to follow on the same line.
2. Press Caps Lock on for appropriate lines.
3. Use the Tab key to place the cursor in the correct column for the Education, Work Experience, Awards, and Special Skills entry labels. PC-Write doesn't adjust columns for font symbols that are inserted in the text when it moves the cursor with the Tab key. The font symbols can be turned off and on, however, by pressing the Alt key and the Space Bar. The Tab key will then ignore the presence of the font symbol in moving from place to place.
4. Use the Tab key before typing the professional goal, "To work . . ."
5. At the end of each entry line in Education and Work Experience, press the Enter key twice. The entries for Awards and Special Skills should be broken with an Enter key since word wrap will continue text at the left margin. The entry for Professional Goal should not be word wrapped.
6. The underlining of text is accomplished in a fashion similar to boldfacing. Press Alt and U, for underlining before you start typing the words to be underlined. The underline symbol ⍖ will appear. The underlining symbol can be hidden/unhidden with the Alt-Space Bar key combination.

SUGGESTIONS FOR MODIFICATION

Harriet Hartley took her résumé to a Career Planning Counselor for the counselor to critique. The counselor suggested several changes to the résumé to convey the most important facts about Harriet's background to potential employers more effectively. Among the changes suggested by the counselor were:

1. The career goal was too vague. It should be specific to a particular vocation.
2. The work experience section emphasized the agencies Harriet had worked for,not the positions that she had held.
3. The work experiences for the University and the retail store should be reversed since they were not in descending chronological order.
4. The two educational experiences should be in reverse chronological order.

Deleting Blocks of Text

Harriet decided to change the Professional Goal to "A marketing position in a computer company." To make this change, place the cursor on the left margin preceding the sentence explaining Harriet's Professional Goal. You will delete the two-line entry with a block delete. Notice that the function key reminder lines show F4 as the delete/mark key. Press,

F4 Function key F4, to change the status line to "Marking"
↓↓ Down arrow twice, to highlight the block defining the old sentence describing the career goal
F4 Function key F4, to delete the block

The deleted block is deleted from the file, but the block is also stored in the computer's memory in what is known as the Hold Area. The contents of the Hold Area are the last block of deleted, copied, or moved characters. You can recall the block of text from the Hold Area by pressing,

Ctrl-F4	Control and Function key F4. If you pressed the Control and F4 key again, additional copies of the Hold Area would be entered into the file. Do *not* do this. The block of retrieved text is still marked as the highlighting shows
F4	Function key F4, to delete the block
Tab	Tab key
A marketing position in a computer company.	The new position objective
↵	Enter key, to separate this section from the next section

Moving Blocks of Text

The F6 key used earlier to mark and center a block of text is also used to mark and move a block of text from one location to another. The date of employment for the student at Smith & Baker Retailers is chronologically earlier than the entry for the University. To place it behind the entry for the University it is not necessary to delete and retype the entry for Smith & Baker. Move it instead. F6 is shown in the reminder lines as the move/mark key.

In order to move the text, place your cursor on the space immediately after the phrase ''WORK EXPERIENCE:'' and press,

F6	Function key F6, to turn ''Marking'' on
↓↓↓↓↓↓	Down Arrow six times, to highlight the block of text, the blank line and the empty space up to the cursor on the line containing ''University of the Mountains''
F6	Function key F6, to ''Mark'' the block. Note the change in highlighting and the phrase, ''MARKED,'' on the status line. Keeping your cursor in the same column, move your cursor to the line on which the entry for ''Flowers Are Forever'' is placed
F6	Function key F6, to complete the move. The marked block is inserted between the University and florist shop entries
F5	Function key F5, to remove the marking

The University entry has a boldface symbol in front of it. This turns off the boldfacing started at the beginning of the line. Similarly, the retailing store line had been boldfaced because it was on the same line as ''WORK EXPERIENCE:'' but now it is no longer boldfaced since it has no boldfacing symbol. Do not correct these errors now.

In the same manner, reverse the two educational experiences as well.

The counselor suggested moving the position titles to the top of each work experience entry to emphasize what Harriet had done, not whom she had worked for. The movement of titles also uses the F6 key. Place the cursor under the underlining symbol for the first position title, ''Student Activities Programming Assistant,'' and press,

F6	Function key F6, to begin marking the block
↓	Down Arrow
F6	Function key F6, to complete the marking. Now move the cursor under the boldfacing symbol in front of the ''U'' in ''University''
F6	Function key F6. The text is re-inserted at the location of the cursor
F5	Function key F5, to remove the marking

Delete the underlining symbol in front of ''Student'' and the boldfacing symbol in front of ''University.'' Boldface the job position with Alt-B. Repeat these steps for the other positions and employers also.

Changing Case

The placement of the job titles at the top of each employment experience satisfies part of the counselor's recommendations. In addition, Harriet would like to capitalize the titles and change the agency names to lowercase except for the first letter. She does not want to have to retype all of this text, however. PC-Write uses the F8 key to change the case of a letter or of a marked block of letters.

Place your cursor on the first "t" in "Student" and press,

F8 Function key F8. The letter changes to uppercase and the cursor places itself under the next letter; ready to change it and advance again with the next pressing of the F8 key. Continue pressing F8 across the line, but using the Right Arrow key to avoid changing the case of letters that are already capitalized

Now place the cursor under the "N" in "UNIVERSITY" and repeat the process, reversing the case of the letters that should be put into lowercase. Continue this process for each of the three entries.

Remove the boldfacing characters from view by pressing the Alternate key and the Space Bar together. The résumé with the boldfacing characters invisible should now look as it does in Figure 5–5.

```
                        HARRIET HARTLEY

                        22 Elm Street
                   West Washington, NV 89888
                         707-555-5665

PROFESSIONAL GOAL:
    A marketing position with a computer company.

EDUCATION:           UNIVERSITY OF THE MOUNTAINS
                     Lake Hicauma CA 12880
                     Bachelor of Science, Business Administration
                     1989

                     WEST WASHINGTON HIGH SCHOOL
                     2100 Parker Drive
                     West Washington, NV 89888
                     Academic Diploma, 1985

WORK EXPERIENCE:     STUDENT ACTIVITIES PROGRAMMING ASSISTANT,
                     University of the Mountains
                     Lake Hicauma, CA 12880
                     Academic Year, 1987-1989

                     ASSISTANT BUYER
                     Smith & Baker Retailers
                     1 Black Oak Lane
                     West Washington, NV 89888
                     Summer, 1986-1986

                     SALES CLERK-FLORAL ARRANGER,
                     Flowers Are Forever
                     Market Square
                     West Washington, NV 89888
                     Academic Year, 1985-1986
```

Figure 5–5. Harriet Hartley's Revised Résumé.

```
AWARDS AND
SCHOOL ACTIVITIES:          Varsity Basketball, Omega Phi Beta,
                            Outstanding Student Volunteer, President's
                            Honor Roll,
                            Crisis Call Volunteer.

SPECIAL SKILLS:             Programming in BASIC and Pascal,
                            Spanish (3 Yrs.)
```

Figure 5–5—*Continued*

Notice that the words "UNIVERSITY," "STUDENT," "Varsity," and "Programming," are pulled to the left when the boldfacing symbols disappear. Insert or delete blank spaces as necessary to position the entries correctly for printing.

SAVING AND PRINTING THE FILE

The résumé is complete. Print it by pressing,

F1 Function key F1, to bring up the help menu

F7 Function key F7, to start the printing process. The file RESUME.RES is created first. You will see the prompt,

```
File to print (Esc:cancel F8:dir): "b:hartley.res"
```

↵ Enter key. If you elected to have several print rulers on the PC-Write diskette, you see the prompt screen,

```
Print control filename (Esc:exit Enter:none): "_"
```

to which you enter the filename for the printer you are currently using. Press Enter. If you have only the default printer file, you will not see this prompt. The next prompt will be,

```
Esc:Exit F9:Print to a file F10:Printer is ready
```

F10 Function key F10 if the printer is turned on and if it is connected to your computer. You will see a menu of choices that you can make while the printing is in process. The top lines of the menu are:

```
Waiting. Print from ''b:resume.res'' to ''PRN'', ready to begin.
F1:Help-screen F3:Finished F5:Input-end F7:Repeat-pages F9:Page-Stop
F2:Exit-to-DOS F4:Dos-command F6:User-Input F8:Skip-pages F10:Continuous
Show help screen, giving dot commands and other information
```

F10 Function key F10 if your printer is using continuous paper, or press F9 if the printer uses a single-sheet feeder

BACKING UP THE FILE AND EXITING THE EDITOR

When you return to the editor, save your file again (it was saved for you during printing) to your backup diskette by removing the diskette from drive B and replacing it with your backup diskette. Save the file on the backup diskette by pressing

F1 Function key F1
F3 Function key F3

Stop working on your document by pressing

F1 Function key F1
F2 Function key F2, to exit to DOS. The DOS prompt will be the next line placed on your screen

EXERCISES

A. Modify Harriet Hartley's résumé so that the two entries for education are reversed.
B. Create the following résumé using ED.RES.

DIXON MARS

557 Waterbrook Farm Rd.
Covington Cove, NH 12111
323-718-9812

PROFESSIONAL GOAL:

To employ my educational skills in the context of an exciting, upper-level, management position within an international corporation.

EMPLOYMENT:	**WEEKLY GAZETTE** Newspaper Delivery Boy, High Falls, MA 37456
	BURGER HEAVEN Short Order Cook, High Falls, MA 37456
EDUCATION:	**JOHNSON COUNT JUNIOR COLLEGE** A. S. in Business Administration, 1987
	WILSON STATE UNIVERSITY B. A. in Public Administration 1989
AWARDS AND SCHOOL ACTIVITIES:	Varsity Track (3 yrs.), Spanish Club (President), Alumni Solicitation Drive Volunteer, Ecology Club, Student Council (2yrs.), Data Processing Management Association
LANGUAGES SPOKEN:	Spanish, Russian, German

Modify the resume to make it stronger by making the following changes:
—change the professional goal to, "To work in the overseas division of an international hotel chain."
—delete the entire, weak employment history and replace it with a functional description of Mr. Mars' skills as follows:

```
FUNCTIONAL SKILLS:

PLANNING:        Developed an organized approach to the distribution
                 of student government funds to approved organizations,
                 reviewed all student organizational plans and projects,
                 served as parliamentarian

DIRECTING:       Started the Ecology Club, created the aluminum can
                 recycling effort, managed a trip to Mexico City during
                 Spring break, served as a student coordinator for
                 statewide telephone marathons

TRAVEL:          Lived in Madrid, Spain for 6 months, toured Japan for 2
                 weeks with family, attended the Study Abroad Program in
                 Bonn, West Germany, organized trip to Mexico City,
                 biked the Appalachian Trail
```

—reverse the entries under education.
—insert a section **INTERNATIONAL STUDIES COURSES:** and list the following courses:

```
ECON.   242 International Economics
MGRS.   342 International Business
PADM.   313 Independent Study-Trade Barriers in the Japanese Trade Market
LANG.   433 Russian Literature in Translation
PADM.   412 Comparative Study of Bureaucracies
Russian—4 language courses
German—6 language courses
Spanish—4 language courses
```

—delete the languages spoken section

C. Use ED.RES to create your own résumé for use in job seeking.

Chapter 6

Advanced Word Processing: A Term Paper

CHAPTER OUTLINE

Creating a Second Ruler
Invoking the Editor
Text Manipulations
    Centering and Boldfacing
    Underlining
    Reading In Use-Specific Rulers
    Indenting Paragraphs
    Returning to the Default Ruler
Saving and Printing the File
Using Dot Commands
    Margins
    Line Spacing
    Page Numbers
    Centering
    Headers and Footers
    Footnotes
    Other Dot Commands
    Using Special Fonts with Blocks of Text
    Cautions
Hiding Dot Commands
Saving and Printing the Document
Page Breaking
    Repaging
    Toggling Page Breaks
Exiting the Editor
Exercises

The documents that you have created thus far have demonstrated many of the features of PC-Write. You are now quite capable of producing many types of documents for your studies and for other purposes. Still, there are other features of which you could take advantage to give your documents a professional look. This chapter will introduce you to some of these features and, while not all of the features present can be dealt with in detail, there is no doubt that you will be able to experiment with the remaining features on your own if you wish to do so. You will

1. Develop and use two different rulers in different portions of a paper,
2. Indent paragraphs so that a number can appear inside of the left margin,

3. Insert special "dot" commands that change the appearance of a page when it is printed. The dot commands introduced can be used for including footnotes, for changing margins, for using header and footer lines and for changing from single to double spacing.

The document to be worked with in this chapter is a short class paper. On the surface it is not an apparently difficult paper to type. It uses some features that you have used before such as font changes and line centering. The indented paragraphs (lettered subsections) are different and, after the initial text has been entered, you will be adding features such as footnotes, headers, and page numbers. These are examples of features that are required for any sophisticated word processing software.

CREATING A SECOND RULER

Figure 6–1 is a short class paper produced by a student in an introduction to computing class. It is obvious by looking at the document that the first three paragraphs of the paper can be created with the default ruler created in chapter 5. That ruler looks like,

```
L--P--T--T--T--T--T--T--T--T--T--T--T---R---
^  ^  ^                       ^
|  |  Tabs every 5 spaces                65
|  5
0
```

Figure 6–1. The Default Ruler.

The default ruler has a paragraph marker "P" that automatically indents five spaces from the left hand margin with each pressing of the Enter key. This ruler will not be useful in the entry of the indented paragraphs, however, because you will have to backspace to the left-hand margin to enter the capital letters, and the text will be word wrapped to the left-hand margin. You could create a ruler from inside the editor that would handle this method of formatting, but PC-Write allows only one ruler in use at a time. This means that you could use the default ruler initially and then use the F2 key to modify the ruler to the second style. When you finish the first outline you will need to return to the default ruler—again modifying the ruler with the F2 key. You would enter but one paragraph with this ruler and then you would have to modify the ruler again.

If this paper were a twenty-page paper with similar formatting changes throughout, the constant changing of the ruler would be time consuming and perhaps inconsistent.

Fortunately, PC-Write allows you to create rulers that can be brought into a file from within the editor. That means that you can create one ruler in a process similar to that with which you created the file ED.DEF. Instead of modifying the ruler time and time again, you may read new rulers into the file whenever you need to switch. Since you are using the rulers that exist already, rather than constantly modifying the one ruler you have to work with, the rulers will be consistent from one usage to the next and it will take less time to go from one format to another.

Before you enter any of the text of the paper, you will create the second ruler that will be used for the indented paragraphs. Copy the file ED.DEF to the diskette on drive B with the command,

`copy ed.def b:ed.001`

↵ Enter key

Then modify ED.001 on drive B with the PC-Write editor. The command,

```
ed b:ed.001
```

↵	Enter key, to invoke the editor
F9	Function key F9, to make a backup file
Scroll Lock	Scroll Lock key, to put the editor into overwrite mode
Caps Lock	Caps Lock on. Modify the ruler so that the paragraph marker, "P," precedes the left margin, "L," so that the ruler looks like,

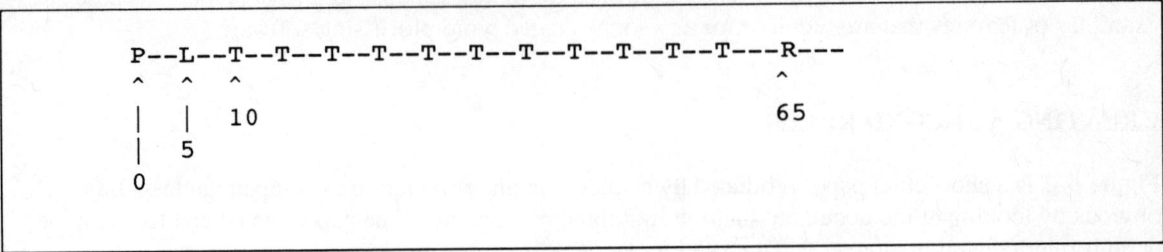

```
P--L--T--T--T--T--T--T--T--T--T--T--T---R---
^  ^  ^                                 ^
|  |  10                                65
|  5
0
```

Figure 6–2. The Modified Ruler, ED.001.

Save the file with the

F1	
F2	Function key F2, to save the file and to exit the editor

The reversal of the two letters, "L" and "P", is important. With ED.DEF when you hit the Enter key, there is an automatic indent of five spaces. As word wrap occurs the words are placed to the left of the initial indentation on the left margin. After pressing Enter with the new ruler, the cursor will go to the paragraph marker on the left. After the first line of a paragraph, word wrap will be to the left margin, which is to the right of the paragraph marker. You will see this when the two rulers are put to work.

INVOKING THE EDITOR

Begin the creation of the new file with the command,

```
ed b:paper
```

↵	Enter key which, since no extension is given, will cause PC-Write to use the default ruler ED.DEF.
F9	Function key F9, to continue when the Registration/Copyright screen appears. If you wish, you can check the appearance of the ruler ED.DEF
F2	Function key F2, to see the default ruler. Notice that the cursor is at the left margin
F2	Function key F2, to put the ruler into the background

Figure 6–3 displays the paper you are going to create. After text has been entered, the ruler will automatically indent the first word of each paragraph. Do not use tabs or the text will automatically indent to the tab mark following the paragraph marker. Read the additional instructions in the section "Text Manipulations" before typing anything.

THE PROS AND CONS OF WORD PROCESSING

JOHN KNOWSIT

I. INTRODUCTION TO WORD PROCESSING

There are many ways in which computers can operate on textual information. Text editors are normally used to create programs or data to be processed by programs. Text editors are not adapted to preparing letters, term papers, and other documents. They have little capability for formatting the text in a variety of styles. Some programming languages, most notably SNOBOL, are adept at analyzing text files, but they are almost useless for preparing normal business and personal communications.

Word processors and text formatters, software designed to produce written documents, are improving steadily. Word processors are generally categorized as displaying a document on the computer monitor in much the same appearance as that of the printed document. Text formatters, on the other hand, produce files in which there are large numbers of ''dot'' commands that will be used by the formatter to guide printing. The file looks substantially different from the eventual printed document since word filling, footnotes, margin settings, and type faces are not arranged by the formatter until the document is printed.

II. ADVANTAGES OF WORD PROCESSING

Word processing software capabilities have been developing rapidly. The number of word processing packages is large and the number of persons who use word processors in their work and for personal usage is also substantial. Many people do not begin to utilize all of the capabilities their word processors possess, but they are likely to realize at least some of the advantages noted by some of the writers who have studied the use of word processing in industry. Among the advantages of word processors and text formatters are the following:

A. Reduced Cost. Errors can be corrected rapidly, greatly reducing the time involved in producing a document. Of greater importance, revisions to documents are significantly less costly than are complete retypings of documents.

B. Reduced Production Time. When documents are revised, the editor need only proofread the altered text for accuracy. Previously acceptable text will not have changed. This is different from typed text in which an entire document must be reread to be certain that new errors have not slipped in.

Figure 6–3. John Knowsit's Paper.

C. Efficient Staff Usage. Documents can be entered by relatively untrained, lower-cost typists. Corrections and complex formatting can be turned over to more skilled word processing operators in later revisions.

D. Higher Quality Output. Because revisions are easy to make, managers and other writers are less hesitant to revise and reprint documents until they are precisely correct.

III. DISADVANTAGES OF WORD PROCESSING

Even though there is almost universal agreement that word processing is an essential element in the modern business environment, there are drawbacks to its usage. These disadvantages include:

A. Cost. Word processors are significantly more expensive to buy and maintain than are standard typewriters. Personnel must be trained to use the word processors.

B. Vendor Dependence. Each word processing software package is unique. Document files cannot be easily shared, if at all, between different word processors or word processing software packages. Once a company has committed itself to one approach, change is costly.

C. Professional Time Lost. Many people who used to dictate or write out documents by hand find that they prefer to type their own drafts of documents. They may then find that they prefer to do the editing themselves because it is faster than writing notes about changes to be made and then having to explain the notes to a secretary. To be certain the document is correct, they print it out. Before you know it a professional being paid $40,000 a year is doing the job of a $15,000 a year secretary.

D. Word Processing Inadequacies. There are many differences among word processors. Even with the best word processors there will be special capabilities like equation formatting, table production and interfaces with type setting equipment that are not available. The production of some documents may be difficult and the organization may find that several different word processors will be needed to meet all of the company's needs, thereby leading to further incompatibilities.

IV. CONCLUSION

It is clear that the introduction of word processors has had a significant impact on the corporate work place. This impact will become even greater in the future. Despite a number of problems associated with word processing, the advantages are notably greater. Although there is no objective way to document this in every respect, it is obvious that industry has concluded that this is the case with every software package purchased.

Figure 6–3—*Continued*

TEXT MANIPULATIONS

Centering and Boldfacing

The first line is boldfaced and centered. Do this by pressing,

Alt-B	Key combination first
Caps Lock	Caps Lock on

THE PROS AND CONS OF WORD PROCESSING

The title of the paper

Shift-F8	Shift and Function key F8, to center the line
↵	Enter key

Enter and center the next line of text (without boldfacing) in the same manner. Press the Enter key twice to move the cursor down two lines.

Because you are using the ED.DEF ruler, each time you press Enter the cursor goes to the indented position for a new paragraph, not to the left margin. Before typing in the heading, ''I. INTRODUCTION TO WORD PROCESSING,'' press

Home	The Home key, to place the cursor on the left margin

Underlining

The line beginning with the Roman numeral ''I'' should be preceded with the typing of the Alt and U key combination to underline the text. The underlining will stop at the end of the line. Use the same technique for underlining the two additional lines with Roman numerals as they occur in the text.

Enter the first three paragraphs and stop when you reach the end of the paragraph immediately before the first subsection, ''A.''

Reading in Use-Specific Rulers

At this point it is desirable to read in the ruler ED.001 that was created specifically to format the indented paragraph portion of the paper. Do this by pressing

F2	Function key F2, to view the default ruler and a ruler menu
F6	Function key F6, to read the ruler (from file), which will give the prompt,

```
control file to read (Esc:cancel F8:dir):"pr.def"
```

b:ed.001	The name of the file containing the replacement ruler
↵	Enter key. The new default ruler appears in the reminder lines
F2	Function key F2, to confirm that the ruler has changed. The paragraph marker is now to the left of the left margin
F2	Function key F2, to put the ruler away

Indenting Paragraphs

Use the new ruler by pressing,

↵↵	Enter key. The cursor moves to the left margin. It does not indent as it did before
`A.`	The label for the paragraph
`Tab`	Tab key
`Alt-U`	Alternate and U pressed simultaneously
`Reduced Cost.`	The subheading
`Alt-U`	Alternate and U pressed simultaneously, to turn underlining off

Continue typing the paragraph. As word wrap occurs, you will see the ruler's left margin (which is to the right of the paragraph marker) is used to keep the paragraph indented. The label "A." is "hanging" inside of the temporary left margin.

In the same way, enter the paragraphs labeled B, C, and D.

Returning to the Default Ruler

At the end of paragraph D of section II, press,

`F2`	Function key F2, to obtain the ruler on the screen
`F6`	Function key F6
`ed.def`	The new ruler name typed in response to the prompt
↵	Enter key

Enter the next subsection. At the end of the paragraph use F2 and F6 to return to ED.001. You will have to retrieve ED.DEF for the concluding subsection.

Keeping these instructions in mind, create the paper.

SAVING AND PRINTING THE FILE

The paper is complete. Print it by pressing,

`F1`	Function key F1, to bring up the help/system menu
`F7`	Function key F7, to start the printing process. You will see the prompt,

```
File to print (Esc:cancel F8:dir): "b:paper"
```

↵ Enter key, If you elected to have several print rulers on the PC-Write diskette, you see the prompt screen,

```
Print control filename (Esc:exit Enter:none): "_"
```

to which you enter the filename for the printer you are currently using; for instance, OKI or EPSON. Then press Enter. If you have only the default printer file, you will not see this prompt. The next prompt will be,

```
Esc:Exit F9:Print to disk F10:Printer is ready
```

`F10` Function key F10. If the printer is turned on, and is connected to your computer. You will see a menu of choices that you can make while the printing is in process The top lines of the menu are:

```
Waiting. Print from "b:paper" to "PRN", ready to begin.
F1:Help-screen F3:Finished F5:Input-end F7:Repeat-pages F9:Page-Stop
F2:Exit-to-DOS F4:Dos-command F6:User-Input F8:Skip-pages F10:Continuous
Show help screen, giving dot commands and other information
```

F10 Function key F10. If your printer is using continuous paper or press F9 if the printer uses a single-sheet feeder

USING DOT COMMANDS

PC-Write is not truly a "What You See Is What You Get" word processor. The documents created so far have printed out as they appeared on the screen with the exception of alternate font symbols. In many ways, as exemplified by the current document, the printed output is crude. You have probably only begun to sense that there are additional controls you would like to have over the final appearance.

Many of these controls are provided by commands that appear in the file, but do not print when the file is printed. The "Dot Commands" are PC-Write commands are on highlighted lines called Guide Lines and begin with a period. Guide Lines are created by pressing the Alt and G keys simultaneously. Guide Lines often are identified with the symbol ♂ which is created by the pressing of Alt and G.

Margins

The rulers used to create files generally place the text in acceptable locations with respect to the left and right margins. They have no effect on the top and bottom margins, however, which are typically too small to be acceptable. To change the top margin of the file PAPER, press,

Shift-↑ Shift and Up Arrow, to bring the cursor to the top line

Shift-← Shift and Left Arrow, to bring the cursor to the left edge of the top line of the file. The dot command for you to type that will control the top margin is,

Alt-G Alternate and G pressed simultaneously. To produce what PC-Write calls a Guide Line for dot commands

.XT:2 The "." designates the start of a dot command, the "XT" stands for "eXtra top margin," and the ":2" stands for two extra top lines before the text of the document begins to be printed. Notice that the title has been moved over

↵ Enter key, to leave the dot command on its own line

Leave two extra blank lines at the bottom of the page by typing on the next line,

Alt-G To produce a Guide Line

.XB:2

↵ Enter key, to complete the insertion of the Guide Line.

Line Spacing

By placing the command "M:2" on a line by itself, the document will be double spaced. The number 2 can be replaced by any reasonable number. If you needed to alternate between double and single spacing, you would use this command and "M:1" to return to single spacing.

You can experiment with this command at another time.

Page Numbers

Any document that exceeds two pages should have its pages numbered. Continue at the same location by entering,

`Alt-G`	To produce a Guide Line
`.N:1`	The command to begin numbering at the top of the first page with the number one.
↵	Enter key
`Alt-G`	To produce a Guide Line
.H: . . . $$$ . . .	The command to set up a header line (*see* following). The pair of ellipses (". . .") places the page number, represented by the "$$$," in the center of the header line. Omission of the first ellipsis will place the number on the left side of the line, while omission of the second ellipsis will place the number on the right side
↵	Enter key

Dot commands that affect whole pages take affect at the top of the page following the command. If page numbering was to begin on the second page (no number on the first page), precede the .H: . . . $$$ . . . line by a completely blank line. To separate the page number from the body of the text, follow the .H . . . $$$ . . . line with one or more .H: lines (with no text following the colon) to create blank header lines after the page number.

Centering

The title has been shifted by the procedures used above. Center the title by placing the cursor behind the title and pressing,

`Shift-F8`	Shift and Function key F8, the centering key

Headers and Footers

On long documents it is often desirable to have common identification lines at the top and/or bottom of each page called headers and footers, respectively. You might want to identify the pages with one or more identifiers as:a date; the words "Draft" or "Top Secret"; or the title of the document. For this paper, include the footer line at the bottom of the page.

`Alt-G`	To produce a Guide Line
`.F: ...`	`Draft ...` The footer line to identify the pages
↵	Enter key, to place the footer line on a line by itself

Header lines would use the ".H:header line" format. Text should not follow a dot command on the same line. The title which shifted to the left margin is placed back in the center of the line by putting the cursor behind the title and pressing,

`Shift-F8`	Shift and F8 pressed simultaneously, to center the title

Footnotes

In typing, the placement of footnotes is always a challenge. You must keep track of the number of lines you have typed and leave enough space to put the footnote(s) at the bottom. Small miscalculations may cause you to have to retype an entire page. PC-Write takes care of these calculations for you.

Assume that you wished to include a footnote citation to document the conclusion in the first paragraph that some forms of word processing don't work well. Do this by placing your cursor immediately behind the last character of the first paragraph and type an asterisk to indicate that a footnote is given. Press,

*	Asterisk, to indicate that a footnote is made for this sentence. A number could be substituted here
↲	Enter key, to start a new line. Then enter the following set of lines at the left edge to create a footnote
Alt-G	To produce a Guide Line
.DB	The dot command for the beginning of a footnote. The "D" stands for "Down" and the "B" stands for "begin"
↲	Enter key

*See Wells, M. T. "Approaches to Word Processing," Journal of Spurious Results, Vol. 10, Number 13, May, 1989, pp. 22–24.

↲	Enter key
Alt-G	To produce a Guide Line
.DQ	The "Q" stands for "Quit," or "End of Footnote." Some of the text is underlined with the Alt and U key combination. Additional footnotes could be added throughout the document in this way

Other Dot Commands

PC-Write uses many dot commands that give it considerable flexibility. A partial list of these commands and the commands described above is given in Figure 6–4. Remember that all dot commands must be created by simultaneously pressing Alt and G before the remainder of the command is entered.

DOT COMMAND	EFFECT
..<test>	Ignored when printing starts
.DB	Begin footnote
.DQ	End footnote
.F:<test>	Footer line including page no. position
.H:<test>	Header line including page no. position
.L:<number>	Page length change
.M:<number>	Line spacing change
.N:<number>	Page number
.X:<number>	Add extra space to left margin on every page
.XB:<number>	Add extra space to bottom margin
.XT:<number>	Add extra space to top margin
.XF:<text>	Add extra footer line
.XH:<text>	Add extra header line
...	Used to separate header/footer entries. The dots will center an entry between dots (e.g. .F: ... Draft ...), or place it on the right if one set of dots is to the left of the entry (e.g. .F: ... Draft)

Figure 6–4. Basic Dot Commands.

Using Special Fonts with Blocks of Text

It is awkward to use the alternate font style characters to begin and stop the font styles when the text to be affected covers multiple lines. It takes time to put in all of the special font symbols and if a paragraph is reformatted the symbols may interfere with one another or may produce incorrect results. Although it is not needed in this paper, the following dot commands could be used to bold an entire paragraph:

```
.R:B
This is a paragraph that is to be bolded. Even though
it covers several lines, each line will be bolded. There
are no special font characters that appear on any of the
lines.
.Q:B
```

In this example, the command, ''.R:B'' turns the bolding on for all text up to the ''.Q:B'' which turns the bolding off.

Cautions

Dot commands must be preceded by the entering of Alternate and G to have any effect. Without the Guide Line highlighting, the command will be treated as though it is regular text—it will be printed.

Some dot commands such as .M, which changes line spacing and .D which creates a footnote, can appear anywhere on a page. They take effect immediately. Other commands that affect the entire appearance of a page must appear before the page begins to print. Header and footer commands, for instance, must be examined by PC-Write before the printing of a page is begun.

HIDING DOT COMMANDS

In an earlier chapter you saw that the pressing of the Alt and Space bar turned off the appearance of the special symbols that indicated the use of special fonts. The same combination of keys will hide the dot commands. Practice this. Before proceeding, examine the appearance of the top of your file. See that it now looks like that pictured in Figure 6–5. If it does not, edit it now.

```
.XT:2
.XB:2
.N:1
.H: ... $$$ ...
.F: ... DRAFT ...

                THE PROS AND CONS OF WORD PROCESSING
                            JOHN KNOWSIT

I. INTRODUCTION TO WORD PROCESSING

     There are many ways in which computers can operate on
textual information. Text editors are normally used to create
programs or data to be processed by programs. Text editors
are not adapted to preparing letters, term papers, and other
documents. They have little capability for formatting the text
in a variety of styles. Some programming languages, most notably
Snobol, are adept at analyzing text files, but they are almost
useless for preparing normal business and personal
communications.*
```

Figure 6–5.

```
|.DB

*See Wells, M. T. "Approaches to Word Processing," Journal of
Spurious Results, Vol. 10, Number 13, May 1989, pp.22-24.

.DQ

Word processors and text formatters, software designed to . . .
```

Figure 6–5—*Continued*

SAVING AND PRINTING THE DOCUMENT

The paper is ready to be printed. Print PAPER by pressing,

F1 Function key F1, to bring up the help/system menu

F7 Function key F7, to start the printing process. You will see the prompt,

File to print (Esc:cancel F8:dir): "b:paper"

↵ Enter key. If you elected to have several print rulers on the PC-Write diskette, you see the prompt screen,

```
Print control filename (Esc:exit Enter:none): "_"
```

to which you enter the filename for the printer you are currently using; for instance, OKI or EPSON. Press Enter. If you have only the default printer file you will not see this prompt. The next prompt will be,

```
Esc:Exit F9:Print to a file F10:Printer is ready
```

F10 Function key F10, if the printer is turned on and is connected to your computer. You will see a menu of choices that you can make while the printing is in process. The top lines of the menu are:

```
Waiting. Print from "b:paper" to "PRN", ready to begin.
F1:Help-screen F3:Finished F5:Input-end F7:Repeat-pages F9:Page-Stop
F2:Exit-to-DOS F4:Dos-command F6:User-Input F8:Skip-pages F10:Continuous
Show help screen, giving dot commands and other information
```

F10 Function key F10, if your printer is using continuous paper, or press F9 if the printer uses a single-sheet feeder

PAGE BREAKING

As you look at your document you will see that at the bottom of page 1, the heading, "DISADVANTAGES OF WORD PROCESSING," appears without the paragraph that follows. A document looks better if at least two lines of the text follow immediately after the heading introducing that section. Since this is not possible, it is desirable to force the printer to move to the next page before this heading appears. If the heading is placed at the top of the next page, the text will appear in association with the heading.

The command for forcing the printer to eject to the next page is called a "hard" page break. A "soft" page break is the page break that is entered by PC-Write when it determines when it has printed as many lines on a page as it can. Put a hard page break in your document by placing your cursor under the first letter in the heading and pressing,

`Alt-T` Alternate and T keys pressed simultaneously. The symbols ♀ ☼ appear signifying that the page will break at that point during printing

Repaging

PC-Write will automatically break the pages when necessary. It does not, however, show you where soft occur unless you ask it to. To see this, press,

`Alt-` Alternate and (non-grey) Minus Sign, to move the cursor to the top of the document
`Alt-F7` The Page Breaks Menu which appears as

```
Esc F1 F5:Menu:All F6.Fill-Page F7.Nex-Page F8.Hard/Soft PgUpDn.Move-UpDn
```

`F5` Function key F5, to select "Menu:All"
`F5` Function key F5, to repage the entire document. The status line returns

Move through the document with the Shift-PgUp/PgDn key combination to see the symbol ♀ followed by page numbers. These are the soft page breaks. The hard page break has a page number appended to it as well.

Toggling Page Breaks

Pressing the Alternate key and the Space Bar not only hides dot commands, but it also changes the appearance of soft and hard page breaks. This action will change the symbols to a row of equal signs. By checking these markings you can determine whether page breaks will occur in correct locations before you take the time and go to the expense of printing your document. If you see that a break occurs in the wrong place, you should force a hard page break above the point of the soft break.

Follow the directions given under "Saving and Printing the Document" section of this chapter to print out your paper.

EXITING THE EDITOR

The printing procedure automatically saved your document. Save the file on your backup diskette by removing the diskette from drive B and replacing it with your backup diskette. Save the file on the backup diskette by pressing,

`F1` Function key F1
`F3` Function key F3, to save the file
`F2` Function key F2, to exit the editor

EXERCISES

A. Use PC-Write to produce your next term paper or class assignment.
B. Select sections of this or some other book that uses underlining, boldfacing, indented paragraphs, columns, or other special formatting features and try to reproduce them with PC-Write.

C. Using the paper, "THE PROS AND CONS OF WORD PROCESSING," produced in this chapter, create a third ruler for indenting four entries under the paragraph entitled, "A. Reduced Cost." Revise the paragraph to include the subentries shown below.

```
A.   Reduced Cost. Errors can be corrected rapidly, greatly
     reducing the time involved in producing a document. Of
     greater importance, revisions to documents are significantly
     less costly than are complete retypings of documents.
     1. Cheap printers can produce draft work,
     2. Laser printers can produce final documents,
     3. Proofreaders do not have to reread entire documents,
     4. Document files can be accessed by some typesetters.
```

Then use the same ruler to add entries beneath the paragraph entitled, "D. Higher Quality Output," so that it appears as,

```
D.   Higher Quality Output. Because revisions are easy to make,
     managers and other writers are less hesitant to revise and reprint
     documents until they are precisely correct.
     1. Laser printers can be acquired,
     2. Spelling checkers and thesauruses can be used,
     3. Documents can be merged and reused,
     4. Data from spreadsheets and databases can be added.
```

Save this file as PAPER2.

Chapter 7

Using the Spelling Checker

CHAPTER OUTLINE

INTRODUCTION TO SPELLING CHECKER

Modern word processing tools have moved beyond simply allowing you to type text into documents. Spelling checkers, thesauruses, and grammar checking programs are also available. Sometimes these programs are provided with a word processor and sometimes they are "add ons" that are acquired separately. PC-Write has a versatile spelling checker that allows you to check the last word you typed for incorrect spelling and to search your document for any misspelled words it may contain. It also lets you catch misspellings automatically as you type. If it finds a misspelled word, it will display a selection of similar correctly spelled words. If one of these is the word you were trying to spell, you can select it and it will replace the misspelled word automatically.

A master word list called WORDS.MAS contains 50,000 words and is located on the working copy of the PC-Write Word List disk. The WORKDISK program copies the file WORDS.MAS on to this working diskette. The original copy of this file is on the PC-Write Reference Disk. The first time you use the spelling checker during the tutorial, the master list is loaded into RAM so PC-Write can access it. You can also create personalized or custom word lists, although only one can be loaded into memory at a time. These "user lists" should be composed of words that you use frequently but are not in the master list, perhaps because the words are proper names or technical terms that are not important to many other people. You may have to use the spelling checker for a while before you determine which words you use often enough to require being added to the master list. When you call up the spelling checker menu the spelling checker has access to the words in these files; you can add more words to the user list as you edit.

The PC-Write spelling checker does not actually identify misspellings. More accurately, it determines whether the word it is checking is in the master or user list. Thus, a word may be correctly spelled but it may be ''flagged'' simply because the spelling checker doesn't recognize it. One and two letter ''words'' are ignored.

In this chapter you will gain knowledge of how to use the spelling checker. Specifically, you will use these spelling checker options:

1. Check the last word you typed;
2. Turn automatic spell checking on and off;
3. Guess at a correction for the misspelled word;
4. Scan for the next or prior word that is not in the master or user list.
5. Create a custom user word list;
6. Load the user list into the computer's memory;
7. Add a word to the user list;
8. Save the user list to a file;

There are three basic ways to use the spelling checker: check the last word you typed, have PC-Write automatically check each word as you type it, or scan the entire file for a misspelling.

USING THE SPELLING CHECKER

Boot your computer, and obtain the ''A'' prompt. Place the working copy of your PC-Write diskette in drive A and your files diskette in drive B. Load PC-Write and create the following document with the filename SPELL.CK on drive B. There are several words deliberately misspelled. These errors should be typed as they appear. You will use the spelling checker to correct them. If you make additional mistakes, they can also be corrected later. The example words in quotation marks are correct and need not be changed.

```
                 SPELLING ERRORS IN THE ENGLISH LANGUAGE

     Several words in the English languag are misspelled every
day. It is very difficult to spell words correctly for many
different reasons. Mistakes are made every day in all typse of
businesses around the country.
     Some words are not spelled as they sound, for exampel,
"laughter," "conscience," "sophomore" and "sergeant."
     Homophones are words that sound exactly the same but are
spelled differently and have different meanings, for example,
"there" and "their," "to," "two," and "too," "capitol" and "capital."
     Many words are pronounced wiht the vowel sound "uh" which is
confusing and jard to speel correctly, for example, "sensible,"
"capable," and "defiant."
     Varous misspellings are doe to mispronunciation over time,
sych as in "accidently" for "accidentally," or "disasterous" for
"disas trous."
     Other misspellings are due to typographical erors or jusf
plan carelessness.
```

Figure 7–1. Spelling Check Test File.

```
    Using the spelling checker featire on persnal computer
ssoftware can practically eliminate thes common spelling problems
and/or errors. Learning such a feature on the copmuter can be
very beneficial and time saving.
```

Figure 7–1—*Continued*

When you have finished typing the paragraph, place your cursor at the top of document by pressing,

Alt-= Alternate and Equal sign keys, to place the cursor at the top of the document

Take the working copy of the PC-Write program diskette out of drive A and place the PCW Word List diskette in drive A. Enter,

Alt-F2 Alternate and F2 keys pressed simultaneously. You will be notified that the master word list is being loaded and that you should wait. Shortly you will see the spelling checker menu appears across the top of the screen as:

`Esc F1 F2:Check F3:Guess F4:Add-word F5:Load F6:Save F7:Auto± Grey±:Sp±`

Esc Escape key. You have now loaded the word list into RAM, have left the spelling checker menu, and are at the main menu

Check the Last Word You Typed

At times you will want to check the spelling of one word, perhaps the last word that you typed. You will now check a word that has already been typed. Place your cursor anywhere under the word ''languag'' on the first line of your article.

Alt-F2 Alternate and F2 key pressed simultaneously, to recall the spelling checker menu.
F2 Function key F2, to check the last word you typed. Since the word is incorrectly spelled it doesn't exist in the master or user list, the top line reads:

Unknown word (Esc:Edit F3:Guess F:4 Add Grey+:Scan): "language"
If the word had been found in the master list, this line would show:
Found in master list: "language"
If the word had been found in the user-developed list, this line would show:
Found in user list: "language"

At this point, all spelling checker options are available: you can press Esc (but not yet) to edit the word yourself; F3 (but don't) to have the spelling checker guess at a correct spelling or; F4 (but don't) to add ''language'' to the user list. Since there is a typing error, correct the word.

Esc The Escape key, to leave the spelling checker menu and to edit the word yourself. The status line returns to the top of the screen. Type the letter ''e'' correctly at the end of the word ''languag'', on the first line

Place the cursor behind the word ''difficult'' in the second line of the paragraph and enter,

Alt-F2 Alternate and the F2 keys pressed simultaneously, the spelling checker menu appears again

F2 Function key F2, to check the last word you typed. Since the word ''difficult'' is on the master word list, the top line reads:

```
Found in master word list:''difficult''
```

Esc Escape key twice, to return to the editor

Turn Automatic Spell Checking On and Off

PC-Write has the ability to check words for correctness as you type them. Before proceeding, notice that the status line displays ''Se-.'' The letter next to the ''S'' indicates whether the grey keys are being used for the *e*ditor or for the *s*peller. The minus or plus sign indicates whether the automatic spell checking function is activated. The options are as follows:

Se-	Normal editing is on and automatic spell checking is off
Se+	Normal editing is on and automatic spell checking is on
Sp-	Spell search is on and automatic spell checking is off
Sp+	Spell search is on and automatic spell checking is on

Figure 7–2. Status Line Options for Spell Status.

Activate it by pressing,

Alt-F2 Alternate and F2 keys pressed simultaneously,to bring up the spelling checker menu

F7 To turn on automatic spell checking. The status line now reads,

```
Esc: Menu Push Wrap+ Se+ R:F 94% 1/1, 1 Edit "b:spell.ck"
```

The plus sign in SP+ or SE+ means that the automatic spelling checker has been toggled on. Now every word that you might type (but don't) will be checked. If a word is not found, the computer beeps at you. Try this by entering,

Space Bar Space Bar, to place a space after the last word

doog The misspelling of the word, ''dog''

Space Bar Space Bar. Listen for the beep noting that the word is misspelled

Backspace Backspace 6 times to erase the misspelled word

Try this feature again with the word, ''spellng,'' but after the misspelling is detected backspace and correct the word as ''spelling.'' Then the spelling checker will not beep. You may leave the word in place.

Alt-F2 Alternate and the F2 keys pressed simultaneously, bringing up the spelling checker menu

F7 Function key F7, to turn the automatic spelling checker off. The status line now reads,

```
Esc: Menu Push Wrap+ Se- R:F 101/530, 1 Edit "B:project.1"
```

The minus sign in Se- or Sp- means that the spelling checker has been toggled off. PC-Write will not beep when a misspelled word is entered.

Guess at a Correction for a Misspelled Word

Place your cursor behind the word ''typse'' in line three of the paragraph.

`Alt-F2`	Alternate and the F2 keys pressed simultaneously. The spelling checker menu appears
`F2`	Function key F2, to check the spelling of the word, ''typse.'' PC-Write reports that the word is unknown
`F3`	Function key F3, to guess at a correction for a misspelled word. The top line reads,

```
Esc F1 Arrows:Select F10:Replace: types tease tense terse these those typed types typos
```

''Typse'' is the misspelled word and ''types'' is PC-Write's best guess at the correctly spelled word. When guessing, the spelling checker only considers words starting with the same letters as the incorrect word. PC-Write selected the correct guess, but if it did not, the right arrow key would be used to select the correct guess

`F10`	Function key F10, to replace ''typse'' with ''types''. Notice the correction is made, you are returned to the editor and the status line reappears

Place the cursor behind ''exampel'' in the second paragraph.

`Alt-F2`	Alternate and the F2 keys pressed simultaneously, the spelling checker menu appears. Since it is apparent that the word, ''exampel,'' is misspelled, you need not press F2 to have PC-Write determine the same thing
`F3`	Function key F3, to guess at a correction for a misspelled word without marking it as being misspelled with the F2 key. Notice at the top of the screen the suggestion of ''example'' for ''exampel''. PC-Write has only one guess to make
`F10`	Function key F10, to replace the incorrect word with the correct word. The incorrect word ''exampel'' is replaced with the correctly spelled word ''example''

Scan a File for the Next Word Not in the Master or User List

Rather than having to visually search for misspelled words, you can have PC-Write find the misspelled words.

`Alt-=`	Alternate and Equal sign pressed simultaneously, to place the cursor at the top of your document
`Alt-F2`	Alternate and the F2 keys pressed simultaneously, bringing up the spelling checker menu
`Grey+`	Grey Plus key, to initiate the search. You will briefly see the prompt,

```
Processing spelling check; 34% thru; Esc:Cancel, F9:Faster
```

The first word in the file, that is not in either the master or the user word list, will be highlighted. The word ''Homophones'' is highlighted. The top line reads,

```
Unknown word (Esc:Edit F3:Guess F4:Add Grey± Scan: "homophones")
```

Since the word ''homophones'' is not on the Master or User Lists; the word is assumed to be incorrect and will be ''flagged.'' If this was a word that you used frequently, you would add it to your personal list and save it for future reference. Since you will not save the word press,

`Grey+`	Grey Plus key, to leave, ''Homophones,'' alone and to move the next misspelled word. The word ''wiht'' is marked. The computer recognizes that the word ''wiht'' is not on either of the spelling lists

F3	Function key F3, to guess at the correct spelling. The spelling checker lists several choices of words to replace the incorrect word
→	Right arrow as necessary until you highlight the correct spelling of the word "with"
F10	Function key F10, to replace "wiht" correctly to "with," and to return to the main menu
Alt-F2	Alternate and the F2 keys pressed simultaneously, to bring up the spelling checker menu
Grey+	Grey Plus key, to find the next misspelled word

The next word identified by the spelling checker is "jard." The spelling checker will not guess at "hard," because the correctly spelled word starts with an "h." The spelling checker will only guess with words that start with a "j."

Esc	Escape key, to edit the word yourself
h	To enter the correct starting letter
Del	To delete the "j" from the word

Scan a File for the First Previous Word Not in the Master or User List

When the spelling checker is toggled on (when the status line displays either Se+ or Sp+), pressing the Grey Plus key finds the first misspelled word toward the bottom of the document. Pressing the Grey Minus key finds the next misspelled word toward the top of the document.

Alt–	Alternate and (non-grey) Minus keys pressed simultaneously, to place the cursor at the bottom of the document
Grey-	Grey Minus key. The first previous word in the file that is not in either list will be highlighted, "copmuter" is highlighted. It should be "computer"
F3	Function key F3, to guess the word. "computer," is highlighted
F10	Function key F10, to replace the misspelled word with the correctly spelled word

USER LISTS

The "User List" is a file of words created by you, the user, that are not in the WORDS.MAS file. These words are words that you use frequently and want to save on a list to be checked by the spelling checker. There is only one user file available and PC-Write uses the filename WORDS.USE as the default filename.

Create Your Own Custom User Word List

With PC-Write, we will create a file on your working diskette. PC-Write automatically looks for and loads a file called WORDS.USE, so you may want to call your main user list this. The first time you used the spelling checker, PC-Write loaded the master list WORDS.MAS in your computer's memory. When you check a word for misspelling, the spelling checker looks in this file and in WORDS.USE to see whether the word is present in either file. If you want the spelling checker to look in a different user word list, you must load that file into memory in place of WORDS.USE. You can only have one user word list in memory at a time.

Load a User List into the Computer's Memory

You need to exit this program and return to drive A to create the WORDS.USE file. To do this you must first save your work, then create the file, then return to your tutorial. Replace the utility disk in drive A with the PC-Write program disk.

F1	Function key F1, to bring up the System/Help menu
F3	To save the file B:SPELL.CK
F1	Function key F1, to bring up the System/Help menu
F6	Function key F6 1, to create the file WORDS.USE without exiting from PC-Write
a:words.use	To create the file WORDS.USE, the user-created list of words
↵	Enter key, to create the file
F9	Function key F9, to create WORDS.USE
F2	Function key F2, to recall the default ruler in use
Scroll Lock	Scroll Lock key, to change the status line to "Over." Change the ruler so that the starting markers are,

```
L----T----T----T----T----
```

The words to be placed in WORDS.USE should be placed on separate lines and all words should begin in column one

F2	Function key F2, to store the new default ruler which will allow the words to be entered at the extreme left hand side of the file

Enter the following list of words with each word typed on a separate line in lowercase and arranged in alphabetical order. Since the spelling checker is on automatic and these words are not in the WORDS.MAS file, you will hear a beep each time you press the Enter key. These words will be the contents of your WORDS.USE file.

```
alt
homophone
words.mas
workdisk
```

Save the file by entering,

F1	Function key F1, to call up the System/Help Menu
F2	Function key F2, to save the file and to exit PC-Write

Retrieve the document SPELL.CK by entering,

ed b:spell.ck	Edit the file named SPELL.CK on drive B
↵	Enter key, to initiate the editing
F9	Function key F9, to make a backup copy

Place the PCW Word List disk in drive A. These are the steps you will follow to load the list:

Alt-F2	Alternate and Function key F2, to recall the spelling checker menu
F7	Function key F7, to turn automatic spell checking on
Alt-F2	Alternate and Function key F2, to recall the spelling checker menu
F5	Function key F5, to load the list. The top line reads,

```
Esc F1 F8:Index search file F9:Shorthand file F10:User wordlist spell file
```

F10	Function key F10, to begin the loading of the file WORDS.USE. The file is loaded into the computer's memory and is available to the spelling checker
↵	Enter key, to accept the default user word list, ".\words.use," suggested by PC-Write. The status line returns to the screen
Alt-	Alternate and non-grey Minus Sign, to place your cursor at the bottom of the file
catt	A misspelled word

`Space Bar`	Space bar. Listen for the beep indicating that the word is misspelled and is not found in either of the two word lists in use
`homophone`	A word that previously would have caused a beep. It is accepted since it is now found in WORDS.USE
`Space Bar`	
`chemotherapy`	A word that is incorrect because it is not in the WORDS.USE list. A beep is heard.
`Space Bar`	
`workdisk`	Another word that previously would have caused a beep. It is accepted since it is now found in WORDS.USE
`Space Bar`	

Add a Word to a User List

If you have many words to add to your WORDS.USE file, it is efficient to add them as a group. As "misspelled" words are encountered, however, they can be added to WORDS.USE at that time. These two techniques enable you customize the spelling checker to your vocabulary and to your word processing needs. It will take some time and practice to find out what is on the WORDS.MAS list and to know which words you will want to add to your own word list, WORDS.USE. To add the word, "chemotherapy," to the WORDS.USE file, place your cursor behind this word and enter,

`Alt-F2`	Alternate and the F2 keys pressed simultaneously, to bring up the spelling checker menu. Place the cursor on the word you want to add to the user list currently loaded in memory
`F4`	Function key F4, to add a word to the list. The top line reads,

```
Add word to user list (Esc:Cancel): "chemotherapy"
```

"Chemotherapy" is identified as the word to be added to the user list. If necessary, you can edit the word to appear as you wish. Editing is not necessary here

↵	Enter key, to complete the addition of the word to the "user list". It is entered in alphabetical order

When you add words to the user list, you should save the file WORDS.USE to the disk.

Save the User List to Disk

`Alt-F2`	Alternate and F2 pressed simultaneously, bringing up the spelling checker menu
`F6`	Function key F6, to save the list. The top line reads,

```
Save word list to file (Esc:cancel F8:dir): "words.use"
```

↵	Enter key, to complete the operation of saving the WORDS.USE. Edit the filename in the quote marks if you are saving a different user list
`F9`	Function key F9, to complete the saving of the revised user list

If you add any words to a user list, PC-Write asks you if you want to save the updated user word files when you exit with F1 then F2, print with F1 then F7, or exit temporarily with F1 then F4.

You can merge your word list WORDS.USE into the compressed master word list WORDS.MAS. Consult the PC-Write manual for instructions on this procedure.

SPELL CHECKING RULES

Here are some of the rules PC-Write follows in applying the spelling checker to a document:

1. Words that are apostrophed with an ''s'' such as it's, Sam's, and 10's, are always accepted.
2. Other apostrophed words (contractions) can be placed in a user list.
3. Single letter and two letter words are always accepted.
4. The spelling checker does not distinguish between upper- and lowercase.
5. Spaces, normal hyphens, and punctuation marks that separate words are not evaluated.
6. The maximum word length is 19 characters.

SAVING AND PRINTING YOUR FILES

The spelling checking of the document is finished for now. The corrected version will be completed in Exercise A. To print out your document, place the working copy of the PCW Program disk in drive A and type,

F1 To bring up the help menu
F7 To start the printing process. The file SPELL.CK is created first. You will see the prompt,

```
File to print (Esc:cancel F8:dir): "SPELL.CK"
```

↲ Enter key

If you elected to have several print rulers on PC-Write diskette, you see the prompt screen,

```
Print control filename (Esc:exit Enter:none):"."
```

to which you enter the filename for the printer you are currently using

↲ Enter key, to complete the filename entered. If you have only the default printer file, you will not see this prompt. The next prompt will be,

```
Esc:Exit F9:Print to a file F10:Printer is ready
```

F10 Function key F10, to print the document

If the printer is turned on and if it is connected to your computer, you will see a menu of choices that you can make while the printing is in process. The top lines of the menu are:

```
Waiting Print from "b:spell.ck" to "PRN", ready to begin.
F1:Help-screen F3:Finished F5:Input-end F7:Repeat-pages
F2:Exit-to-DOS F4:DOS-comm F6:User-Input F8:Skip-pages
Show help screen, giving dot commands and other information
```

F10 Function key F10, if your printer is using continuous paper, or F9 if the printer is using a single-sheet feeder

BACKING UP YOUR FILE

When you return to the editor, save your file again to your backup diskette by removing the diskette from drive B and replacing it with your backup diskette. Save the file on the backup diskette by entering,

F1 Function key F1, the Help Menu key
F3 Function key F3, the Save File key

EXITING PC-Write

Exit PC-Write and return to DOS by pressing,

F1 The Help Menu key
F2 The Exit Key

EXERCISES

A. Retrieve the document, B:SPELL.CK and make these spelling corrections:

speel	spell
Varous	Various
doe	due
sych	such
erors	errors
jusf	just
plan	plain
featire	feature
persnal	personal
ssoftware	software
thes	these

Make any other spelling corrections that may need to be made.

B. Create a one page letter to a principal asking for something to be ordered. For example computers, software, smaller class sizes, money, gym equipment. Use the automatic spelling checker during your letter as a proofreader.

C. Create and load your own custom user word list. Follow the directions in this chapter. Find at least 15 words that you may want to include on the WORDS.USE list that may be beneficial to you in the future. Save this file to the disk.

D. Add 10 more words to your ''User List'' and save the file to the disk.

E. Obtain the PC-Write Manual and determine how to merge the ''User Lists'' titled WORDS.USE, and the ''Master List'' titled WORDS.MAS to a single list using WORDS.EXE on the PC-Write Words List diskette.

F. Retype the spelling checker rules making at least 20 mistakes. Print a copy. Go back and correct your mistakes using the spelling checker. Print a copy of the revised version of the rules.

Part III

Worksheets with As-Easy-As

Chapter 8

The Basics of As-Easy-As

CHAPTER OUTLINE

An Orientation
Loading As-Easy-As
The As-Easy-As Worksheet Screen
Cell Pointer Movement Keys
An Exercise
Function Keys
An Exercise
Special Purpose Keys
- Enter (Return)
- Backspace
- Space Bar
- Esc
- Caps Lock
- Control
- Alternate
- Number Lock
- Delete
- Insert

Entering Data into Worksheet Cells
- Labels

An Exercise
- Values

An Exercise
An Exercise
Built-In Functions
An Exercise
Pointing Versus Cell Address Naming
An Exercise
Entry Lengths
Column Widths
An Exercise
Correcting Mistaken Entries
- Retyping
- Editing

An Exercise
An Exercise
As-Easy-As Command Menus
An Exercise

Files
An Exercise
Worksheet Erasing
Quit
Exercises

AN ORIENTATION

This chapter is intended to be a brief introduction to the nature of worksheets and to the techniques of working with As-Easy-As. It has been designed as a tutorial guide you should work through on the computer as you read. If you find that you have to exit before this chapter is completed, skip to the section, Quit, at the end of the chapter.

Additional information will be given to you about the intricacies of 1–2-3 as you work through future chapters. This chapter is provided in order to give you a preliminary feeling for the layout of the microcomputer keyboard as it relates to As-Easy-As and to introduce terms and concepts you need to know before you start to construct worksheets in the chapters that follow. For more complete details of this nature, consult the As-Easy-As manual or other texts about 1–2-3.

LOADING AS-EASY-AS

If your copy of As-Easy-As has been properly installed, the entry into As-Easy-As should be easy. Consult your manual for instructions on the correct method of installation if this process has not been completed. Boot your computer if necessary, and obtain the ''A>'' prompt. Place the As-Easy-As diskette in disk drive A and place a formatted diskette with available space for saving your As-Easy-As worksheet files in disk drive B. Enter

`aseasy` The command for loading As-Easy-As. Following a brief message displaying, ''Loading As-Easy-As from . . . A:\'' you will see the registration screen like the one shown in Figure 8–1.

↵ Enter Key

```
You are encouraged to copy and share this program (BUT NOT THE
MANUAL) with other users under the conditions that the program is
not modified, no fee or consideration is charged, and that this
notice is not bypassed or removed.
```

```
As-Easy-As is a POWERFUL and LARGE spreadsheet of 1,024 rows x 256
columns. Create GRAPHS on screen or a printer, manipulate
DATABASES, PRINT formatted reports, execute programmable MACROS,
or calculate sophisticated models with a generous selection of
Finance, Statistic, Logic, and Science functions. And much more!!
```

Figure 8–1. As-Easy-As Registration Screen.

```
If you find As-Easy-As useful, we encourage you to register your
copy. Registration costs $30.00 US and provides you with the
current As-Easy-As DISK, printed MANUAL, and on-line HELP SCREENS.
Manuals may be purchased separately in quantities of 10 or more.
School or college? Ask about site licenses . . .

  Make check  \          TRIUS Inc.,         15 Atkinson St.
  payable to  /                              Lynn, MA, 01905.
```

Figure 8–1—*Continued*

↵ Enter key, to continue. A cursor is flashing inside of the cell pointer located in a matrix of rows labeled 1 through 20 and columns labeled A through H. The As-Easy-As worksheet screen as shown in Figure 8–2. Upon entry into As-Easy-As a new, blank worksheet is always provided.

```
—F1:Help—F2:Edit—F5:Goto—<Ready!>—F6:Window—F9:Calc—F10:Graph—
A1:

........A/........B/........C/........D/........E/........F/........G/........H/

 1
 2
 3
 4
 5
 6
 7
 8
 9
10
11
12
13
14
15
16
17
18
19
20

—Free:99.7% [373k]—Auto—2:27:45 pm —
```

Figure 8–2. As-Easy-As Screen.

THE AS-EASY-AS WORKSHEET SCREEN

The As-Easy-As screen consists of two sections, a work area or window that is bounded by a highlighted (reverse video) column of numbers, beginning with the number 1, which identify each of the 1,024 rows, and a highlighted row of letters, beginning with "A," which identify the 256 columns into which a worksheet can be divided. A cell is the location in the grid of a row and a column. For instance, the cell address C13 uniquely identifies the cell found in column C and in row 13. The portion of an As-Easy-As worksheet that you can see on the twenty rows on your screen is called a window because you cannot always see all of the active part of the worksheet at one time. You must move the window to see different parts of the worksheet.

A worksheet consists of 262,144 cells (256 x 1,024). Although this provides a large number of theoretically available cells, many microcomputers do not have enough random access memory to take advantage of even a large fraction of this space.

Inside of the window, probably at cell address A1, if you did not accidentally touch a cell pointer movement key, you will see a highlighted cell pointer. Movement of the cell pointer activates the cell on which it is placed. When you enter data, it will be entered into the active cell.

There are three lines above the window. The top line displays the function key menu choices. Pressing one of the function keys will carry out the named commands. At the center of this line you will see the word "READY" in a highlighted block. This is called the mode block indicator. The word inside the mode block changes from time to time in order to inform you about what As-Easy-As is doing or about the type of response As-Easy-As is expecting.

The second line is called a status line. On the left of this line is an address noting where the cell pointer is currently located. This is the address of the active cell. Next to the cell address may appear: a) a notation to guide the display of a number assigned to that cell; b) a notation to express the width of a column; c) a notation to indicate that the cell is unprotected; and d) the actual contents of the cell. The portion of a sample worksheet screen in Figure 8–3 displays the information that cell B2 contains the number 27.5, but the formatting notation [C2] displays the number as currency with two decimal places (i.e., $27.50).

```
    F1:Help-F2:Edit-F5:Goto-<Ready>! -F6:Window -F9:Calc-F10:Graph-
    B2: [C2]: 27.5

........A/........B/........C/........D/........E/........F/........G/........H/

        1
        2     $27.50
        3
```

Figure 8–3.

The third line, the entry line, is used for three different purposes. If you are typing data to be placed in a cell, this line serves as an entry line which displays what you have typed before this data is actually entered with the Enter key. If you have already entered data into a cell, this data can be recalled to the entry line with the edit key, F2. The data can then be edited and reentered. Figure 8–4 illustrates how part of the control panel appears when data is being entered.

```
F1:Help-F2:Edit-F5:Goto-<Ready!>-F6:Window-F9:Calc-F10:Graph-B A1:
This is data about to be entered.

........A/.......B/.......C/.......D/.......E/.......F/.......G/.......H/

1
2          $27.50
3
4
```

Figure 8–4.

A line beneath the worksheet window is reserved for the display of information about the amount and percentage of memory available for the worksheet being built (the numbers will be different for different computers) and for the signaling that selected key functions have been turned on. For instance, if the Caps Lock has been activated, the block with the word ''Cap'' will appear. There are similar displays for the Num Lock, and Scroll Lock keys. Indicator blocks are eliminated with the pressing of the appropriate key a second time.

CELL POINTER MOVEMENT KEYS

Nine keys (see Figure 8–5) located on the right-hand side of the keyboard of your microcomputer are used for moving the cell pointer within the worksheet.

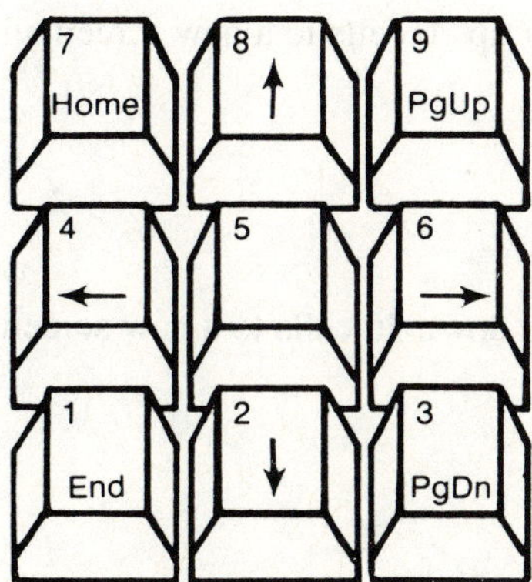

Figure 8–5. Cell Pointer Movement Keys.

Be sure to notice that the numbers are in the uppercase position. The lowercase positions are used by the directional arrows and the commands Home, End, PgUp, and PgDn. The uppercase numbers can be accessed by depressing the Shift key or by depressing the Num Lock key. Generally, having the numbers in the keypad readily available and not the directional arrows is undesirable. Use the numbers on the top row of the keyboard instead. The directional keys are used in the following manner:

Moves the cell pointer down one cell.

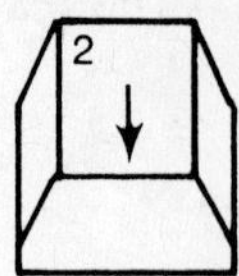

Moves the cell pointer up one cell.

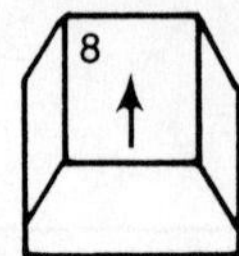

Moves the cell pointer right one cell.

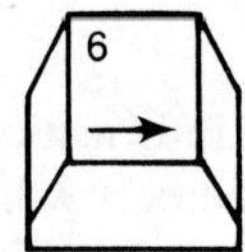

Moves the cell pointer left one cell.

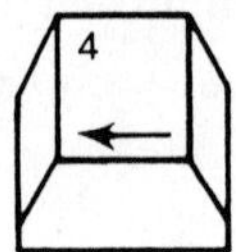

Returns the cell pointer to the cell located at address A1, the top left corner of the worksheet.

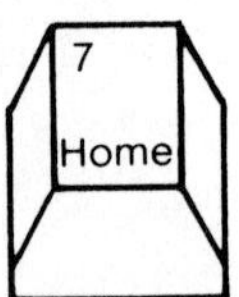

Moves the cell pointer up 20 cells to a new screen with no overlapping of cells.

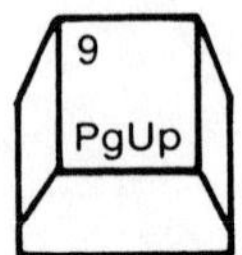

Moves the cell pointer down 20 cells to a new screen with no overlapping of cells.

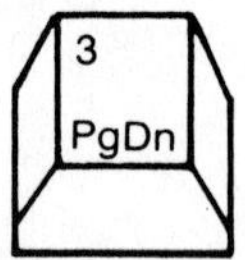

When End precedes the use of any arrow key, the cell pointer moves to the next boundary position in the direction of the arrow key pressed after the End key. A boundary position is a point where one group of cells with contents (i.e., data in them) are next to cells that are empty (i.e., have no data in them).

Another key, the Tab key, is useful for moving around the keyboard. The Tab key is located to the left of the letter "Q." This key is not labeled, but appears as:

Moves the cell pointer to the column immediately to the right of the current screen. Shift and Tab together move the cell pointer to the left in the same fashion.

AN EXERCISE

Try moving the cell pointer with these directional keys. You will probably notice several things as you experiment with moving the cell pointer. You will notice that,

1. You cannot move the cell pointer across an edge of the worksheet.
2. The cell address in the control panel changes as the cell is moved around.
3. The row numbers and column letters change as the cell pointer crosses window boundaries. The column letters advance from A to Z, to AA, AB, AC, to AZ, to BA, BB, BC, to BZ, and so on until they stop at IV.
4. The End key followed by a right arrow will take you to the IV column since there are no boundaries other than a worksheet edge in a new worksheet.
5. The End key followed by a down arrow will take you to row number 8,192 since there are no boundaries other than a worksheet edge in a new worksheet.

FUNCTION KEYS

On the left-hand side of the keyboard are ten keys marked F1 through F10 as shown in Figure 8–6.

On some microcomputers the function keys are located across the top of the keyboard. Wherever these keys are physically positioned, their functions remain the same. Generally, function keys are used by computer programs to carry out relatively complicated actions quickly. This is the case with function keys in As-Easy-As also. The most commonly used function keys will be further described within the context of the worksheets that are developed in this book.

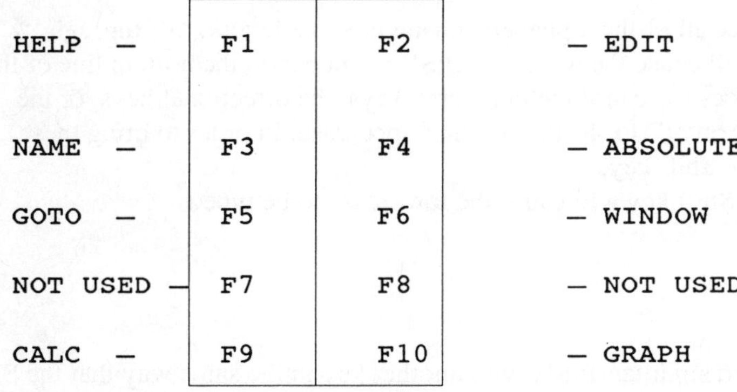

Figure 8–6. Function Keys.

AN EXERCISE

Place the As-Easy-As Help disk in drive A. Press the F1 key. This is the Help key that provides fast explanations of what choices you have available to you at any point. Use of the Help key is said to be context sensitive because the information it provides changes depending on the menu commands (described below) As-Easy-As is displaying.

Return to As-Easy-As by pressing Q, for "Quit," or the Escape (Esc) key.

SPECIAL PURPOSE KEYS

Several of the remaining keys have special functions to perform.

Enter (Return)

The Enter key is used to place data that is typed on the entry line of the control panel into the cell on which the cell pointer is currently located.

Backspace

The Backspace key is used in the editing of data on the entry line. Use of the Backspace key deletes the character to the left of the cursor.

Space Bar

The space bar is used to enter blanks (spaces) on entry lines. A blank is a character just as are the letters ''a'' and ''Z.'' If a cell contains only blanks, a cell may appear to be empty, but actually it has contents.

Esc

The Escape key is useful because it enables you to back out of mistakes you may make in the selection of menu choices and to erase data from the entry line.

Caps Lock

The key marked ''Caps Lock'' will place all of the alphabetic characters, the letters ''a'' through ''z'', into uppercase. Setting Caps Lock on will cause the word ''CAPS'' to appear on the bottom line of the worksheet. Use of the Caps Lock key does not cause the numbered keys, the directional keys, or the keys with special operators such as ''.'' or ''/'' to shift to become uppercase. In order to bring these keys to uppercase requires the use of the Shift key.

If Caps Lock is on, the use of the Shift key will cause the lowercase to be typed.

Control

The Control key, marked ''Ctrl,'' is used simultaneously with another key in the same way that the Shift key is used. In As-Easy-As the most important function the Control key has is in conjunction with the key marked ''Break / Scroll Lock.'' This combination of keys cancels some operations such as the printing of a worksheet or the stopping of a keyboard macro.

Alternate

The Alternate key, marked ''Alt,'' is used to give keys an alternative meaning in As-Easy-As. This key is used to invoke keyboard macros, complex commands that you can build that As-Easy-As can carry out for you automatically. Macros are an advanced feature of As-Easy-As that are not dealt with in this book.

Number Lock

The key marked, ''Num Lock,'' puts the light-colored key pad on the right side of the keyboard in uppercase. The directional arrows and commands such as PgUp then become available only through the use of the Shift key. When Number Lock is on, the word ''NUM'' appears on the last line of the worksheet.

Delete

The Delete key is used when data on the entry line of the control panel is being edited. The Delete key will delete the character that is immediately above the cursor. This is a different effect than that of the Backspace key which deletes the character to the left of the cursor.

Although the Backspace key can be used when you are originally entering data on the entry line, the Delete key cannot be used here because it is always found to the right of any characters that have been typed. None are above it. The Delete key can only be used when you are in what As-Easy-As calls the edit mode.

Insert

The key marked “Ins” is used to switch between insert (default mode) and overwrite when you are editing cell contents.

ENTERING DATA INTO WORKSHEET CELLS

Labels

The term “labels” is used by As-Easy-As to describe character data. Labels are strings of 1 or more characters. For instance, “a,” “Dog,” “Name,” “B69C,” and “Address” are labels. As soon as you type a cell entry beginning with a character from “A” to “Z” (upper- or lowercase), a space or any other character that has no mathematical meaning, the mode indicator block which is located in the upper right-hand corner of the control panel changes from “READY” to “LABEL.” This means that the entire entry will be treated as character data, even if it contains numbers.

AN EXERCISE

Place your cell pointer in cell address A1 using the arrow keys if necessary. If you are far from this location, remember that the “Home” key will take you to A1 rapidly. Then type

`Jack` As you type, the name does not initially appear in the cell where the cell pointer is located. It appears on the entry line. Note that the mode block in the top line reads “ ’LABEL ”.

↵ Enter key. If you look in the control panel, you will see that the entry line has been cleared. Now the name “Jack” appears in cell A1 of the window and on the status line of the control panel, next to the cell address of the currently active cell. You should also see that the name is preceded by an apostrophe. The apostrophe is automatically put in front of any label entered into a cell. The apostrophe is called a *label prefix* and is used by As-Easy-As to begin displaying the label from the left-hand side of the cell it is entered into. The label prefix does not appear in the display in cell A1. You can right-justify the label with the quote, ”, or center the label with a caret, ^, if you choose.

After the entry is complete, the word on the top line returns to “<READY>.”

Values

When you begin an entry with a number or with a plus, minus, multiply (asterisk, *) , or divide sign (slash, /), or with any of the several special characters,

- (@ #

the mode block will display " <+VALUE> ." This indicates that the entry you are creating can contain any of the following:

1. a number
2. a formula
3. a cell address

Characters which are not part of one of these entries are not permitted. If you type an illegal character such as the letter "D" and that letter is not part of a valid cell address, the entry will be kept on the entry line and the worksheet is placed in edit mode when you hit the Enter key. The top line displays "<EDIT>? ." You must correct the entry.

AN EXERCISE

Using your arrow keys, place the cell pointer on cell B1. Type

123	The number one hundred twenty-three (123). Notice that the mode block indicator on the top line reads "< +VALUE>."
↲	Enter key. In addition to the entry line having been cleared, the number appears next to the cell address. There is no apostrophe in front of the number, however. This is because you have entered a value and not a label. Numbers are not prefixed with apostrophes. They are right-justified.
↓	Down arrow to move your cell pointer to cell address B2
456a	Type the number four hundred fifty-six followed by the deliberate error of the addition of an "a."
↲	Enter key. Listen for a beep that signals an error. Notice that the mode block now displays "<EDIT>? " because of the presence of the character in the number. The cursor is to the right of the "a," the offending character in the formula.
Backspace	Backspace key, to remove the "a"
↲	Enter key. The number will be accepted as legal. Stop for the moment. You shall return to the worksheet shortly.
Formulas	If As-Easy-As could only enter labels and numbers in rows and columns, it would have rather limited capabilities. It would be a poor word processor that could only help you in structuring the appearance of rows and columns of data. It does far more. You can also enter formulas that contain correctly organized combinations of any of the following:

1. numbers
2. mathematical operators (* / - + =)
3. built-in functions
4. parentheses
5. logical operators such as #AND# and #NOT#

Discussion of the last two elements will be deferred until they are needed in the worksheet exercises.

AN EXERCISE

Type:

↓	Down arrow to move to cell B3
+	The plus sign (if your keyboard has two plus sign keys, you may use either one) notifies

As-Easy-As a value is being entered. Note the "< +VALUE >" in the mode block in the control panel. A plus sign, a number, or some other mathematical notation must precede a cell address that begins a value entry. Otherwise the leading letter will cause the entire entry to be treated as a string of characters (i.e., as a label).

↑ Up arrow, to move the cell pointer to cell address B2. The mode block indicator will have changed to read "< Refer >" indicating that a cell address will appear on the entry line of the control panel. You will see that "B2" has been entered for you next to the plus sign.

\+ A second plus sign indicates that another value will be added to the value found in cell B2. The cell pointer returns to the active cell B3. The mode block changes to "< +VALUE >."

↑ Up arrow, to move up one cell. The mode block changes to "< Refer >" and a second "B2" has been entered.

↑ Up arrow to move one more cell to arrive at cell B1. At this point you will note that the entry line reads,

+B2+B1 that is, "find the value in the cell with the coordinates B and 2 and add that value to the value in the cell with the coordinates B and 1 and enter the result in the active cell, B3. Blanks or spaces should never be entered into a formula because the contents and the display will both be incorrect.

↵ Enter key, to enter the formula into cell B3, the "active" cell on which the cell pointer was located when you began.

Upon entry of the formula into the cell, you will see that cell B3 displays the result 579 which is obtained by adding 123 and 456. If you look at the status line, however, you will see the formula you created next to the cell address. As-Easy-As remembers the formula as its contents. However, in the worksheet window, As-Easy-As displays the number that is created by evaluating the formula. The distinction between a cell's display and a cell's contents is an important one. To illustrate why, do the following:

↑ To move to cell B2. Note that you have not begun a formula so the use of the arrow does not cause the mode block to change from "READY" to "< Refer >."

↑ To move to cell B1.

789 To create the value seven hundred eighty-nine on the entry line.

↵ To enter the value into cell B1, thereby replacing the value 123.

You will see that As-Easy-As almost immediately recalculates the results computed by the formula in cell B3 even though the change was made in cell B1. This is because the content of cell B3 is the formula, not the number it displayed earlier.

BUILT-IN FUNCTIONS

As-Easy-As provides a group of techniques for carrying out complex operations on cells automatically. For instance, if you wished to add up the values found in the first ten cells of column A, you could create a formula similar to this

A1+A2+A3+A4+A5+A6+A7+A8+A9+A10

This is difficult to do, however, for several reasons. The typing of such a long formula requires many keystrokes. This takes time and you may make errors in typing. It is also not always clear whether all of the cells you wished to include are actually included. Further, you may have duplicated a cell address unwittingly. Some operations such as finding the standard deviation for a group of values or the determination of the internal rate of return on an investment may require the writing of difficult formulas that most people would not wish to create.

Functions are operations, usually mathematical or logical, that reduce or eliminate all of these problems. With a function the lengthy formula above can be reduced to

@SUM(A1 . . A10) which can be read as, "Sum up all of the values found in the cells from cell address A1 through cell address A10 and display the result." Built-in functions enable you to develop very complex worksheets rapidly and accurately.

The structure, or syntax, of a built-in function includes five elements. A function always begins with the "at" sign (@) which is followed by the name of the function. This is followed by an opening parenthesis.

Between the parentheses are arguments. The number of arguments in functions varies among the functions. Arguments typically are individual cell addresses, rectangularly-shaped groups of cells called ranges, numbers, or a combination of ranges, numbers, and cells. A closing parenthesis terminates the function.

As you become knowledgeable about As-Easy-As you will find that built-in functions can save you considerable amounts of time and allow you to complete operations that might otherwise be very difficult to accomplish.

AN EXERCISE

Using the arrow keys if necessary, move your cell pointer to cell address B3 and type

@SUM(	Begin the summing function
B1	To add the value found in B1
. .	Through
B2	Cell address B2
)	Terminate the list of cell values to be summed, as well as the function. There are no spaces allowed in formulas. The formula now reads as,
@SUM(B1 . . B2)	
↵	Enter key

When you entered the formula with the **@SUM** function into the active cell, cell B3, this formula calculated the same result calculated by addition.

POINTING VERSUS CELL ADDRESS NAMING

There are two ways of entering cell addresses in formulas. The first way is by "pointing" to cells as you type a formula on the entry line. Once a formula has been started you point by moving any of the directional keys. As you move the cell pointer, the cell address in the formula changes to reflect its current location. This method of cell addressing is most useful when you have to search for the correct cell to be used in the formula.

Whenever you begin to point to cell addresses as a part of formula building, the mode block indicator changes to read " Refer ."

The second method of entering a cell address is to simply type the cell address on the entry line. This may be the fastest method of cell address entry if you can see the cell on the screen or, if you remember or have written down the address. Most of the exercises presented in this book will direct you to type the cell addresses directly; however, you can interpret an instruction to enter +A20 as being equivalent to typing a plus sign and "pointing" to A20 by moving the cell pointer to that cell. While typing @SUM(A8 . . B10), entering A8 . . B10 is being equivalent to pressing the plus sign, pointing to cell A8, pressing the period, pointing to B10 and pressing the Enter key.

AN EXERCISE

Move your cell pointer to cell address B4 and type

+	Begin a formula and change the mode block from "READY" to "< +VALUE >"

↑ Up arrow, to move to B3. Notice the appearance of the cell address on the entry line of the control panel and the word " Refer " in the mode indicator block.

`Esc` Escape key, to remove the formula from the entry line. The function key menu line still reads "< Refer >."

`Esc` Escape key, to exit from point mode and to return the word to "< READY >"

ENTRY LENGTHS

Whether you are entering formulas, numbers, or labels into active cells, there is a 78 character limit to the entry line. Your entry may not exceed this limit. Numbers may not exceed 11 significant digits.

COLUMN WIDTHS

Whenever As-Easy-As calls up a fresh worksheet, it provides an automatic column-width of 9 characters. This is a default value. A default value is a value that is built into a computer program to take effect if the user does not explicitly change it. As-Easy-As uses other default values in other contexts. The default value for column width can be changed. Column width is important in several ways:

1. When you type alphabetic character data (labels), they will be displayed continuously into the adjacent columns as long as the characters do not interfere with the display of data already present in the cells in those columns.
2. A number which is too large to appear in a cell will be displayed as a block of asterisks (*). This forces you to see that the data cannot be displayed correctly. If As-Easy-As did not do this, it would have to truncate the number. The results would then appear to be correct, but would, in fact, be incorrect. When asterisks are displayed, the column width must be widened. As soon as the width is expanded sufficiently, the complete number will be displayed. At no time will an inadequate display width cause the loss of data.

AN EXERCISE

Move your cell pointer to cell A5. Type

THIS IS A VERY LONG LINE ENTRY.
An entry to cell A5

↵ Enter the label. Note that the status line displays the entire entry as the contents of A5.

→ Right arrow to move to cell B5. See that the status line shows no contents for B5, even though the label for A5 overlaps this cell.

→ Right arrow, to move to cell C5

INTERFERENCE
An Entry to cell C5

↵ Enter key to insert the word "INTERFERENCE" into C5. Note how the label in A5 continues to be displayed in columns A and B where the word placed in C5 does not appear. The word in C5 overlaps into column D.

Move the cell pointer to cell B7 and enter

`123456789.456` A number too large for the 9 character display.

↲ Enter key. Note the asterisks that are displayed. The number you entered in the cell appears on the status line with scientific notation since it is larger than 11 digits. As-Easy-As has not forgotten the value of the entry.

CORRECTING MISTAKEN ENTRIES

Retyping

When you are entering data into a worksheet, it is inevitable that you will make mistakes. Certainly you will find that even if cell entries were made correctly, some data will have to be updated or some new information will require you to modify your formulas.

If the original entries are short, or if these entries must be totally reworked so that there is little point in editing them, then the best way to make them correct is to simply type them over. This is accomplished by making the cell active by placing the cell pointer on it, typing, and entering the new entry.

Editing

A second and often preferred method is to edit the cell's contents. The F2 key is called the Edit key. To use the Edit key, you make the cell containing the entry to be corrected active, press the F2 key and edit the entry line. The following keys are the basic keys used in editing:

Del	To delete the character above the cursor
Backspace	To delete the character to the left of the cursor
→	Right arrow to move nondestructively right
←	Left arrow to move nondestructively left
Home	To move nondestructively to the leftmost character
End	To move nondestructively to the rightmost character
Esc	Escape key to delete the entire entry. Esc must be pressed before an Enter key clears the entry line by placing the data in the active cell. Escaping twice leaves the contents of the active cell unchanged.
Ins	To toggle between insert and overwrite. The insertion or overwriting of characters is identical to that found in PC-Write.

Figure 8–6. Editing Keys.

When the entry line has been corrected, it is re-entered with the Enter key.

Exiting From An Initial Entry

It will occur to you that an entry you have started is being placed in the wrong cell. If you have entered a word, "Thomas," for instance, you can erase the entry by pressing the Escape key twice. The first Escape will erase the letters from the entry line. Although the letters are gone, As-Easy-As retains the prefix character for a label. Consequently, the word " Label " still appears on the function key menu line. The pressing of the Escape key will remove the prefix character and return " Ready ! " to the function key menu line.

AN EXERCISE

This exercise will familiarize you with the editing capabilities of As-Easy-As Move the cell pointer to cell D6 and enter

ABC CORP. BUDGET	A label to be typed in. Note the entry on the entry line.
↲	Enter key to place the label in the active cell. Note the apostrophe label-prefix that was added to what you typed, as well as the empty entry line. The cell pointer remains on cell D6.
F2	Edit key, to put the entry back on the entry line. The word changes to "< EDIT >? ." The cursor is to the right of the entry.
←	Ten left arrows to place the cursor under the "R" in "CORP"
Del	Press three times to delete the alphabetic character string "RP."
MPANY	Insert the letters "MPANY" to form "COMPANY." Notice that the letters typed were automatically inserted at the location of the cursor. Characters above and to the right of the cursor were moved to the right.

Before entering the revised label "ABC COMPANY BUDGET," experiment with the other movement keys to see their effect.

Home	Home key to go to the extreme left
End	End key to go to the extreme right
←←←	Three left arrows
→→→	Three right arrows
↲	Enter key. This replaces the cell's previous contents with the new entry.

AN EXERCISE

Return your cell pointer to cell D6 if it was moved, then type

F2	Edit key, to recall "ABC COMPANY BUDGET" to the entry line
Esc	Escape key, to delete the entry. Observe the mode block. One escape does not exit you from the edit mode.
Esc	Escape key, to exit from edit mode and to return to "< READY >." There is no change in the contents of cell D6. If you wished to delete the contents of a cell, you would use a different approach to be described below.

AS-EASY-AS COMMAND MENUS

Thus far you have been shown how to move the cell pointer from cell to cell and how to make entries in the cells. Another major category of support comes from the As-Easy-As command menu structure. As-Easy-As commands are initiated with the Slash key. The Slash key, located to the right of the period, is not to be confused with the Backslash key which is located immediately to the left of the space bar. The Backslash has a markedly different purpose.

AN EXERCISE

Be certain that the mode block indicator displays "< READY >." If this indicator does not appear, strike the Escape key repeatedly until it does. Then type

/ Slash key, to invoke the initial menu. Your menu should look like that pictured in Figure 8–7.

Notice that the word reads "<MainMenu>." It is only permissible to make a menu choice, to press the Escape key to exit the menu, or to respond to a prompt. You may not enter data while "<MainMenu>" is displayed.

```
Wsheet
Range
CopyCell
MoveCell
Array
Data
File
Graphics
PrintTo
Exit
```

Figure 8–7. As-Easy-As Main Menu.

↓ Down arrow to highlight the menu choice "RANGE." Note that the prompt line of the control panel changes as the cursor moves from menu choice to menu choice. This line describes what the highlighted choice will help you to do if it is selected.
↵ Enter key to select the Range choice. A new submenu with different choices appears.
E Erase is chosen with the typing of the first letter
↵ Enter key, to erase the currently active cell identified in the prompt, "ERASE range is :D6 . . D6." There is no change made to the other cells.

Another illustration will show how you can reverse menu decisions. Move your cell pointer to B7 and type

/ Slash to invoke the initial menu
R Range
Esc Escape key, to back up to initial menu
Esc Escape key, to clear the control panel of menus and to return to the READY mode. No change was made to the cell on which the range command was begun, but not completed.

The command menu sequences open to you are diverse and numerous. At first the variations may seem to be overwhelming. As you work with As-Easy-As you will find that the seemingly foreign and hard to remember command sequences will become easier and easier to recall without reference to manuals or guidebooks. For now it is sufficient to know that until an action is actually initiated, you can always use the Escape key to reverse yourself.

Any time you make an "error" by typing a character that is not on the menu, As-Easy-As will "beep" at you. A beep does not make any changes to your worksheet. Rather, it calls attention to your attempt to make As-Easy-As do something that you are not allowed to do.

FILES

So far we have worked, albeit awkwardly, with a worksheet that is resident in the microcomputer's random access memory (RAM). The worksheet in RAM is said to be transient because it has no permanent existence. If the computer is turned off, the results of your typing will be lost. This may not seem like much of a tragedy given the screen in front of you, but in other circumstances this will be important indeed.

In order to save the worksheet so that you can recall it a day or a month from now, you have to use the command structure to save it to a diskette. Again, the exercise that follows assumes that the As-Easy-As system diskette has been correctly adapted to your computer and that it appropriately saves your files to the right disk drive and, if necessary, to the correct directory. If it does not, consult your As-Easy-As manual to assure that it works correctly. Check to be certain that a formatted disk is in drive B.

AN EXERCISE

As-Easy-As is distributed to save and retrieve files from disk drive A. If As-Easy-As has been installed on the hard drive, or if you have a single disk drive system, this is acceptable. If you have a dual drive system, you can remove As-Easy-As from drive A and replace it with your files disk. You can also change the default drive so that it will carry out all file operations on the B drive by entering

/	Slash
F	File
D	Directory
Esc	Escape Key, to remove the old default of A:\
B:	New default directory
↵	Enter Key. Drive B will be the default drive for the remainder of this session. It will have to be reset as the default drive in each session.

The cell pointer can be in any location on the worksheet when the worksheet is saved to disk. The following typing sequence can be initiated from any location:

/	Slash, to invoke the main menu
F	File
S	Store, to save the worksheet to disk
JUNK	The name of the file, given in response to the prompt "STORE:Name of file ?," you chose any name that describes the worksheet in a manner that will help you to recall its contents.
↵	Enter key. Observe 1) the red light that appears on the disk drive receiving the permanent copy of the worksheet, and 2) the word changes to "## WAIT ##." While the red light is on, As-Easy-As is actively writing out the file.

When saving a revised version of a worksheet, another choice must be made. A prompt requests confirmation. Select "R" to "Replace" an earlier version with the new one.

Filenames are limited to lengths of eight characters, a limitation that restricts the degree of descriptiveness the name can have. Because a floppy diskette, or to a still greater degree, a hard disk, can store a large number of files, it is important to assign each file a name that can help you to recall it without your having to search files at random looking for the one you need.

A very important point to remember regards the red light that appears when the computer is writing a file to disk. As the file is being written out, the mode block reads "WAIT." "WAIT" is replaced by "READY" as soon as As-Easy-As is finished. It takes the computer somewhat longer to write the file out so the red light stays on longer. Remember: Do not turn the machine off or take the diskette out of the disk drive until the red light goes off.

The reason for this is that As-Easy-As destroys the old file before it writes out the new one. If the new file has not been completely written out, it will not be recoverable by As-Easy-As in subsequent sessions. If you have lost the old file and you have an incomplete new file, you have lost all of your efforts.

WORKSHEET ERASING

Worksheet Erase

Saving a file does not erase it from the worksheet window that appears on your screen. To remove the current worksheet from the window and to remove it from the computer's memory, though not from the diskette, type

/	Slash
W	Worksheet
E	Erase
Y	Yes

This command sequence will clear your screen.

QUIT

Before exiting from As-Easy-As, be sure to save your file first. In this case there is no need to save your file. To quit As-Easy-As, type

/	Slash
E	Exit
Y	Yes, to confirm that you wish to exit As-Easy-As

EXERCISES

A. Create the following monthly sales report for an automobile distributor. The report lists the sales by individual sales person. The first name, ''R. Jones'' should be placed in cell A4 and the number 126 should be placed in B4. Total the column with the formula, **+B4+B5+B6+B7+B8.**

MONTHLY SALES REPORT

NAME	SALES
R. Jones	126
B. Smith	251
T. Kelp	182
A. Herter	178
M. Mills	224
TOTAL	961

—Change the name, ''R. Jones,'' to ''R. Lister'' by overtyping
—Use the edit key (F2) to change ''M. Mills'' to ''M. Wiley''
—Change the sales reported for ''T. Kelp'' to 128.

B. Create the following quarterly report for refrigerator sales at 5 stores. The first store name, ''Fifth St.'' should be placed in cell A4 and the number 126 should be placed in B4. Total the numbers in column B with the formula, **+B4+B5+B6+B7+B8.** Total the numbers in column C with the formula, **+C4+C5+C6+C7+C8.** Total the numbers in column D with the formula, **+D4+D5+D6+D7+D8.**

QUARTERLY SUMMARY OF REFRIGERATOR SALES

STORE	MONTH 1	MONTH 2	MONTH 3
Fifth St.	11	8	12
Lone Pine	19	16	15
MacKay's	27	13	18
Wilson's	17	19	20
Big W	29	23	25
TOTAL	103	79	90

—Change the store name, ''MacKay's,'' to ''Shop Fast,'' by overtyping
—Use the edit key (F2) to change ''Wilson's,'' to ''LoCost''
—Change the sales reported for ''Fifth St.'' in the three months to 12, 18, and 21.

Chapter 9

Getting Acquainted with Worksheets

CHAPTER OUTLINE

Some analysts cite the availability of electronic worksheets as the key reason for the initial popularity of microcomputers. Worksheet programs are useful in organizing data that is normally displayed in rows and columns. Unlike word processors that only use tab markers for aligning columns of data, worksheet programs have powerful mathematical capabilities that allow the user to manipulate data rather than simply record data. The difference is significant.

In this chapter you will

1. Learn the basic components of a worksheet screen;
2. Move the cell pointer around the worksheet;
3. Enter text, numerical data, and formulas into cells;
4. Execute worksheet commands;
5. Learn the difference between cell and range addresses;
6. Change the appearance of a cell's contents;
7. Copy cells;
8. Change the width of a column of cells;
9. Save and retrieve a file.

WHY WORKSHEETS?

Think about the production of a company's annual budget without a worksheet program. Someone must compute the values for a company's various expense and income categories with a calculator. Subtotals and totals must also be computed by hand. The last step in what may be a laborious process will be the passing of hand-written budget sheets to a secretary for typing. If the numbers used in calculations must be changed for any reason, the entire typed copy is likely to have to be redone to reflect the changes that are felt throughout the budget. In a worksheet, as you will see, a change can be made and the worksheet automatically recalculates all formulas in the budget to bring it up to date.

Worksheets, also called spreadsheets, can be employed to organize and experiment with data required to solve a variety of problems. Among the problems this software can help to solve are the production of financial statements of all types: budgets, income analyses, cash flow analyses, break even and start-up cost analyses, income tax reporting, and investment analyses. Worksheets can be especially useful in making projections of sales and income, utility costs and other expenses, and the impact of external factors on the internal financing of a company.

Not all worksheets involve monetary data. Many quantitative problems not involving money can be addressed with worksheets. Some worksheets actually use little quantitative data.

WHAT IS A WORKSHEET?

Assume that you are constructing a computer sales projection for a small manufacturing firm. The firm sells three models of microcomputers that have been introduced at different times and confront different levels of competition from other computer manufacturers. Among the factors that must be taken into account in producing a projection are the following:

1. The Hacker 1 model computer is cost competitive and is popular with certain banking institutions. Last quarter sales of this model were at 15,500 and sales are expected to grow at 3% per sales quarter over the next year.
2. The Hacker 2 model has been discontinued, but an inventory remains. With a discounted price, the company expects to be able to sell these models at levels that decrease by 50% in each quarter. In the last quarter 7,300 Hacker 2s were sold.

HARDWARE ASSOCIATES

QUARTERLY SALES BY SALES OFFICE

OFFICE	QTR 1	QTR 2	QTR 3	QTR 4	YEARLY TOTAL	PERCENT OF TOTAL
SOUTHWEST	10,329	8,790	7,834	7,903	34,856	31%
SOUTHEAST	2,900	4,376	4,502	4,678	16,456	14$
NORTHWEST	4,567	4,500	4,325	5,605	18,997	17%
NORTHEAST	10,654	10,834	10,839	10,854	43,181	38%
TOTAL SALES	28,450	28,500	27,500	29,040	113,490	
MINIMUM	2,900	4,376	4,325	4,678	16,456	
MAXIMUM	10,654	10,834	10,839	10,854	43,181	
AVERAGE	7,113	7,125	6,875	7,260	28,373	

Figure 9–1.

3. The Hacker 3 model is popular due to its high speed and large hard disk subsystem. Unfortunately, the supplier of the hard disks can only gear up to provide an increase of 450 disks in each quarter. 5,500 Hacker 3s were sold in the last quarter.

Without a worksheet program, a typical approach to projecting the company's probable sales over the next four quarters would be to sit down with a pencil, paper, and calculator to do the projections manually. The result is Figure 9–1.

To construct this projection manually is not an overwhelming task although it does take time to perform the twenty-one calculations by hand. Miscalculations are possible. The major problem with manually preparing this forecast is the prospect that it may have to be changed. The supplier of hard disks could announce that it is able to increase its production by 100 each quarter. The company may begin a new relationship with a chain distributor that will increase Hacker 1 sales by 200 per quarter. A new model computer might be introduced. Each of these changes requires that some, if not all, of the twenty-one calculations in this worksheet need to be recomputed.

A worksheet is a computer model that will look like the hand-produced projection shown. The worksheet will be organized in a grid with rows and columns. Unlike the hand-produced projection, the computer model will be easily modified to accommodate changes.

LOADING AS-EASY-AS

To start As-Easy-As, your computer must have been booted with DOS. The "A" prompt should be visible. Entry into As-Easy-As is begun by placing the As-Easy-As system disk into drive A. Then type

aseasy	The command will take several seconds to execute. First you will see the loading message, then a copyright screen and then your screen (see Figure 8–2) will display.
↵	Enter key, to retrieve the As-Easy-As window screen.

DATA ENTRY

Begin to enter the data in the worksheet by placing your cell pointer on D1 and pressing,

Caps Lock	To enter text in uppercase
HARDWARE ASSOCIATES	The text to be entered
↵	Enter key

If you enter incorrect text into a cell, you can simply edit or retype the entry. The new entry will replace the old entry. If you put the entry into the wrong cell, you can erase the contents of the cell by placing your cell pointer on the cell and typing

/	Slash
R	Range
E	Erase
↵	Enter key to empty the currently active cell

When you are entering data, you need not always press the Enter key. Pressing any of the directional keys (arrows, Home, Enter, Tab, PgUp, PgDn) will automatically enter the data typed on the entry line before the cell pointer is moved. For example, if you are entering a column of numbers by typing a number and pressing Down arrow, instead of typing a number, pressing Enter, and then pressing the Down arrow, you will save one key stroke with each entry. If the column had 300 numbers, you would save 300 key strokes.

Using your directional keys to change to different cell addresses, make the following text entries:

Cell Coordinate	**Entry**
D3	SALES FORECAST
B5	LAST
C5	'1ST
D5	'2ND
E5	'3RD
F5	'4TH
G5	YRLY
A6	MODEL
B6	QTR.
C6	QTR.
D6	QTR.
E6	QTR.
F6	QTR.
G6	TOTAL
A8	HACKER 1
A9	HACKER 2
A10	HACKER 3
A12	TOTALS
B8	15500
B9	7300
B10	5500

When entering labels that start with a numeric digit, you must enter a label-prefix character before the first label character. That is why the apostrophe is required. Other label-prefixes would also work. If you enter a number with text behind it, the entry is put into edit mode.

FORMULA ENTRIES

Formulas can contain: 1) numbers; 2) mathematical operators including, but not limited to:

^	Exponentiation
×	Multiplication
/	Division
+	Addition
–	Subtraction

3) cell addresses such as A10 and B15 which are interpreted to mean the value contained in the cells located at the coordinates stated; and 4) built-in functions that result in mathematical values. An example of a relatively complex formula is

(A5×C10+AVG(B2 . . B5))/2 which if it were entered into a cell would be read as

Multiply the value of the cell A5 by the value of the cell in C10 and
Add that result to the average of the values in the cells B2, B3, B4, and B5 and then
Divide the result by two, and
Display the result in the active cell.

Place your cell pointer on cell B12 and type the formula

+B8+B9+B10

The formula to calculate the annual sum.

After entering the formula with the Enter key, you will see that the cell displays the number 28300, but its contents are seen on the status line to be a formula, **+B8+B9+B10.** The distinction between display and content is important. Move your cell pointer to B9 and type

8500 A new value for sales of the Hacker 2

↵ Enter key. Notice that the total for the column changes, seemingly immediately. The changes are made because the content of B12 is a formula that is recalculated every time a new entry is made in the worksheet.

Type and re-enter the number 7,300 in B9. Your worksheet should now look like Figure 9–2.

```
                         HARDWARE ASSOCIATES

                           SALES FORECAST

           LAST            1ST       2ND       3RD       4TH       YRLY
MODEL      QTR.            QTR.      QTR.      QTR.      QTR.      TOTAL

HACKER 1        15500
HACKER 2         7300
HACKER 2         5500

TOTALS          28300
```

Figure 9–2.

As long as the formula you type contains correctly formed cell addresses and numbers, the entry will be treated as a value. If you press Return and the formula appears in the cell, you have made a mistake in the entry; probably a missing plus sign as the first character. At times you may hear a "beep" and the mode indicator may display "<EDIT?>." This signal indicates that you began entering a value with the first character but a later character was a label. Common errors that put the entry into edit mode are using an "l" instead of a 1 and an "o" instead of a 0. Incorrect cell addresses and illegal operators will also cause the entry to be put into edit.

CELL DISPLAYS THAT ARE TOO LARGE *Worksheet Column-width*

The default width of a cell is 9 characters. Although text entered in cells may overlap to adjoining columns, numbers that are too large to display correctly will not overlap. Whenever As-Easy-As encounters this situation, you will see the cell filled with "*********" symbols. This is a special display. It is not an indication that the contents are incorrect. The "*********" characters may appear after a number has displayed correctly if you change the display. For instance, if a cell displaying 1234567 was formatted to display the number as currency with two decimal places, thirteen characters must be displayed since the formatting adds a dollar sign, two commas, a period, and two zeros to look like $1,234,567.00. Since this is too large, the "*********" characters are displayed. By looking on the entry line, you will be able to see that the original contents remain. Again, there is a difference between a cell's contents and its display.

To replace the "*********" characters, you must change the width of the cell by typing,

/	Slash
W	WSheet
C	ColWidth
S	Set
14	Or any number large enough to display the number
↵	Enter key

The **W**orksheet-**C**olumn-width command allows you to set the width in two ways. In the exercise just completed you typed 14 and pressed the Enter key. This is the approach to take when you are confident you know what the width should be. Sometimes you do not know the width you should have. When this is the case, instead of typing a new number, use the Right and Left arrow keys. As you press the arrows, the width of the column widens and contracts interactively. Expand the column to the width you desire and then press the Enter key.

USING CELL AND RANGE ADDRESSES

The cell address B6 is a reference to a single cell. The value stored in B6 is returned to a formula that references it.

The reference to B2 . . B5 in the sample formula is a range address. It refers to a rectangular group of cells which has the cell B2 in one corner and the cell B5 in the opposing corner and includes all the cells in the block. B2 and B5 are the end points of the range. A range address could reference,

A single cell	A1 . . A1	with 1 cell
A column of cells	A1 . . A10	with 10 cells
A row of cells	A1 . . G1	with 7 cells
A block of cells	A1 . . G10	with 70 cells

Some of the command menu choices will ask you to indicate which cell or range of cells is to be affected. When initiating these commands, if you can see or you know where the cells and ranges are, you can type them in response to a prompt.

In the pages that follow, you are often asked to ''anchor'' a range. This is accomplished with the period. Pressing the periods changes a cell address like C10 . . C10 which will change as the cell pointer is moved, to a range address in which one corner is anchored. This enables you to move the cell pointer to create a rectangular block of cells such as C10 . . D20. Use the Escape Key to ''unanchor,'' the range.

THE COMMAND MENU

In addition to entering data in cells, there are many operations that are conducted through a command menu. The main command menu is obtained by pressing the Slash key (uppercase is a question mark). The main menu appears as:

```
Wsheet
Range
CopyCell
MoveCell
Array
Data
File
Graphics
PrintTo
Exit
```

Figure 9–3. As-Easy-As Main Menu.

Each of the choices on the menu begins with a unique character. ''Range,'' for instance, is the only choice that begins with the character ''R.'' Once this menu or any submenu appears, you make choices by typing the first letter of the word of choice you wish to make, or by responding to prompts (questions) that some of the choices will lead to.

The commands included in the command menu serve the functions noted in Figure 9–4.

You will use the command menu shortly. To exit from the menu whenever you are finished using it, or whenever you enter it in error, press the Escape key. **Do so now.**

`WSheet`	Insert and delete rows and columns, erase the worksheet, create windows and titles, set global worksheet characteristics
`Range`	Change the display of cell ranges, erase, protect, and unprotect cells
`CopyCell`	Duplicate a cell or range of cells
`MoveCell`	Relocate a cell or range of cells
`Array`	Manipulate arrays of numbers with operations such as multiplication, subtraction, division, addition, transposition, and inversion.
`Data`	Sort rows, database operations such as sort, extract, and deletion, frequency counting
`File`	Save, erase, and retrieve worksheets
`Graphics`	Create bar, stacked bar, X-Y, line, and pie charts from worksheet data
`PrintTo`	Print a file and specify the printout's range, margins, and other characteristics. Also used to write the file to disk.
`Exit`	Exit from As-Easy-As
`.`	The period will move the MainMenu to opposite sides of the screen.

Figure 9–4. As-Easy-As Commands.

TEXT JUSTIFICATION AND FORMATTING *Range Label-Prefix/Range Format*

As numbers are entered, they are right-justified; text is left-justified. Often it will be necessary, for better appearance, to change the justification of either numbers or text. Change the justification of the column headings in columns B through G by placing the cell pointer on cell B5 and typing

`/` Slash, to call up the command menu
`R` Range
`P` Prefix
`R` Right, to set right justify
→ Right arrow, five times to highlight the range B5 through G5
↓ Down arrow once, to highlight B5 through G6
↲ Enter key, to complete the range designation. Observe that a quote has replaced the apostrophe in cell B5

Use the formatting procedure to change the appearance of the numbers that appear as the sales for the last quarter and for future quarters by placing the cell pointer on cell B8 and typing,

`/` Slash, to call up the command menu
`R` Range
`F` Format, to change the display of a cell's contents
`C` Currency format
`0` `0,` for the number of decimal places

↲	Enter key
→	Right arrow five times to highlight B8 through G8
↓	Down arrow four times to expand coverage to B8 through G12
↲	Enter key. Observe the designation of "[C0]" on the status line which identifies the formatting as currency, zero decimal places.

The cells B8 through G9 have now been formatted to display numbers in a currency format. New numbers entered in these cells and numbers created by formulas will follow this formatting and not the general format provided by default by As-Easy-As.

CREATING AND USING FORMULAS

You have already created one formula that summed the sales for the last quarter. Now you must create formulas for projecting the sales of each computer model and for summing the 1st quarter sales. For each model of computer sold, there is a different assumption that is used to project (guess) the sales. To project the sales for the Hacker 1, place your cell pointer on C8 and without entering any spaces in the formula type

+B8	The cell address for the value representing the sales of the Hacker 1 computer in the last quarter
×	The multiplication symbol
1.03	to increase the previous sales by 3%
↲	Enter key, to enter the formula **B8*1.03** currently on the entry line into active cell, C8, giving the projected sales of $15,965

Now project the sales for the Hacker 2. Move to C9 and type

+B9/2	To reduce the value in B9, the last quarter sales for the Hacker 2, by 50%
↲	Enter key, to enter the formula which produces the value $3,650

Project the sales of the Hacker 3. Move to C10 and type

+B10+450	To increase the last quarter sales of the Hacker 3 by a fixed amount of 450 units
↲	Enter key, to enter the formula created. This produces the value 5,950

COPYING

Range Copy

These three formulas provide you with the first quarter's projected sales. You could (but don't) continue to create additional formulas of the same type throughout the remaining columns for quarterly sales. You could also type a formula for totaling the last quarter's sales at the bottom of each column. In each case, you would use the same formula, but you would adjust the cell addresses. To project the 2nd quarter's sales, for illustration, you could type C8*1.03, instead of B8*1.03. This duplication of formulas could lead to mistakes, however. The time that it takes to duplicate the formulas could be substantial if a worksheet is large.

As-Easy-As provides a command for copying these formulas that will save you time and assure you that the formulas have been copied correctly. To copy the formulas, place the cell pointer on cell C8 and type

/	Slash
c	CopyCell
↓	Down arrow twice to enter range to copy "from" as C8 . . C10
↲	Enter key
.	Period to "anchor" the range. The cell address is converted to a range address

→ Right arrow three times to enter horizontal range which highlights C8 through F8
↵ Enter key, to complete the copy

USING BUILT-IN FUNCTIONS

The total annual sales for each model of computer is to be computed in column G. You could follow the approach taken in totaling the last quarter's sales by adding the individual cells to one another. A formula like C8+D8+E8+F8 is awkward to use because it takes time to type, you may mistype, omit, or duplicate a cell address, or a new column may be added and the formula would have to be retyped. As-Easy-As provides a group of operations called functions that enable you to carry out complex operations easily. To compute the annual total, place your cell pointer on G8 and type

@SUM(C8 . . F8)
↵ Enter key

which uses the @SUM function to sum the values in the cells C8, D8, E8, and F8; all the cells between and including C8 and F8.The result is 66,792 (includes a roundup of one). The range address could include a large group of cells, for instance, C8 through Z8, yet it takes no more effort to create a formula with this range than with a small range.

@SUM is only one built-in function. You will use others later.

MORE COPYING *Copy*

Now you should copy the formula by placing your cell pointer on G8 (if it has been moved) and typing,

/	Slash
c	CopyCell
↵	Enter key, to accept G8 as the default "from" range of cells to be copied. It is legal to type a cell address, to type a range address, or to press the Enter key to accept the active cell as the default address.
.	Period to anchor the range of copy "to."
↓	Down arrow twice to set the range to G8 through G10
↵	Enter key

Complete the worksheet by copying the formula in B12 so the totals for the remaining columns are also displayed. Place the cell pointer on cell B12 and type

/	Slash
c	Copy
↵	Enter key
.	Period to anchor the range.
→	Right arrow five times
↵	Enter key

Your worksheet should now look like that pictured in Figure 9–5.

HARDWARE ASSOCIATES

SALES FORECAST

MODEL	LAST QTR.	1ST QTR.	2ND QTR.	3RD QTR.	4TH QTR.	YRLY TOTAL
HACKER 1	15,500	15,965	16,444	16,937	17,445	66,792
HACKER 2	7,300	3,650	1,825	912	456	6,844
HACKER 2	5,500	5,950	6,400	6,850	7,300	26,500
TOTALS	28,300	25,565	24,669	24,700	25,202	100,135

Figure 9–5.

SAVING A FILE *File Save*

The worksheet you have been building is in the computer's RAM, or main memory. It has not yet been stored on the diskette where it can be recalled later. Be sure to save your work when it has been completed. When you are constructing a large worksheet, you should save your file periodically to avoid the possibility of accidental loss through a power loss or through a failure to save the file before the machine was turned off. Save your worksheet by typing,

/	Slash
F	File
S	Store
Computer	Or any filename chosen by you
↲	Enter key

Saving a worksheet does not exit you from As-Easy-As. You can save a worksheet and then continue working on it. Replace the diskette in drive B with your backup diskette and repeat the save procedure.

RETRIEVING A FILE *File Retrieve*

If you wish to return to the file COMPUTER to work on it at a later time, do so with the following command sequence:

/	Slash
F	File
R	Retrieve. The execution of this command displays a menu of filenames on the default drive. You can retrieve a file by using the right and left arrow keys to highlight the filename you want and then pressing Return. You will see that As-Easy-As has appended the file extension .WK1 to the filenames. Alternatively, you can simply type the filename you want, without the extension. If your files diskette is not in the default drive, you will have to use the command sequence, /File **D**irectory **B:** ↲, to change the default.

COMPUTER	The filename for the saved worksheet
↲	Enter key

When a worksheet file is retrieved, it replaces any other worksheet that is in the computer's memory. If a worksheet you have been working on is to be saved, it must be saved before a second worksheet is retrieved.

LISTING WORKSHEET NAMES

To determine which files are on your disk, press

/	Slash
F	File
L	List
W	Worksheet, to see worksheet and not graph or print files
↲	Enter Key, to return the mode indicator block to ''<File>''
Esc	Escape Key
Esc	Escape Key, to return to ''<Ready>''

PRINTING

Print

To print your worksheet type

/	Slash
P	PrintTo
P	Printer
R	Range
Home	Home key
.	Period, to ''anchor'' the range at A1
↓	Down arrow 11 times, to highlight a vertical range A1 through A12
→	Right arrow six times to highlight a horizontal range A1 through G12
↲	Enter key, to close the range
A	Adjust, to print top of worksheet at the top of page. Check the printer to see that the paper is at the top of the printer head.
G	Go, to execute the printing
P	Page, to move to a new page
Q	Quit the print menu

Printing Cell Contents

Often, it is desirable to print out the contents of the cells so formulas can be checked for accuracy. This can be done with the sequence,

/	Slash
P	PrintTo
P	Printer
R	Range. The print range used previously is a ''remembered'' range. You can skip this step if the print range has been defined and need not be changed. Press the Enter key to reconfirm the range if you pressed ''R.''
O	Options, to change or modify the usual print characteristics
T	Type
C	Cells, to print the cells' contents, not the cells' display

Q Quit, to return to the next higher menu. Escape would return you to the same menu.
A Adjust
G Go

EXITING *Quit*

Now that you have saved and printed your worksheet, exit the As-Easy-As program. Place the DOS disk in drive A and type

/ Slash
E Exit
Y Yes

EXERCISES

A. A small book company produces specialty cook books for local bookstores. The sales of last year are already known, but only estimates can be made of the future sales for each volume. Its book, Cooking With Gas, is expected to increase in sales annually by 15%. Serving Cold Foods is expected to drop to 90% of each previous year's sales. Fish & Fowl will increase its sales by 45 per year, while Meat & Potatoes is anticipated to sell 300 fewer copies per year. The publisher prepared the following worksheet to illustrate the results of a two-year projection.
Reproduce the results obtained by the publisher.

BOOK SALES

TITLE	LAST YEAR	THIS YEAR	YEAR AFTER	3-YEAR TOTAL
COOKING WITH GAS	2,578	2,965	3,409	8,952
SERVING COLD FOODS	1,145	1,030	927	3,103
FISH & FOWL	980	1,025	1,070	3,075
MEAT & POTATOES	1,577	1,277	977	3,831
TOTALS	6,280	6,297	6,384	18,961

B. An oil producing company has four oil fields that have different prospects for continuing to yield oil. The Great Gusher field has not reached its peak and will be increasing by 7% each year. Oilmen's Acres will increase by 1,300 barrels per year as new wells are drilled. Black Gold Hills will drop production by 1,400 barrels per year and Well Mountain will decrease by 12% per year. The chief geologist produced the following worksheet. Reproduce it using appropriate formulas and formatting.

OIL OUTPUT
(IN BARRELS)
============

OIL FIELD	CURRENT YEAR	NEXT YEAR	YEAR AFTER	3-YEAR TOTAL
GREAT GUSHER	20,500	21,935	23,470	65,905
OILMEN'S ACRES	15,800	17,100	18,400	51,300
BLACK GOLD HILLS	19,700	18,300	16,900	54,900
WELL MT.	29,500	25,960	22,845	78,305
TOTALS	85,500	83,295	81,615	250,410

C. A small city school district has four high schools that have been experiencing different growth patterns. East High had 2,101 students in 1987 and was expected to increase its enrollment by 7% in each of the next three years. In the same period West High would increase its enrollment of 3,224 students by 5% each year. North High will increase from 2,768 at a 2% annual rate. South High will experience a decline of 3% each year from its 1987 level of 2,346. Prepare a worksheet that displays the expected enrollment for each of the high schools and a yearly total for the combined schools.

D. In the first quarter of a year, a manufacturer of computer hardware sold 210, 356, 275, 156, and 142 units each of printers, tape drives, disk drives, card punches, and card readers. Printers, tape drives, and disk drives are expected to increase by 5%, 5%, and 3% respectively each of the following 3 quarters. Card punch sales will be decreasing by 15% and card reader sales will be decreasing by 11%. Prepare a worksheet that projects the sales for each device each quarter and that displays the total sales for each device over the one-year period.

Chapter 10

Using Worksheets: A Sales Analysis

CHAPTER OUTLINE

Worksheets like As-Easy-As make a wide range of techniques available for calculating and displaying data in a form that is useful to decision-makers. Keeping a worksheet useful often means that the worksheet must be changed as demands change. Usefulness also requires that complex formulas must be developed to address complex problems. In this chapter, you will apply previously learned skills and you will

1. Utilize built-in functions for analyzing data;
2. Add and delete rows and columns;
3. Examine the need to adjust cell formulas when the number of rows and columns change;
4. Edit, rather than retype, a cell's contents;
5. See the need for distinguishing between absolute, mixed, and relative cell and range addresses during the copying process.

THE PROBLEM

The manufacturing company that produces the three Hacker model computers distributes its machines through regional sales offices. The president of the company needs to see sales statistics on the relative productivity of these offices. These statistics help top management to evaluate the degree to which staffing changes are needed, additional promotion and publicity campaigns should be mounted, and marketing analyses should be undertaken. The Assistant to the President assembles these statistics from quarterly reports submitted by the managers of each of the regional offices. Unlike the first worksheet, which projected sales based on assumptions made by management, this report is more analytical. The Assistant wishes to produce a report that looks like Figure 10–1.

```
                 HARDWARE ASSOCIATES
                 ===================

               QUARTERLY SALES BY SALES OFFICE
                                                       YEARLY     PERCENT
OFFICE         QTR 1    QTR 2     QTR 3     QTR 4       TOTAL    OF TOTAL
-------------------------------------------------------------------------
SOUTHWEST     10,329    8,790     7,834     7,903      34,856         31%
SOUTHEAST      2,900    4,376     4,502     4,678      16,456         14%
NORTHWEST      4,567    4,500     4,325     5,605      18,997         17%
NORTHEAST     10,654   10,834    10,839    10,854      43,181         38%

TOTAL SALES   28,450   28,500    27,500    29,040     113,490
MINIMUM        2,900    4,376     4,325     4,678      16,456
MAXIMUM       10,654   10,834    10,839    10,854      43,181
AVERAGE        7,113    7,125     6,875     7,260      28,373
```

Figure 10–1.

The report should be created on a worksheet like As-Easy-As because this reporting format could be reused every year. Also, the Assistant believes that once the report is shared with the regional managers, they may have corrections to make in the sales data. By using a worksheet, the formulas will automatically update the calculations based on revisions of the reported sales.

INITIAL ENTRIES

After loading As-Easy-As, make the following numerical and text entries:

Cell Coordinate	Entry
C1	HARDWARE ASSOCIATES
C2	'= (Apostrophe, 19 Equal Signs)
B4	QUARTERLY SALES BY SALES OFFICE
F5	YEARLY
G5	PERCENT
A6	OFFICE
B6	QTR 1
C6	QTR 2
D6	QTR 3
E6	QTR 4
F6	TOTAL
G6	OF TOTAL
A7	'– (Apostrophe, 66 Minus Signs)
A8	SOUTHWEST
B8	10329
C8	8790
D8	7834
E8	7903
A9	SOUTHEAST
B9	2900
C9	4376
D9	4502
E9	4678
A10	NORTHWEST
B10	4567
C10	4500
D10	4325
E10	5605
A11	NORTHEAST
B11	10654
C11	10834
D11	10839
E11	10854
A13	TOTAL SALES
A14	MINIMUM
A15	MAXIMUM
A16	AVERAGE

FORMATTING

Range Label-Prefix

The column headings can be right-justified to align the headings with the numbers below by placing the cell pointer on cell B6 and typing

/	Slash
R	Range
P	Prefix, to alter the display of a label
R	Right
↑	Up arrow once, to highlight B6 through B5
→	Right arrow five times, to highlight B6 through G5
↲	Enter key, to complete the Range Prefix command

Column-Width ***Worksheet Col-width***

The text entries in column A, especially A13, are too wide to display properly in a nine character cell. Widen this column by placing your cell pointer anywhere in column A and typing

/	Slash
W	WSheet
C	ColWidth
S	Set, a return here will suffice since the command cursor is already on Set-Width
→	Right arrow 3 times, the column expands to a width of 12
↲	Enter key, to complete the WSheet ColWidth command

The Range Format command is used to alter the display of numbers. Since the sales figures represent the number of units sold, they should be displayed with commas, but no decimal places. Do this by placing your cell pointer on B8 and typing

/	Slash
R	Range
F	Format
,	Comma, to select the comma formatting style. The comma is needed because the typing of a "C" would have formatted the range of cells as *C*urrency.
0	Zero, no decimal places
↲	Enter key, to accept the zero. The prompt, **FORMAT range is:** displays B8 . . B8.
↓	Down arrow 8 times to highlight B8 through B16
→	Right arrow 4 times to highlight B8 through F16
↲	Enter key, to complete the command

USING BUILT-IN FUNCTIONS

The first worksheet you constructed was a projection of sales that illustrated some of the primary features of worksheet software. In that model, you used the @SUM function to total the values in each row of sales figures. The @SUM function is similar to other functions that As-Easy-As possesses. The built-in function @AVG, for instance, could be used to average the sales in each year and the function @MIN could be used to determine what the lowest number was in each year. To use these functions on identical ranges, you need only alter the function name and retain the range addresses that appear in the totals column. @SUM(C8 . . F8) displays a total of the values in the 4 cells C8, D8, E8, and F8, whereas AVG(C8 . . F8) displays the average of the same cells.

To address the current problem, the development of a sales analysis model, will involve the @SUM function and several additional, similar built-in functions. Place your cell pointer on B13 and type

@SUM(B8..B11)	The formula
↲	Enter key

which displays 28,450, the sum of the sales for the four offices for the first quarter. The determination of the minimum, maximum, and average sales per office per quarter will be similar. Type

CELL COORDINATE	ENTRY	DISPLAYS
B14	@MIN(B8..B11)	2,900
B15	@MAX(B8..B11)	10,654
B16	@AVG(B8..B11)	7,112

The yearly total column (F) utilizes the @SUM function, but the range of cells being summed is horizontal, rather than vertical. Place your cell pointer on F8 and type

@SUM(B8 . . E8)
↵ Enter key, which produces 34,856

Selected Built-In Functions

As-Easy-As has many built-in functions that can assist you in the development of sophisticated worksheets. Figure 10–2 identifies thirteen of these functions. There are others that are described in the As-Easy-As manual.

Function	Description
@ABS(NUMBER)	Returns the absolute value of a number
@AVG(list)	Returns the average of all values in a list, does not count empty cells
@COUNT(list)	Returns the count of the number of nonempty cells, including labels, in a list
@IF(logical expression,result1,result2)	Returns result1 if the logical expression is true or returns result2 if the logical expression is false
@INT(number)	Returns the integer portion of a number
@HTABLE(key,range,offset)	Looks up the key value in the horizontal lookup range and returns thevalue in the cell above or below specified by the offset
@VTABLE(key,range,offset)	Looks up the key value in the vertical lookup range and returns the value in the column in the cell to the right specified by the offset
@MAX(list)	Returns the largest value in a list
@MIN(list)	Returns the smallest value in a list
@ROUND(number,place)	Returns the value of a number rounded to a specified number of decimal places
@SQRT(number)	Returns the square root of a number
@STD(list)	Returns the standard deviation for all numbers in a list
@SUM(list)	Returns the sum of a list of numbers

Figure 10–2. Selected As-Easy-As Built-in Functions.

COPYING

Range Copy

Copy the formulas for total, minimum, maximum, and average sales per quarter in column B, across the next four columns by placing the cell pointer in cell B13, followed by the command sequence

/ Slash
C CopyCell
↓ Down arrow 3 times
↵ Enter key, to define the copy "from" range as B13 . . B16
. Period to anchor the copy "to" range
→ Right arrow 4 times, to highlight the cells B13 through F13
↵ Enter key to execute the copy command.

Copy the formula for the annual total of sales found in F8 for the other three offices by placing your cell pointer on F8 and typing

/ Slash
c CopyCell
↵ Enter key, to accept the current cell as the single cell to be copied. Since the range address F8 . . F8 was shown, only a single cell composes the range.
. Period to anchor the copy "to" range
↓ Down arrow three times
↵ Enter key to execute the copy command

Look at the formulas that were created in F9 by moving your cell pointer to F9. Observe on the status line how the cell addresses in the formula that was copied were changed from B8 to B9 and from E8 to E9.

ABSOLUTE AND RELATIVE CELL ADDRESSES

As-Easy-As allows for three types of cell addresses: relative, absolute, and mixed. When a cell address in a copied formula is adjusted, the row and column coordinates are changed relative to the direction in which the cell address is being copied. For instance, if cell address C10 is contained in a formula found in D20 and this formula is copied to E21, and if C10 is allowed to be adjusted because it is a relative address, it will be changed to D11. The C is adjusted to D because the formula was copied one column to the right. The 10 is changed to 11 because the formula was copied one row down.

```
      A          B          C          D          E
 20                                 +C10*2
 21 Original cell reference ----┘                 +D11*2
 22                   Address after adjustment ─┘
```

Cell addresses are made absolute by placing a dollar sign in front of both the row and column coordinates. If an absolute cell address is copied from one cell to another, the cell address is copied unchanged. An absolute cell address prevents adjustment so that the cell "absolutely" refers to the same cell it did before copying. If the formula $C$10*2 is copied, no adjustment is permitted, and the cell address will remain unchanged regardless of the number of rows or columns that separate the original cell from the copy.

```
      A          B          C          D          E
 20                                 +$C$10*2
 21 Original cell reference ----┘                 +$D$11*2
 22                   Address after adjustment ─┘
```

The dollar sign in front of the column coordinate C means, "if this formula is copied, absolutely do not adjust the column coordinate." The dollar sign in front of the row number has a similar meaning, but holds the row coordinate constant. If a cell address will not allow either the column or row to be adjusted, copies of it will always refer to the same location.

A mixed cell address holds either the column or the row absolute but not both. $C10 and C$10 are mixed addresses.

The differences between relative, absolute, and mixed cell addresses is critical to the successful development of worksheets. In many formulas, there will be addresses of each type. After copying formulas, you should always examine the products of the formulas copied to be sure that they are returning the correct answers; don't assume that they are! If the correct answers are not present, but the original formula was correct, look closely at the formulas in the cells to which the formula was copied and check the cell references to be sure that they refer to the appropriate cells. If they do not, reset the cell addresses correctly.

Column G calculates the percentage each office's sales are of the total sales for the company. To create this combination absolute and relative formula for the first office, place your cell pointer on G8 and enter

+F8/$F$13 a formula to calculate the percentage of sales coming from this office

This divides the Southwest office's "relative" sales by the company's "absolute" sales. The dollar signs imbedded in the column and row address F13 designate an absolute reference to the total sales cell for the year.

FORMATTING *Range Format*

To format this number as a percentage, type

/ Slash
R Range
F Format
P Percent
0 To suppress the display of any fractional parts
↵ Enter key
↵ Enter key, to execute the Range Format command which displays 31%

COPYING *Range Copy*

Copy the formula in G8 by leaving your cell pointer on G8 and typing

/ Slash
C CopyCell
↵ Enter key, to accept the current cell as the cell to be duplicated
. Period to anchor the copy "to" range
↓ Down arrow 3 times
↵ Enter key, to execute the copy command

Since the formula in G8 is referencing both absolute and relative columns and rows, the formulas in G9 through G11 will adhere to the same addressing modes.

Your worksheet should now look like that pictured in Figure 10–3.

HARDWARE ASSOCIATES
====================

QUARTERLY SALES BY SALES OFFICE

OFFICE	QRT 1	QTR 2	QTR 3	QTR 4	YEARLY TOTAL	PERCENT OF TOTAL
SOUTHWEST	10,329	8,790	7,834	7,903	34,856	31%
SOUTHEAST	2,900	4,376	4,502	4,678	16,456	14%
NORTHWEST	4,567	4,500	4,325	5,605	18,997	17%
NORTHEAST	10,654	10,834	10,839	10,854	43,181	38%
TOTAL SALES	28,450	28,500	27,500	29,040	113,490	
MINIMUM	2,900	4,376	4,325	4,678	16,456	
MAXIMUM	10,654	10,834	10,839	10,854	43,181	
AVERAGE	7,112	7,125	6,875	7,260	28,372	

Figure 10–3.

ADDING ROWS

Worksheet Insert

Adding Rows within Ranges

One of the great values of worksheets is the rapidity with which they can be modified. Suppose that after the Assistant to the President completed the annual sales analysis model, it was found that the company had actually sold 2,205 more computers than were reflected in the sales in each region. The difference is found to be the failure to include sales by two sales representatives who report to the main office of Hardware Associates, rather than to a regional office. One of these sales people is in Alaska and the other is based in Kansas City. Since the company is contemplating opening full-scale offices in both locations, the Assistant decides to add two new rows to the worksheet.

For illustrative purposes, the two rows will be added in two separate locations. To create the first entry for the "Central" office in Kansas, place your cell pointer on A10 (although the cell pointer could be anywhere on this row), and type

/	Slash
W	WSheet
I	Insert, to create a new row 10 and to move row 10 and other rows below it underneath the new row
R	Row
↵	Enter key, to choose row 10 as the location at which a new row will be inserted. If you wished to insert more than one row, you would press the Down arrow key once for each additional row needed

The new row appears, but more changes have been made to the worksheet than is apparent. Move your cell pointer to B14 and look at the contents of the cell as they appear next to the prompt line. The range of cells being summed, which you entered as B8 . . B11 is now shown as B8 . . B12. The end points of the range of cells were automatically adjusted by As-Easy-As to include the inserted row. This is because the new row was located between the two range corner cells B8 and B11. This adjustment was made to all the formulas that are now found in rows 14 through 17. Had a column been inserted, the ranges found in column F would also have been adjusted.

The information you should now enter in the blank row is

Cell Coordinate	Entry
A10	**CENTRAL**
B10	**379**
C10	**334**
D10	**311**
E10	**323**

Entries in this row change the column totals, averages, and minimums. This data is taken into account by the formulas on rows 14 through 17 as soon as it is entered. The yearly total and the percent of total columns for Central remain empty because no formulas have been put in them. The formulas will be added shortly.

Adding Rows Outside Ranges

The Assistant to the President decides to add the Alaskan entry at line 13, a line that is currently blank. A blank line is still needed to separate the data from the results of the analysis. To add the new row, place your cell pointer on row 13, and type

/	Slash
W	WSheet
I	Insert, to create a new row 13 and to move row 13 and other rows below it down
R	Row
↵	Enter key, to choose row 13 as the location of the row to be inserted

Make the following entries:

Cell Coordinate	Entry
A13	ALASKA
B13	<LEAVE BLANK>
C13	256
D13	295
E13	297

ADDING COLUMNS *Worksheet Insert*

This exercise demonstrated how rows are inserted in worksheets. The insertion of a column is essentially the same. The completion of the insertion command causes a new column to be inserted at the location of the cell pointer. The column the cell pointer was on is pushed to the right, along with any other columns to the right of the cell pointer. When columns or rows are inserted, you should examine relevant formulas closely to be sure that the new column is included in the intended formula ranges.

DELETING ROWS AND COLUMNS *Worksheet Delete*

The command sequence for deleting columns and rows can also affect the validity of formulas contained in other columns and rows. For instance, the deletion of column F can cause a formula in column G that reads @SUM(A8 . . F8) to display an error. As-Easy-As keeps track of the two end points of a range and not the entire range. Thus, when one of the end points is eliminated, As-Easy-As does not assume that there is a new end point such as E8. An error is displayed.

The deletion of a row or column in the middle of a range is automatically accommodated by formulas that had that row or column in the middle of its range.

EDITING CELL CONTENTS *F2*

Notice that total sales for the last three quarters have not changed even though there were sales in Alaska. Neither have the minimum or the average sales changed. Move your cell pointer to B15 and look at the range address on the contents line. The range being summed is still defined as B8 . . B12 so the row that was just added was not included in this or in any of the formulas on rows 15 through 18. The formulas must all be edited to reflect the inclusion of this row.

It is not necessary to retype a cell's contents completely if much of it is correct. Retyping might introduce new errors. Edit the contents with the Edit key, F2, instead. With your cell pointer on B15, type the following:

`F2`	Edit key
←	Left arrow to place the cursor under the ")"
`Backspace`	Backspace key, to remove the 2
`3`	To insert a 3 to make the range B8 . . B13
↵	Enter key

The total does not change because B13 is blank. An empty cell is not treated as a zero. It is ignored. Notice that an empty cell is not treated as a zero by the minimum function. An empty cell is different from a cell with a zero in it. A zero would be evaluated in all four functions used here.

Edit the cells in B16 through B18 with the same key strokes.

The formulas in the total column (F) and the four analytical rows (B15 through B18) must be recopied. Do this by placing the cell pointer on B15 and typing

`/`	Slash
`C`	CopyCell

↓ Down arrow 3 times to set the copy "from" range
↲ Enter key
. Period to anchor the copy "to" range
→ Right arrow 4 times to set the copy "to" range
↲ Enter key for execution of the CopyCell command

Recalculate the annual totals and the percent of totals figures for each of the offices by placing your cell pointer on F8 and entering

/ Slash
C CopyCell
→ Right arrow once to set the copy "from" range
↲ Enter key
. Period to anchor the range
↓ Down arrow 5 times to set the copy "to" range
↲ Enter key to execute the CopyCell command

Your worksheet is complete and should look like Figure 10–4.

HARDWARE ASSOCIATES
===================

QUARTERLY SALES BY SALES OFFICE

OFFICE	QRT 1	QTR 2	QTR 3	QTR 4	YEARLY TOTAL	PERCENT OF TOTAL
SOUTHWEST	10,329	8,790	7,834	7,903	34,856	30%
SOUTHEAST	2,900	4,376	4,502	4,678	16,456	14%
CENTRAL	379	334	311	323	1,347	1%
NORTHWEST	4,567	4,500	4,325	5,605	18,997	16%
NORTHEAST	10,654	10,834	10,839	10,854	43,181	37%
ALASKA		256	295	297	848	1%
TOTAL SALES	28,829	29,090	28,106	29,660	115,685	
MINIMUM	379	256	295	297	848	
MAXIMUM	10,654	10,834	10,839	10,854	43,181	
AVERAGE	5,766	4,848	4,684	4,943	19,281	

Figure 10–4.

The percentage column does not add up correctly because of round-off error. The percentages could be displayed to reflect a 100% total if fractional parts were displayed.

SAVING YOUR WORKSHEET *File Save*

Save your worksheet by typing

/ Slash
F File
S Store

SALES	To assign **SALES** as the filename. If you have already saved SALES once, the name will automatically appear. You need not retype the name. Go on to the next step instead.
↵	Enter key, to enter the save filename

Replace the diskette in drive B with your backup diskette and repeat the file save procedure.

PRINTING YOUR WORKSHEET *Print Printer*

To print your worksheet, type

/	Slash
P	Print
P	Printer
R	Range
Home	Home key
.	Period to anchor the copy "to" range
↓	Down arrow 17 times for the vertical range
→	Right arrow 6 times for the horizontal range
↵	Enter key, to complete the print range
A	Adjust. Set the paper crease at the top of the print head.
G	Go, to execute the printing of the worksheet
P	Page, advance to the top of the next page
Q	Quit, to return to As-Easy-As

PRINTING A WORKSHEET TO DISK *Print File*

Normally to say that you are printing a file implies that you are sending the file to the printer to get hardcopy output. It is also possible to print a file to the disk. When you do this, a line-by-line image of the worksheet is sent to a new file. Unlike the worksheet file in which all of the formatting commands, column widths, and cell contents are known, the printed disk file only contains the characters that you see on the screen inside of the worksheet. For example, a single cell that contains a formula "B2*C3/20" might display "$20.13" because the number created by the formula is displayed as currency, two decimal places. A print file only contains leading spaces, if any, the dollar sign, the period, and the numerals as part of a larger line. There is nothing to indicate how these characters came to become part of the line printed within the file.

Print to disk files are primarily used to create files that are accessible to word processing and other programs. Worksheet files by themselves cannot be read into most other programs directly. Worksheet files contain information and control characters that the user does not want to become a part of the receiving file and that the receiving program does not know how to handle. By creating a print file, only the display of the worksheet is saved. These print lines can be added to a word processing or other program file later.

You are going to print a file to disk now that will be used in chapter 18. In that chapter, you will create a memorandum using PC-Write. The memorandum will include information from the worksheet you have just completed, as well as data from a PC-File+.

To print a file to disk, type

/	Slash
P	Print
F	File
SALES	The filename to be used. The extension .PRN will be added to the filename automatically.
↵	Enter key
G	Go, to print the worksheet image to a file
Q	Quit, to return to As-Easy-As 123

PRINTING WORKSHEETS AS FORMULAS *Print Printer Options Other*

At times it is necessary to examine the contents of cells rather than the displays of the cells. If results are inaccurate, it may be that the formulas contained in some of the cells are incorrect. It may be difficult to evaluate all of the formulas if you are restricted to a single screen of the worksheet since many worksheets contain hundreds of formulas which are found throughout thousands of cells. Printing the formulas allows you the flexibility of having the formulas close at hand while you examine a print out of the display organized by rows and columns to see whether correct references are being made to cell and range addresses. Print out the formulas for this worksheet by typing

- / Slash
- P Print
- P Printer
- O Options
- T Type
- C Cells
- Q Quit, to return to a higher command level
- G Go, to print out the cell formulas
- P Page, advance to the top of the next page
- Q Quit, to return to As-Easy-As 123

EXITING AS-EASY-AS *Exit*

Save your file as you did earlier, so that the print range is preserved. Exit the As-Easy-As program. Type

- / Slash
- E Exit
- Y Yes, to confirm exit

and load the DOS diskette if prompted to do so.

EXERCISES

A. A college professor is keeping student grades in an As-Easy-As worksheet. Copy the following seminar class grade book. The cumulative total column represents the sum of each student's grades for the semester, while the final column averages all scores.

GRADE BOOK
CIS 450
==========

NAME	TEST 1	TEST 2	TEST 3	TEST 4	FINAL	CUM. TOTAL	AVERAGE
SMITH, S.	89	92	90	92	99	462	92
JONES	78	85	82	70	80	395	79
BLACK, B.	98	93	92	90	91	464	93
WHITE, W.	77	80	86	78	88	409	82
THOMAS, T.	85	87	87	83	90	432	86
WRIGHT, W.	85	73	84	87	84	413	83
AVERAGE	85	85	87	83	89	429	
MINIMUM	77	73	82	70	80	395	
MAXIMUM	98	93	92	92	99	464	

Print out this worksheet as it appears and as formulas. Also print this worksheet to a file with the filename GRADES.PRN (As-Easy-As appends the .PRN). This file will be used in an exercise in chapter 18.

B. A motor vehicle sales office manager breaks down the dollars earned through the sales of vehicles in four categories: sedans, station wagons, vans, and trucks. In addition to totaling the sales, the manager wishes to determine the percentage of the total each amount represents. The sales for each half-year and the percentage of the total for each is shown below. Reconstruct the worksheet.

INCOME ANALYSIS

PRODUCT	FIRST HALF	% OF TOTAL	SECOND HALF	% OF TOTAL
SEDANS	$2,456,686	43.91%	$3,112,800	45.59%
STA. WAGONS	$1,233,345	22.05%	$1,577,380	23.10%
VANS	$114,567	2.05%	$134,677	1.97%
TRUCKS	$1,789,655	31.99%	$2,003,456	29.34%
TOTALS	$5,594,253	100.00%	$6,828,313	100.00%

The dollar signs are displayed with the use of the Range Format command. Select "C" to display the dollar sign and the comma for the specified range.

The sales office began to sell subcompact cars in the second half of the year. Modify the worksheet to reflect $57,657 of income realized from the sale of subcompacts as a fifth category.

Print out this worksheet as it appears and as formulas. Also print this worksheet to a file with the filename INCOME.PRN. This file will be used in an exercise in chapter 18.

C. A superintendent of a small rural school district has been asked to prepare a table that reflects the number and percent of the total of males and females employed at each school level in the district. At the elementary school level, there are 26 males and 67 females. At the middle school level, there are 28 males and 24 females. At the high school level, there are 32 males and 24 females. Prepare a worksheet that displays this information, the totals for each grade level and the percentage each sex contributes to the total of 100% for each grade level. For instance, the 26 males at the elementary school level are 27% of the total of 93 teachers employed at the elementary level. Also display the total numbers of males and females for the district and the composite percentages each group makes up of the total. Print this worksheet as it appears and as formulas. Also print the worksheet to a file named MFRATIO.PRN for use in an exercise in chapter 18.

D. The Watson County School district's budget is composed of expenditures of $1,609,370 for instruction, $327,058 for administration, $346,600 for maintenance, and $172,630 for transportation. A comparative study of 10 other school districts showed their average expenditures for the same items to be $1,472,300, $313,980, $256,780, and $142,890 respectively. Build a worksheet that displays the percent of support each item is of the total for both the school district and the comparative sample. Display the four items in thousands of dollars (e.g., $313,980 is displayed as $313.98).

E. The Ace taxi cab company has five vehicles. The mileage for each vehicle is tracked carefully. The mileages for one quarter are:

VEHICLE	JAN.	FEB.	MAR.
123-ABH	2056	3004	2768
345-XYG	2344	3021	2856
455-XYH	1589	1468	1290
231-ABH	2788	2234	1121
346-XYG	2700	2344	1903

Create a worksheet that identifies the average, total, minimum, and maximum mileages for each month, as well as for the quarter. Also, display the percent of the total that each cab was driven.

A sixth vehicle with the license plate 311-BMW is acquired in March. Add this vehicle to the list as well as its March mileage of 1,250 miles. Adjust the formulas to accurately reflect this addition.

Chapter 11
As-Easy-As Graphing

CHAPTER OUTLINE

Numerical presentations like that of the projected sales for each regional office of Hardware Associates are useful to management in that the data presented offers a quantitative basis for planning. Discussion of the assumptions made in the projection enable managers to question whether the projections are realistic or not. If data needs to be changed, this can be done quickly and easily. Unfortunately, it is difficult for many people to fully grasp the implications of the projections. Which of the several regions are increasing their sales? Are overall sales increasing or decreasing? Graphs and charts portraying numerical data are often more useful in presenting data in a form that is suitable for human understanding than are raw numbers. In this chapter, you will learn how to

1. Construct and save As-Easy-As graphs;
2. Save graphs and to print them out;
3. Name graph settings so the graph can be recalled for adjustment in the future;
4. Use the Graph key;
5. Reset graph settings to facilitate the development of new graphs.

RETRIEVING A WORKSHEET *File Retrieve*

In the last chapter, you created a worksheet with the filename SALES. If you have been working with As-Easy-As, you will want to save the file you have been working with before you retrieve the file SALES because this file will totally replace the worksheet currently in view. If you are starting anew, boot the computer with DOS and type

aseasy
↵ Enter key, to load As-Easy-As. The Registration screen appears
↵ Enter key, to enter As-Easy-As

When you have obtained the blank worksheet screen, retrieve the worksheet SALES by typing

/	Slash
F	File
R	Retrieve
SALES	The name of the file to be retrieved
↵	Enter key

The graph to be created first will be a pie chart that displays the first quarter's sales. Each sector, or pie piece, will represent the sales by one sales office. Together, the sales of all of the offices will total 100% of the sales. As-Easy-As has difficulty printing labels on graphs with as many letters as the office names. Change these names to their abbreviated names: "SW," "SE," "CNT," "NW," "NE" and "AL" before proceeding.

THE GRAPH COMMAND *Graph*

Before initiating the graph command, place your cell pointer on A8, the label "SW." Once you have begun to execute a command sequence, it is awkward to move the cell pointer to a desired location. You are restricted to making choices from the menu or to responding to prompts. The prompts frequently assume that the currently active cell is the starting point for a range. If the current cell is not the starting point, you must relocate the cell pointer to the new location. The Graph command is initiated by typing

Caps Lock	Put Caps Lock on
/	Slash
.	Period, to move the menu to the right side of the screen. Pressing the period again would toggle the menu to the left side of the screen.
G	Graphics, which displays the following menu:

```
GRAPHICS
Type
X
A
B
C
D
E
F
Options
Reset
Name
View
Plot
Quit
```

The default choice, Type (default because it is already highlighted), is used to select the style of graph you would like to prepare. Press

↵ Enter key, to select "Type." Notice that there are five types of charts that are possible: line, bar, pie, XY charts, and stacked bar charts
P Pie, to create a pie chart

Notice that after As-Easy-As accepted the pie chart choice, the graph menu returned to the control panel. This is a "sticky" menu that assumes that you will need to continue working with it since the construction of a graph is a multistep process. A sticky menu saves you the trouble of retyping the "/" and "G" to return to this menu many times.

The X on the menu represents the choice to use to identify the range of cells that will compose the identifying labels for the pie's sectors. In this graph, you would like to have the office names (SW, SE, etc.) be these labels. The letters A through F are used to designate the data ranges that will be used to construct the graphs. In a pie chart, you need only set the X and A ranges. As-Easy-As allows only one chart per screen. Therefore, only one set of data can be graphed. To set the two ranges, type

X To select the X range. A prompt shows the default cell to be A8. A8 is a "free" cell address because it is not anchored. If necessary, you could move the pointer and only highlight the currently active cell. This is the correct cell to begin with since the X range should highlight the office names.
. Period, to anchor the range and to display "A8 . . A8"
↓ Down arrow 5 times to highlight the office names and to display the X range as "A8 . . A13"
↵ Enter key
A To select the A range. Again, the default cell is A8, which is not correct.
→ Right arrow, to begin the A data range at B8
. Period, to anchor the range and to display "B8 . . B8"
↓ Down arrow 5 times to highlight the sales figures and to display the A range as "B8 . . B13." It is important to note that the X and A data ranges parallel one another. As-Easy-As will make the association between "SW" and the number 10,329, as well as between the other office names and their corresponding sales figures.
↵ Enter key
V View, to see the pie chart. Observe the labels that were selected as the X range. The numbers of the A range were automatically converted to percentages which are also displayed. "AL" does not appear since this office had no sales in this quarter

GRAPH OPTIONS

Graph Options

Titles

The pie chart is accurately produced, but it is lacking some vital information. Namely, there are no titles indicating what the graph portrays. Add titles by pressing

Esc	Escape key, to cancel the graphic display
O	Options, to enhance the graph with some additional information
T	Titles, to incorporate one of the possible titles on the graph
F	First, to create a banner title that will go across the top of the graph
HARDWARE ASSOCIATES	The main title
↵	Enter key, to enter the title
Caps Lock	Put Caps Lock off
S	Second, to enter a subtitle just beneath the main title
First Quarter Sales	The subtitle

↵ Enter key. A pie chart does not use X-axis and Y-axis titles so these choices will not be selected
Q Quit, to return to the graphics options menu.
Q Quit, to return to the graphics menu.
V View, to see the graph with the titles, as displayed in Graph 11–1.
Esc Escape, to return to the graph menu

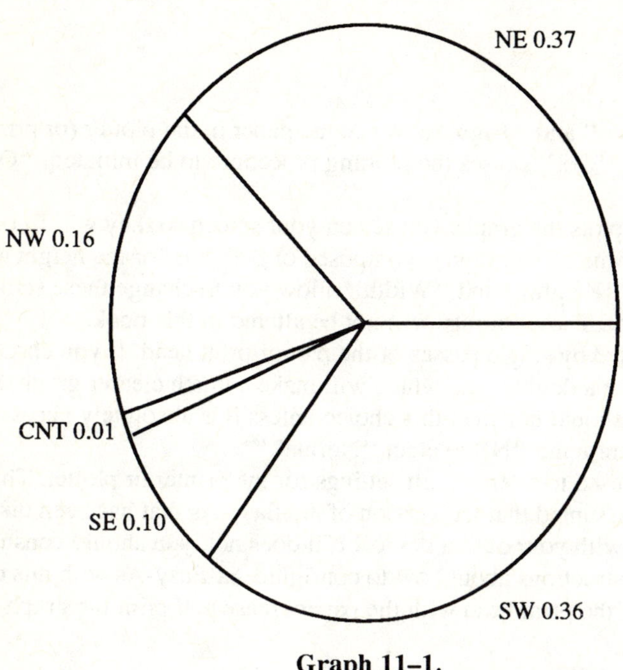

Graph 11–1.

NAMING THE GRAPH *Graph Name*

Another choice on the graph menu is "Name." The Name command does not save a picture. Neither does it create a separate file. It is used to identify and retain for future use the settings that can reproduce graphs on the screen. By naming a graph, you associate a series of graph settings with the name selected. Name the graph by typing

N Name
C Create
QTR1A The graph settings name
↵ Enter key. Notice how quickly control returns to the graph menu and that the red light did not go on. No new files were created.

Once the graph settings have been named, you can reuse the graph name and recall the graph at any time. You will do this shortly.

PLOTTING THE GRAPH

As-Easy-As allows you to plot or print your graph from the graphic menu. Press,

P Plot, to enter the graphics plot menu which appears as,

```
GRAPHICS
PLOT
Height
Width
Normal
Double
Setup
Line
Page
Go
Quit
```

The menu choices ''Line,'' and ''Page'' advance the paper in the plotter (or printer) in the same way that the print menu does. ''Go,'' causes the plotting procedure to be initiated. ''Quit;'' exits you from the plot menu.

Normally, As-Easy-As plots the graphs you see on your screen so they will fit on one half of an 8 1/2 inch by 11 inch sheet of paper. The graph is composed of 800 dots for the height and 800 dots for the width. The menu choices ''Height,'' and ''Width'' allow you to change these settings, within limits, to change the height and width. These settings will not be altered in this book.

The default plot is created by single passes of the plot or print head. If you choose the ''Double'' option, the plot head will make a double pass which will make a much clearer graph. Since the plot procedure is a slow one, you should not elect this choice unless it is absolutely necessary. If there is a diamond next to ''double,'' press the ''N'' to elect ''Normal.''

The ''setup'' choice is used to alter default settings for the printer or plotter. This topic is beyond the scope of this text so it is assumed that the version of As-Easy-As that has been distributed with this book functions satisfactorily with your output device. If it does not, you should consult the As-Easy-As manual for more complete instructions about how to configure As-Easy-As with this device.

Check the alignment of the print head with the paper crease and print the graph by entering,

G Go, to initiate the plot.
Q Quit, to exit the graphics plot menu.

MODIFYING THE GRAPH

The pie chart is only one of the possible displays available. Change the chart type by pressing

T Type, or Enter, to select a new style
B Bar, the new style (displayed in Graph 11–2)
V View, to see the altered graph style
Esc Escape key, to cancel the graph's display

Plot the graph as described in the ''Plotting a Graph'' section above. Name the graph settings with the name QTRIB also.

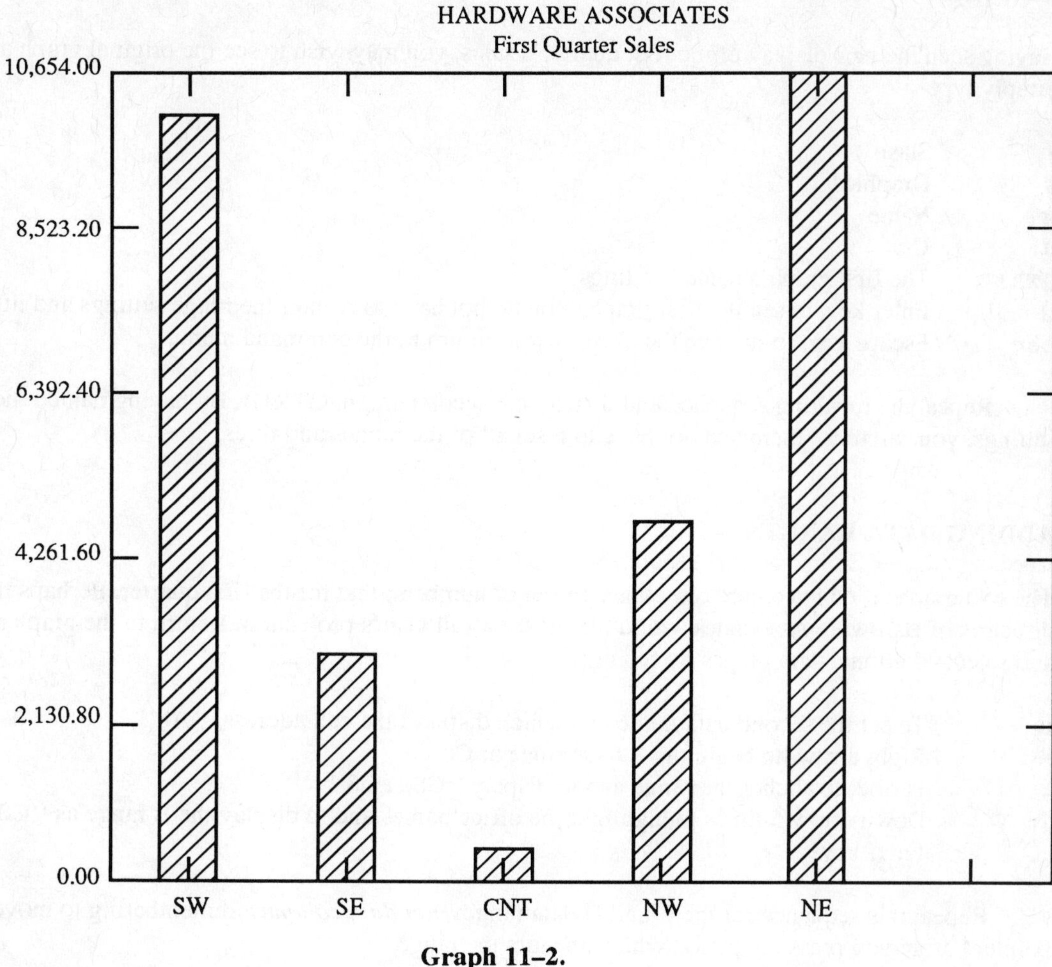

Graph 11–2.

THE GRAPH KEY *F10*

As-Easy-As keeps track of the last settings used in a graph display. The function key F10 is called the graph key because it recreates a graph from the READY state with the last graph settings used. This allows you to change the specific values in the X and A ranges, for instance, and to reproduce the graph without reentering the graph menu. The graph displayed will be reorganized to reflect the changes. Obtain a clear control panel and change the mode block to " <Ready> !" by pressing

Q Quit, to quit the plot menu
Q Quit, to quit the graphics menu

Change the sales for the SW office for QTR1 to 9,000. Then see the difference this makes by pressing

F10 The Graph key, to see the revised graph
Esc Escape key, to remove the graph and to return to the command menu

Print the graph following the instructions for plotting given earlier. After printing the graph, change the sales for the SW office back to 10,329.

RECALLING NAMED GRAPHS

Graph Name

Having seen the new display of the first quarter's sales, you may wish to see the original graph again. Simply type

/	Slash
G	Graphics
N	Name
U	Use
QTR1A	The first graph's named settings
↵	Enter key, to see the first graph. You do not have to reenter the range settings and titles
Esc	Escape key, to remove the graph and to return to the command menu.

Repeat the recalling sequence and display the second graph, QTR1B. By having named the settings, you can reuse them and not have to reset all of the ranges and titles.

ADDING DATA RANGES

The two graphs used have used only one column of numbers; that for the first quarter. Perhaps the directors of Hardware Associates would like to see a full year's projection. Return to the graph menu and select additional data ranges by typing

B	To set the second data range and which displays the cell address, ''A8''
→	Right arrow, to begin the B data range at C8
.	Period, to anchor the range and to display ''C8 . . C8''
↓	Down arrow 5 times to highlight the office names and to display the B range as ''C8 . . C13''
↵	Enter key

Repeat this sequence for the C and D data ranges, *not data columns,* remembering to move the cell pointer before you press the period which anchors the range.

UNANCHORING A DATA RANGE

If you mistakenly press the period, you can ''unanchor'' the range by pressing the Escape key. Also, if you set a range incorrectly, you can cause As-Easy-As to ''forget'' a remembered, incorrect range, by pressing the Escape key.

VIEWING THE GRAPH

When you have set the four data ranges, change the graph style and view the graph by typing

T	Type
B	Bar
V	View, to see the graph. Notice that with 4 data ranges, 4 different patterns are used to display the data
↵	Enter key, to return to the graph menu.

ADDING TITLES AND LEGENDS

Graph Options

The new graph has two ambiguities associated with it. First, it is not immediately obvious what the four patterns stand for. Second, the height of the bars is marked by numbers on the vertical dimension (the Y-axis) and each group of bars is labeled with two-letter abbreviations. If you had not constructed the graph, would you know what the numbers and the abbreviations represented? In three months will you remember? Identify these labels more accurately by typing

O	Options, to enhance the graph with some additional information
T	Titles, to incorporate additional titles
S	Second, to change the original subtitle
Quarterly Sales	
↵	Enter key
X	**X,** to create a title that will go across the bottom of the graph
Regional Offices	The X-axis title, to identify the X-range labels
↵	Enter key, to enter the title
Y	**Y,** to enter a title that will appear vertically along the left-hand side of the graph to identify the significance of bar heights
Level of Sales	The title
↵	Enter key
Q	Quit, to exit the graphics titles' options menu
L	Legend, to identify the data range patterns
A	The legend title for the A data range
1st	The title
↵	Enter key
L	Legend, to identify the data range patterns
B	The legend title for the B data range
2nd	The title
↵	Enter key
L	Legend, to identify the data range patterns
C	The legend title for the C data range
3rd	The title
↵	Enter key
L	Legend, to identify the data range patterns
D	The legend title for the D data range
4th	The title
↵	Enter key
Q	Quit, to return to the graph menu
V	View, to see the graph with the new titles and legends (displayed in Graph 11–3)
Esc	Escape, to return to the graph menu

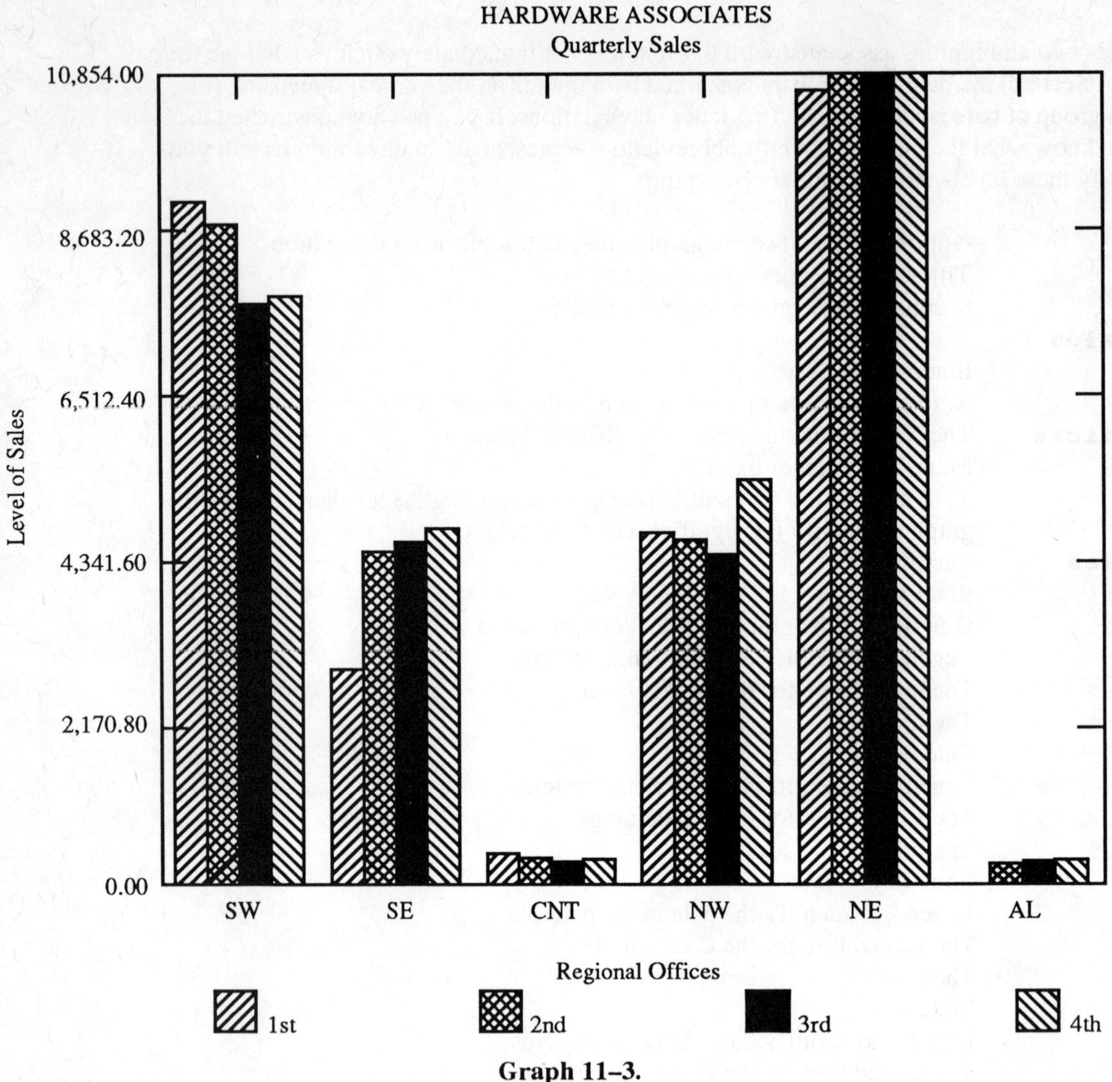

Graph 11–3.

Name the graph with the following commands:

N	Name
C	Create
ANNUAL	The graph settings name
↵	Enter key
Q	Quit, to exit the graph menu

Print the graph using the instructions shown in the section, "Plotting a Graph."

SAVING NAMED GRAPHS

When graphs have been created and named, the named settings become part of the worksheet. The worksheet file must be saved to the disk if you plan to reuse the graphs in the future. If the file is not saved, the settings will be lost.

SAVING YOUR WORKSHEET

Graph Save

Save your worksheet by typing

- / Slash
- F File
- S Store
- ↲ Enter key, to accept **SALES** as the filename. Since you have already saved SALES once, the name will automatically appear. You need not retype the name. Go on to the next step instead
- R Replace, to overwrite the old file with the new file

Replace the diskette in drive B with your backup diskette and repeat the file save procedure.

EXERCISES

A. Using the SALES worksheet, create and print pie graphs for quarters 2, 3 and 4.

B. Retrieve the file GRADES and produce a bar chart displaying the class's average grades over the semester. Add titles and legends.

C. Retrieve the file INCOME and produce a pie chart displaying the sales of the four vehicle types in the first half of the year. Add titles. Create a bar chart with titles and legends displaying the two half-years' sales.

Chapter 12

Using Built-In Functions and Formulas: A Project Costing Model

CHAPTER OUTLINE

The worksheet in this chapter will extend your knowledge of how to employ a worksheet program effectively. You will see how a worksheet can be used to test out what a project will cost given assumptions about costs for various project tasks. In doing this worksheet, you will

1. Set column widths;
2. Justify and format cell displays;
3. Utilize the powerful @VTABLE function;
4. Alter cost assumptions in order to see what impact staffing decisions have on a project's costs.

THE PROBLEM

The worksheet focuses on the need for a manager to determine the costs involved in undertaking a project that has been proposed. The project involves eight activities: (1) the writing of specifications for a computer program, (2) the writing and testing of computer program code, (3) the gathering of data, (4) the entering of data into the program, (5) the revision and correction of data, (6) the editing of a final report, (7) the printing of a catalog, and (8) the distribution of the catalog. Each phase of the project involves different types of employees who earn different salaries.

The manager has a good idea about how the project's financial requirements could be estimated. There are several other projects that are being discussed that will also need to be evaluated carefully before they are implemented. Consequently, the manager has decided to build a worksheet model that could also be used to examine these projects as they arrive.

INITIAL ENTRIES

Figure 12–1, Part A, outlines the basic appearance of the model. To cost out a project requires that the manager identify, for each phase of the project, what type of employee is to be involved, how many days that type of employee is involved, how much those employees will be paid, what other non-personnel related costs are required (paper, travel, books, etc.) and, finally, how much the personnel and non-personnel costs will total. Once the model has been constructed, data specific to each of the coming project proposals can be inserted in the model so she can evaluate the costs accordingly.

Part B of the model is an employee charge schedule. The table identifies some of the firm's employee categories and, on the same line as each job title, is a number which identifies each type of position, an average annual salary and compensation cost for position and a daily rate at which the time for a person in that category could be charged.

Begin to set up the worksheet shown in Figure 12–1 by loading As-Easy-As and making the following cell entries. The entries in column A will not appear in their entirety now.

Cell Coordinate	Entry
C1	PROJECT COST MODEL
C2	PART A
B4	EMP.
C4	TASK
D4	DAILY
E4	PERS.
F4	OTHER
G4	TOTAL
A5	ACTIVITY
B5	TYPE
C5	DAYS
D5	RATE
E5	COST
F5	COST
G5	COST
A7	PREPARE SPEC'S
B7	3
C7	3
A8	WRITE & TEST CODE
B8	4
C8	6
A9	GATHER DATA
B9	1
C9	20
A10	DATA ENTRY
B10	2
C10	15
A11	REVISE ENTRIES
B11	5

```
                              PROJECT COST MODEL
                                    PART A

                          EMP.     TASK     DAILY    PERS.    OTHER    TOTAL
ACTIVITY                  TYPE     DAYS      RATE    COST      COST     COST

PREPARE SPEC'S              3        3
WRITE & TEST CODE           4        6
GATHER DATA                 1       20
DATA ENTRY                  2       15
REVISE ENTRIES              5        5
EDIT FINAL COPY             6        2
PRINT CATALOG               0        0
DISTRIBUTE                  1        2
=================

                          EMPLOYEE CHARGE SCHEDULE
                                    PART B

DESCRIPTION               EMP.      ANN.    DAILY
                          TYPE      SAL.     RATE

NO PERSONNEL                0         $0       $0
HOURLY WORKER               1   $16,000      $64
DATA ENTRY CLERK            2   $20,000      $80
SYSTEMS ANALYST             3   $32,000     $128
PROGRAMMER                  4   $29,000     $116
JR. EDITOR                  5   $24,500      $98
SR. EDITOR                  6   $31,500     $126
TEAM LEADER                 7   $29,000     $116
```

Figure 12–1.

C11	**5**
A12	**EDIT FINAL COPY**
B12	**6**
C12	**2**
A13	**PRINT CATALOG**
B13	**0**
C13	**0**
A14	**DISTRIBUTE**
B14	**1**
C14	**2**
A16	**\= (Backslash, Equal Sign)**
C18	**EMPLOYEE CHARGE SCHEDULE**
C19	**PART B**
B21	**EMP.**
C21	**ANN.**
D21	**DAILY**
A22	**DESCRIPTION**
B22	**TYPE**
C22	**SAL.**
D22	**RATE**
A24	**NO. PERSONNEL**
B24	**0**
C24	**0**

D24	**0**
A25	**HOURLY WORKER**
B25	**1**
C25	**16000**
A26	**DATA ENTRY CLERK**
B26	**2**
C26	**20000**
A27	**SYSTEMS ANALYST**
B27	**3**
C27	**32000**
A28	**PROGRAMMER**
B28	**4**
C28	**29000**
A29	**JR. EDITOR**
B29	**5**
C29	**24500**
A30	**SR. EDITOR**
B30	**6**
C30	**31500**
A31	**TEAM LEADER**
B31	**7**
C31	**29000**

FORMATTING THE WORKSHEET *WSheet ColWidth*

Setting Column Widths

As-Easy-As uses a default column width of 9 characters to display cell entries. The first column is too narrow to display the labels contained in its cells. The other columns will be reduced to a width of 8. There are two methods of changing column widths: globally and individually.

Columns D, E, F, and G should be 8 characters wide. These columns can be set all at once by setting all the columns in the worksheet to 8. The remaining column widths can be set individually. To set the global column width, type

/	Slash
W	WSheet
G	General
C	Column
8	To set column width to 8
↵	Enter key

Column A is too narrow to display the complete text placed in the column of cells. It should be widened by placing the cell pointer in column A and typing

/	Slash
W	WSheet
C	ColWidth
S	Set
19	To set column width to 19, the width of ''WRITE AND TEST CODE'' plus 1
↵	Enter key

Justifying Labels *Range Label*

The headings would look better if those in columns B through G were right-justified. The headings will then have the same justification as the numbers that will appear beneath them. Justify the headings in Part A by moving your cell pointer to B4 and typing

/ Slash
R Range
P Prefix
R Right, to right-justify
↓ Down arrow once
→ Right arrow 5 times to set range
↵ Enter key

Justify the Employee Charge Schedule headings by moving your cell pointer to B21 and typing

/ Slash
R Range
P Prefix
R Right, to right justify
↓ Down arrow once
→ Right arrow 2 times to set range
↵ Enter key

USING FORMULAS AND BUILT-IN FUNCTIONS

To have As-Easy-As compute the daily rate of pay in column D of the Employee Charge Schedule, you need to divide the annual salary by the number of working days in a year (250). Place your cell pointer on D24 and enter

+C24/250

which returns the value of 0. Next, copy the formula down the column by keeping the cell pointer on D24 and using the copy command.

/ Slash
C CopyCell
↵ Enter key, to accept D24 as the default cell to be duplicated
. Period to anchor the range
↓ Down arrow 7 times to complete the copy "to" range
↵ Enter key

Column D of Part A, the daily rate column, presents a more difficult cell entry to develop. If you were filling in the column by hand, you would look in the employee type column (B) to see what job category number was assigned to the position responsible for that phase of the project. Then you would visually find the employee type number in the Employee Charge Schedule and search across to the daily rate column to find the per day charge. This amount would then be entered in the daily rate column for Part A. You would repeat this for each of the phases.

Before proceeding, check to see that your worksheet looks like Figure 12–2.

PROJECT COST MODEL
PART A

ACTIVITY	EMP. TYPE	TASK DAYS	DAILY RATE	PERS. COST	OTHER COST	TOTAL COST
PREPARE SPEC'S	3	3				
WRITE AND TEST CODE	4	6				
GATHER DATA	1	20				
DATA ENTRY	2	15				
REVISE ENTRIES	5	5				
EDIT FINAL COPY	6	2				
PRINT CATALOG	0	0				
DISTRIBUTE	1	2				

===================

EMPLOYEE CHARGE SCHEDULE
PART B

DESCRIPTION	EMP. TYPE	ANN. SAL.	DAILY RATE
NO PERSONNEL	0	0	0
HOURLY WORKER	1	16,000	64
DATA ENTRY CLERK	2	20,000	80
SYSTEMS ANALYST	3	32,000	128
PROGRAMMER	4	29,000	116
JR. EDITOR	5	24,500	98
SR. EDITOR	6	31,500	126
TEAM LEADER	7	29,000	116

Figure 12–2.

The Vertical Table Function *@VTABLE*

The manual operation described would suffice for some purposes, but since the manager wishes to use the worksheet over again for other projects and since the type of employees used for some phases might change, it is preferable to insert a formula with a built-in function to complete this operation automatically and, perhaps, more accurately. The built-in function for this purpose is the @VTABLE function. This function has these parts:

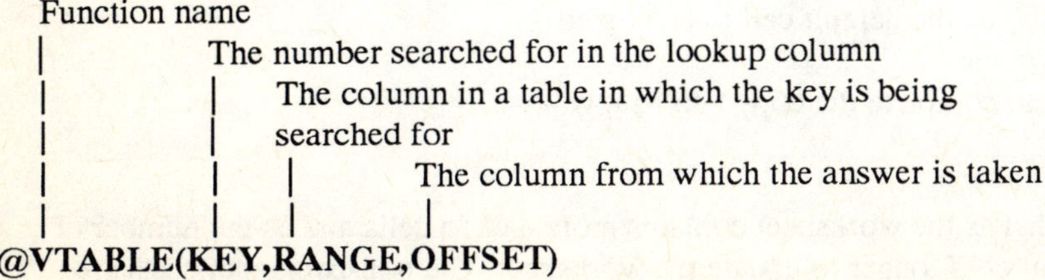

To illustrate with an example, place your cell pointer on D7 and type the following entry without blanks:

@VTABLE(	The name of the function
B7,	The cell with the number for the first employee type

$B$24 . . $D$31,	The range of cells to be searched (employee type). Remember the absolute addressing of cells discussed in chapter 7 with the Function 4 key and don't forget to type the commas separating the three elements within the parentheses.
2)	Return the number found in the second column to the right of the index range. The formula appears as, @VTABLE(B7$B$24 . . $D$31,2)
↵	Enter key, which returns the daily rate of 128

The function entered "looks up" the number 3 (found in B7) by searching down the range. The numbers in the range are, and must be, in ascending order. When the function finds the first entry in the search range that is larger than the number being searched for, it "looks" across from the previous entry. @VTABLE searches down until it finds a 4, a number larger than the 3 being searched for, and then searches across the previous row by the amount of the offset.

@VTABLE does not find that 3 is equal to 3. The method of searching used by @VTABLE allows you to search for an 18 in a list that increments by 5 (0, 5, 10, 15, 20 . . .) and return a value from the row beginning with 15, the last number that was not larger than 18.

The offset column is the number of the column to the right of the index range. The index column is considered to be column number zero. The column to the right is column 1, the next is column 2, and so on. In this example, As-Easy-As will search the second column to the right of the index range.

Copy this formula, keeping the cell pointer on D7, by typing

/	Slash
C	CopyCell
↵	Enter key, to accept D7 as the default cell to be duplicated
.	Period to anchor the range
↓	Down arrow 7 times to complete the copy "to" range
↵	Enter key

The absolute references of the range of cells in the lookup table kept the copied formulas from changing. If you allowed As-Easy-As to adjust the addresses by using relative cell addresses, the first copy of the formula would reference B25 through B32, the second would reference B26 through B33, and so on. Incorrect answers or error messages would be returned as the top of the list, and eventually the entire list would be lost. The personnel cost for each phase is computed by multiplying the daily rate (column D) by the number of days each type of employee is involved. Place your cell pointer on E7 and enter

+C7*D7

↵	Enter key

which returns 384. Copy this formula by keeping the cell pointer on E7 and typing the command sequence

/	Slash
C	CopyCell
↵	Enter key, to accept E7 as the default cell to be copied
.	Period to anchor the range
↓	Down arrow 7 times to complete the copy "to" range
↵	Enter key

You may begin to notice that as the worksheet contains more data in cells and as the number of formulas increase, it takes As-Easy-As longer to update the worksheet. The non-personnel costs are estimated, rather than computed costs, and must be entered as follows:

F7	**250**
F8	**150**
F9	**150**
F10	**50**
F11	**50**
F12	**50**
F13	**2500**
F14	**200**

The next task is to compute the cost for each phase of the project. The cost for each phase is the total of the personnel and non-personnel costs. Place your cell pointer on G7 and enter

+E7+F7
↲ Enter key

which creates the value, 634. Copy the formula with the command sequence

/	Slash
C	CopyCell
↲	Enter key, to accept G7 as the default cell to be copied
.	Period to anchor the range
↓	Down arrow 7 times to complete the copy "to" range
↲	Enter key

The total cost of the project is computed in G15. The entry to this cell is

@SUM(G7 . . G14) which returns 7830.

FORMATTING

Range Format

Many of the columns contain numbers that represent currency. The use of the Range Format command changes the appearance of numbers. If a cell with a label is formatted as a number, the display is left unchanged. Place your cell pointer on cell G7 and enter

/	Slash
R	Range
F	Format
C	Currency
0	Zero
↲	Enter key, to accept the zero
←	Left arrow 3 times
PgDn	Page Down key, to rapidly highlight G7 through D27. The highlighting covers some cells with text but these will not be affected by the formatting change. Do not move the cursor to column C. Movement of the cursor to column C will also highlight the number of days for each task in Part A.
↓	Down arrow 4 times
↲	Enter key

Use of the End Key

End

The End key is one means of rapidly moving the cell pointer through cells in order to relocate it. The End key will be used to format cells C24 through C31. Place your cell pointer on C24 and enter

/	Slash
R	Range
F	Format
C	Currency
0	Zero
↵	Enter key, to accept the zero. The range is displayed as being C24 through C24.
End	End key. Note the word, "End," in the bottom of the screen.
↓	Down arrow once. The highlighting covers all of the cells up to the boundary where filled cells abut an empty cell.
↵	Enter key, to complete the formatting

The model as it appears in Figure 12–3 is now complete.

WHAT IF?

The great advantage of using a worksheet is that as conditions change, data in the model can be changed and the computer can recalculate the formulas immediately to give you revised projections. For instance, suppose that it was determined that the gathering of data could not be handled by unskilled, hourly-paid workers, but had to be conducted by systems analysts. Change the employee type in B9 from 1 to 3. Note the changes throughout your worksheet.

Experiment with other possible changes, but be careful. You can replace numbers with numbers and character strings with strings. If you replace a formula with a number, you are likely to lose some of the accuracy of the model.

PROJECT COST MODEL
PART A

ACTIVITY	EMP. TYPE	TASK DAYS	DAILY RATE	PERS. COST	OTHER COST	TOTAL COST
PREPARE SPEC'S	3	3	$128	$384	$250	$634
WRITE & TEST CODE	4	6	$116	$696	$150	$846
GATHER DATA	1	20	$64	$1,280	$150	$1,430
DATA ENTRY	2	15	$80	$1,200	$50	$1,250
REVISE ENTRIES	5	5	$98	$490	$50	$540
EDIT FINAL COPY	6	2	$126	$252	$50	$302
PRINT CATALOG	0	0	$0	$0	$2,500	$2,500
DISTRIBUTE	1	2	$64	$128	$200	$328
==================						$7,830

EMPLOYEE CHARGE SCHEDULE
PART B

DESCRIPTION	EMP. TYPE	ANN. SAL.	DAILY RATE
NO PERSONNEL	0	$0	$0
HOURLY WORKER	1	$16,000	$64
DATA ENTRY CLERK	2	$20,000	$80
SYSTEMS ANALYST	3	$32,000	$128
PROGRAMMER	4	$29,000	$116
JR. EDITOR	5	$24,500	$98
SR. EDITOR	6	$31,500	$126
TEAM LEADER	7	$29,000	$116

Figure 12–3. Completed Project Cost Model (Screen 2).

SAVING YOUR WORKSHEET

File Save

The worksheet is now complete. Save the file on the files diskette with the following command sequence:

/	Slash
F	File
S	Store
PROJECT	The drive destination and filename of the worksheet
↵	Enter key

Backup your worksheet by placing your backup diskette in drive B and repeating the save procedure.

PRINTING YOUR WORKSHEET

Print Printer

Print your file with the command sequence

/	Slash
P	Print
P	Printer, or Enter key since the cursor is located on Printer by default
R	Range
Home	Home key
.	Period to anchor the range
↓	Down arrow 30 times to cover the vertical range
→	Right arrow 6 times to cover the horizontal range
↵	Enter key, to specify the entire worksheet
A	Adjust
G	Go, to execute to printing
Q	Quit, to return to As-Easy-As

ERASING YOUR WORKSHEET

WSheet Erase

The file PROJECT has been safely stored on the diskette. The next command sequence should be used only if you have carefully considered whether the file is still useful to you and has been saved, or whether it can be erased from the computer's RAM memory because it is either not needed, or a more desirable version already exists on the diskette.

The WSheet-Erase command erases the worksheet seen on your monitor from RAM. It does not delete the worksheet file from the diskette if it has been saved. Erasing a worksheet erases the contents of the cells, returns all default values of the worksheet to the state they would be in if you entered As-Easy-As from DOS. All column widths would be reset to 9.

Erase your file to see the effect with the sequence

/	Slash
W	WSheet
E	Erase
Y	Yes

EXITING AS-EASY-AS

Exit

Exit from As-Easy-As by typing

/	Slash
E	Exit

Y Yes

and replace the As-Easy-As disk in drive A with the DOS disk and hit any key to return to the DOS "A>" prompt.

EXERCISES

A. A corporate accountant has developed a table for determining the cost for a motor vehicle's depreciation in a given year. Knowing the cost and age of a vehicle, the depreciation table can be used to determine the cost to be deducted from corporate taxes that year. The cell displaying the depreciation cost contains a formula with a lookup function multiplied by the original cost of the vehicle. Whenever the age and cost of a vehicle are entered, the depreciation costs are recalculated. The appearance of the accountant's worksheet is shown.

```
                    VEHICLE DEPRECIATION CALCULATOR

                                   DEPRECIATION TABLE
                                   ------------------
YRS. OLD                   3
ORIG. COST           $12,200         VEHICLE          AGE

DEPRECIATION          $2,440               1          30%
                                           2          25%
                                           3          20%
                                           4          15%
                                           5          10%
```

Reproduce this worksheet and test it for a vehicle one year old and costing $15,327. For a four-year-old vehicle costing $11,287.

B. A sales manager computes the monthly commission for the company's sales personnel with the help of a sales commission lookup table. A salesperson's commission is based on the length of time the person has worked for the company. The worksheet used for this assessment is shown below.

```
                         SALES COMMISSIONS CALCULATOR

                               COMMISSION TABLE
                               ----------------
YRS. OF SERVICE              7      YEARS    RESPONSIBILITY
SALES TOTAL            $24,000      SERVICE LEVEL

COMMISSION RATE           5.0%          0        4.5%
COMPUTED COMMISSION     $1,200          5        5.0%
                                       10        5.5%
                                       15        6.0%
                                       20        6.5%
```

Prepare the worksheet so that when new years of service and sales total entries are made, the worksheet automatically computes the commission earned. Test the worksheet with three different sets of values for sales totals and years of service. Note that the years of service entry of 0 includes all persons with between 0 and 4.9 years of service.

C. The personnel office secretary is often asked for the total cost of compensation for hiring a new employee at any one of 16 ranks of pay. Total compensation consists of the salary plus the fringe benefits. The lowest salary is $10,000 and each rank receives an increase of $1,000 over the preceding rank. Fringe benefits are computed as being 28% of the salary. Prepare a worksheet with lookup table in which there are three columns: the lookup column which contains the ranks 15 through 30, the salary column with salaries ranging from $10,000 through $25,000, and the fringe benefits column computed at 28% of the salary. Identify a cell in which the rank is entered, a cell in which the salary is looked up, and a cell in which the fringe benefits are looked up. Add a cell in which the total compensation is computed.

D. A heavy equipment sales organization pays a commission to the salesperson, the salesperson's local sales agency, and the regional sales agency on every order placed. The commissions vary with the size of the order. The table involved looks like the following:

Construct a worksheet that uses a sale amount entered in one cell as the lookup amount. Three separate cells should display the amount of commission paid to each entity (looked-up commission times the amount of sale), as well as the total amount of the commissions paid.

Chapter 13
What If . . .?

CHAPTER OUTLINE

A Project Budget
Some Internal Documentation
- Filename
- Parameters
- Projections

Formatting
The @IF Function
Protection
What If . . . ?
Printing Your Worksheet
Saving Your Worksheet
Exiting As-Easy-As
Exercises

This chapter provides you with another worksheet designed to demonstrate how managers can test ''what if'' changes in a worksheet model. The results of the changes can be analyzed and assessed for decision-making. In particular, this worksheet will enable you to

1. See how including a filename inside of a worksheet can help you to identify a file when you do a directory listing from DOS;
2. Set aside assumptions in identifiable locations so various alternatives can be examined without your having to modify or add formulas to the worksheet;
3. Examine the use of the @IF function;
4. Protect cells from inadvertent changes.

A PROJECT BUDGET

The director of the management information systems department of a medium-sized firm was asked by the firm's vice president for finance to develop a microcomputer literacy project for key people in each of the firm's departments. The MIS director agreed to put together a cost estimate. Arriving at a definitive cost estimate proved to be difficult as the director thought about the problem. The difficulty was not only due to the lack of information about the cost of particular items, but also to the lack of clarity about how many people would participate, how much the departments would be willing to pay toward the project, and how many days of training would be involved. The MIS director also knew that after a project budget was prepared, the vice president and others would make suggestions for changes that would affect the budget. The director decided to put the budget together with As-Easy-As so that the effect of suggested changes could be analyzed.

SOME INTERNAL DOCUMENTATION

Filename

After booting up the microcomputer and loading As-Easy-As, begin to create the worksheet by entering

Cell Coordinate	Entry
A1	PRJTBUDT
A2	DISK #1

These two cell entries are used for internal documentation. Many users of worksheets produce a variety of models that are stored on many diskettes. It can be difficult to remember where a file is stored when you need to use it again. Since DOS allows the user to use only eight characters in a filename, many worksheet names are cryptic. These two cells, if they are printed out along with the key portions of the worksheet, will provide you with the documentation you need to find the worksheet again. A1 gives the name of the file as it is known to DOS and to As-Easy-As. You can use this name to retrieve it. A2 gives the number of the diskette on which the file is stored so you can avoid searching through one diskette after another looking for the file.

Parameters

In constructing formulas within the worksheets completed in earlier chapters, it was difficult, once the worksheet was completed, to see how a number was arrived at. This ambiguity is frequently the case. For instance, a formula in a worksheet might be +C6*B8*.07. Simply looking at the formula is no assurance that you can tell what the formula is attempting to do, so there is no way to be certain that the formula is arriving at a correct answer. When part of the formula is .07, there is no clear indication of why .07 was chosen and not some other percentage. If you knew that somewhere within a worksheet there were references to the inflation rate, you would have no way to tell whether this percentage represented an inflation rate, the expected increase in the Consumer Price Index, the anticipated growth in base salaries, or growth in the projected value of the dollar overseas.

This ambiguity in formulas gets worse over time as you forget how you constructed a worksheet. It is made even worse when the worksheet is used by someone else. You can see why it is that some analysts suggest that as many as 30% of the worksheets used to make major decisions are incorrect, but decision makers do not know it because the displays ''hide'' the formulas that create the displays. Often all they see is the printed worksheet.

To lessen some of the problems, divide the worksheet into two primary parts: a parameter portion and a projection portion. The parameter portion will consist of the most basic pieces of the problem and their values. For this worksheet, enter

Cell Coordinate	Entry
B3	PROJECT BUDGET
B4	\= (Backslash, Equal Sign)
C4	\=
A6	PARAMETERS
A7	\- (Backslash, Minus Sign)
B6	PARAMETER VALUES
B7	\-
A8	NO. OF PARTICIPANTS
B8	15
A9	DAILY PARTICIPANT EXPENSES
B9	20

A10	**NO. OF TRAINING DAYS**
B10	**10**
A11	**COMPUTER COSTS**
A12	**' MICROCOMPUTER**
B12	**2000**
A13	**' PRINTER**
B13	**450**
A14	**' FURNITURE**
B14	**400**
A15	**' SOFTWARE**
B15	**750**
A16	**TRAINER FEE PER DAY**
B16	**500**
A17	**TRAINING ASSISTANT**
B17	**200**
A18	**DEPT. CHARGE-BACK**
B18	**1500**

These cells document the assumptions the director is making about the project. There are ten basic building blocks for determining the costs of the project. The specific values that are entered into column B are not especially important because they can easily be changed. It is much more important to identify all the elements that go into the training project and then to determine how these elements relate to one another. For example, it is important to know that the number of days of training will affect the cost of hiring a trainer who is paid on a per day basis, as well as the total of the daily costs for the participants. It is less important to know precisely how much the trainer will be paid, than that a trainer will be paid on the number of days worked.

Notice that the entries in column B are all numbers. There are no calculations made here. The director will be able to change these numbers to test different cost alternatives without having to worry that an important formula is being overwritten.

Projections

The second portion of the worksheet will be the cost projection for the project. The entries in column B of this portion of the worksheet will avoid the use of typed in numbers. Instead cell addresses will be used. This will enable the director to avoid having to revise and copy the formulas continuously. For example, if a cell is to compute the cost for the trainer, its contents will not be +10*500. Instead, its contents should be +B10*B16. Then the director can try out different numbers of days and different daily pay rates as these are suggested and As-Easy-As will redo the calculation.

Enter the following:

Cell Coordinate	Entry	Meaning
A21	**COST PROJECTION**	
A22	**\- (Backslash, Minus Sign)**	
B22	**\- (Backslash, Minus Sign)**	
A23	**TRAINER**	
B23	**+B10*B16**	**NO. OF TRAINING DAYS × TRAINER FEE PER DAY, Displays 5000**
A24	**TRAINING ASSISTANT**	
B24	**@IF(B8>=10,B17*B10,0)**	**If the NO. OF PARTICIPANTS is greater than or equal to 10, then display the result of multiplying the NO. OF TRAINING DAYS × TRAINING ASSIST., Displays 2000**

A25	**COMPUTER COSTS**	
B25	**@SUM(B12..B15)*B8**	**The total cost for a MICROCOMPUTER, a PRINTER, FURNITURE, and SOFTWARE × the NO. OF PARTICIPANTS, Displays 54000**
A26	**DAILY EXPENSES**	
B26	**+B8*B9*B10**	**The NO. OF PARTICIPANTS × DAILY PARTICIPANT EXPENSES × NO. OF TRAINING DAYS, Displays 3000**
B27	**\– (Backslash, Minus Sign)**	
A28	**TOTAL EXPENSES**	
B28	**@SUM(B23..B26)**	**The total of the expenses computed for TRAINER, TRAINING ASSISTANT, COMPUTER COSTS, and DAILY EXPENSES, Displays 64000**
A29	**TOTAL CHARGE-BACK**	
B29	**+B18*B8**	**The DEPT. CHARGE-BACK × NO. OF PARTICIPANTS. Displays 22500**
A30	**TOTAL TO CENTRAL OFFICE**	
B30	**+B28–B29**	**TOTAL EXPENSES – TOTAL CHARGE-BACK. Displays 41500**

Alter the width of column A to display all the text it contains by placing the cell pointer in column A and typing

/	Slash Format
W	WSheet
C	ColWidth
S	Set
26	A number large enough for the widest entry
↵	Enter key

Your worksheet now looks like Figure 13–1.

```
                         PROJECT BUDGET
                      =====================

PARAMETERS                        PARAMETER VALUES
---------------------------------------
NUM. OF PARTICIPANTS                    15
DAILY PARTICIPANT EXPENSES              20
NUM. OF TRAINING DAYS                   10
COMPUTER COSTS
  MICROCOMPUTER                       2000
  PRINTER                              450
  FURNITURE                            400
  SOFTWARE                             750
TRAINER FEE PER DAY                    500
TRAINING ASSIST. PER DAY               200
DEPT. CHARGE-BACK                     1500
```

Figure 13–1. Screen 1.

```
PARAMETERS                    PARAMETER VALUES
------------------------------------------------
COST PROJECTION
------------------------------------------------
TRAINER                                   5000
TRAINING ASSISTANT                        2000
COMPUTER COSTS                           54000
DAILY EXPENSES                            3000
                                     ---------
TOTAL EXPENSES                           64000
TOTAL CHARGE-BACK                        22500
TOTAL TO CENTRAL OFFICE                  41500
```

Figure 13–1.—*Continued*

For illustrative purposes, the cell in B24 uses the @IF function, to be described below, and contains the number 10. This is the only ''hard'' number in the projection of expenses. Even this number could be replaced with a parameter address. The other formulas that have gone into producing the worksheet only utilize cell addresses. If it was decided that an assistant trainer would only be needed if the number of participants was 12, the formula in B24 would have to be edited. The other cells from B23 to B26 would need to be edited only if the formulas they contain were incorrect in their cell references or if new parameters were added later.

FORMATTING

Range Format

The numbers in column B should virtually all be formatted as currency with no decimal places. Format most of these numbers by moving the cell pointer to B8 and typing

/	Slash
R	**R**ange
F	**F**ormat, or return key since Format is highlighted by the cursor
C	**C**urrency format
0	The number of decimal places
↵	Enter key
PgDn	Page Down key
↓	Down arrow three times to highlight the entire column
↵	Enter key

```
                  PROJECT BUDGET
              =====================

PARAMETERS                 PARAMETER VALUES
----------------------------------------
NUM. OF PARTICIPANTS                  15
DAILY PARTICIPANT EXPENSES            20
NUM. OF TRAINING DAYS                 10
COMPUTER COSTS
    MICROCOMPUTER                  $2000
    PRINTER                         $450
    FURNITURE                       $400
    SOFTWARE                        $750
TRAINER FEE PER DAY                 $500
TRAINING ASSIST. PER DAY            $200
DEPT. CHARGE-BACK                 $1,500
```

Figure 13–2.

```
PARAMETERS                  PARAMETER VALUES
---------------------------------
COST PROJECTION
---------------------------------
TRAINER                          $5000
TRAINING ASSISTANT               $2000
COMPUTER COSTS                  $54000
DAILY EXPENSES                   $3000
                               -------
TOTAL EXPENSES                  $64000
TOTAL CHARGE-BACK         $22500
TOTAL TO CENTRAL OFFICE         $41500
```

Figure 13–2.—*Continued*

Cells B8 and B10 should not be formatted as currency. Place the cell pointer on B8 and type

/	Slash
R	Range
F	Format, or return key since Format is highlighted by the cursor
,	Comma
0	The number of decimal places
↵	Enter key
↵	Enter key to accept cell B8 as the format range and to execute the format change.

Repeat this series of key strokes on B10 also. Your worksheet should now look like Figure 13–2.

THE @IF FUNCTION

The formula in B24 uses the @IF function. The general structure of the @IF function involves three elements, or operands, that are found between the parentheses. The first operand is a logical condition. This condition is evaluated as being either true or false. Examples of possible conditions that could appear in an @IF function are:

1=10	An obviously false relation since 1 does not equal 10
A1<3	True if the value of A1 is less than 3, but false if the value in A1 is 3 or greater

The equal sign and the less than sign are called relational operators. The relational operators that can be used in the @IF statement are:

Symbol	Meaning	Example	Value
=	Equal to	A1=10	True if A1 equals 10
>	Greater than	A2>5	False if A2 equals 3
<	Less than	A3<9	True if A3 contains 2
=	Greater than or equal to	A4>=14	True if A4 contains 14
<=	Less than or equal to	A5<=16	True if A5 contains 16
<>	Not equal to	A6<>20	False if A6 contains 20

The second element in the @IF function is the value the function will return (display in the cell) if the logical condition is evaluated as being true. In B24, the formula returns the value calculated by multiplying B17 by B10. The value returned can be a number, a value obtained from a cell address, a character string, another function that returns a numerical value, or a formula.

The third element in the @IF function is the value the function will return if the logical condition is evaluated as being false. In B24, the formula returns a zero. The value returned could also be a number, a numerical value obtained from a cell address, a character string, another function that returns a numerical value, or a formula.The formula in B24

```
@IF(B8>=10,B17*B10,0)
```

is read as "If it is true that the value of B8 is greater than or equal to 10, then return the value calculated by multiplying the values in B17 and B10, else return the value zero." If the number of participants changes to less than 10, then the cost for a training assistant will be zero (i.e., one is not needed).

Other examples of @IF functions are:

@IF(C10<>45,5,9)	If C10 is not 45, return 5, else return 9
@IF(C1=Z15,@SUM(B1 . . B3),0)	If C1 is equal to Z15, return the sum of cells B1, B2, and B3, else return zero
@IF(W3<500,A1,A2)	If W3 is less than 500, return the value of A1, else return the value of A2

PROTECTION

Range Protect
WSheet Global Protection

By default, As-Easy-As leaves cells unprotected. You, or whoever uses your worksheet, can change any or all cells at will. When you have developed a worksheet, however, you may wish to be sure that certain cells are not changed inadvertently. Changes made may well make the results displayed dangerously inaccurate. Since you are primarily aware of the displays of cells, if an underlying formula is changed or replaced by a number, you may never know that an improper change has been made.

You want to be able to change the parameters, but you also want to be sure that you cannot change cells B23 through B30 since these cells contain formulas that should remain unchanged unless you decide to edit them. First, protect every cell in the worksheet by typing

/ Slash
W WSheet
G General
P Protect
E Enable

Second, unprotect the parameters sections of the worksheet by placing the cell pointer on B8 and typing

/ Slash
R Range
L Lock
N No. Unlock the range to be identified.
↓ Down arrow 10 times to cover the range to be unprotected
↵ Enter key.

Move your cell pointer over the cells from B23 through B30. Try to change one of these cells by trying to replace the contents with some other entry. You will not be allowed to do so.

WHAT IF . . .?

A major advantage of creating this type of worksheet is the ability a decision maker gains to test various alternatives. The initial worksheet displays the costs involved in one possible scenario. Hundreds of others can be tested by changing the values for each of the parameters.

Try changing any of the values in B8 through B18 to see what effect a change has on the total expenses, the total charge-back, and the total cost to the central office. Use the PgUp and PgDn keys to move back and forth. Notice that even though you protected cells B23 through B30, their displays change. The contents of the cell are not permitted to change, but the display is allowed to change.

Find a cost alternative (there are many possibilities), in which the number of participants is greater than 20 and the cost to the central office is less than $40,000 by changing other variables.

PRINTING YOUR WORKSHEET *Print Printer*

Print the alternative cost estimate you locate by typing

/	Slash
P	Print
P	Printer
R	Range
Home	Home key to find the top of the worksheet
.	Period to anchor the range
↓	Down arrow 29 times to cover the vertical range of the worksheet
→	Right arrow once to cover both columns of the worksheet
↵	Enter key, submit the range just set
A	Adjust
G	Go, to print the worksheet
P	Page
Q	Quit, to return to As-Easy-As

SAVING YOUR WORKSHEET *File Save*

Save the file on the files diskette with the command sequence,

/	Slash
F	File
S	Store
PRJTBDGT	The filename of the worksheet
↵	Enter key

Make a backup copy of your file by putting your backup files diskette in drive B and repeating the save process.

EXITING AS-EASY-AS *Exit*

Exit the As-Easy-As program. Type

/	Slash
E	Exit
Y	Yes

and load the DOS diskette when prompted to do so.

EXERCISES

A. A store manager wishes to use a daily inventory of stock on hand to determine whether any items have to be reordered. The manager has determined, for each item in stock, what the minimum number on hand should be for each item in inventory. An assessment has also been made to determine the maximum number of each item that the store should have on hand at any one time. This maximum allows the manager to place an order that brings an economically desirable cost break based on volume, but it prevents the ordering of stock that will simply sit on a shelf. An order is made whenever the stock on hand is less than or equal to the minimum. If an order is made, the amount ordered is the maximum amount allowed minus the amount on hand.

Develop an economic order quantity worksheet for the manager using the following data as your test case:

ECONOMIC ORDER QUANTITY CHART

NO.	NAME	ON-HAND	MIN	MAX	EOQ
100	5 1/4" DISKETTES SS/SD	30	100	500	470
101	5 1/4" DISKETTES SS/DD	100	100	500	0
102	5 1/4" DISKETTES DS/SD	210	100	500	0
103	5 1/4" DISKETTES DS/DD	500	100	500	0
104	8" DISKETTES	49	50	300	251
105	3 1/2" HARD DISKETTES	25	25	100	0
106	10 DISKETTE FILE BOX	10	15	35	25
107	25 DISKETTE FILE BOX	15	15	35	0
108	50 DISKETTE FILE BOX	25	15	35	0
109	8 1/2 x 11" COMPUTER PAPER PLAIN	35	25	50	0
110	1/2 x 11" COMPUTER PAPER LINED	45	25	50	0
111	11 x 8 1/2" COMPUTER PAPER PLAIN	15	25	50	35
112	11 x 8 1/2" COMPUTER PAPER LINED	22	25	50	28
113	11 x 14" COMPUTER PAPER PLAIN	27	25	50	0
114	11 x 14" COMPUTER PAPER LINED	35	25	50	0
115	RIBBONS—CARBON	6	10	40	34
116	RIBBONS—CLOTH	12	10	40	0

B. A motor bicycle company produces three different motor bicycles that have different levels of capability. Consequently, the three models have their own sales history, sales picture, and pricing. The basic model sells for $1,500 and sold 20,150 units last year. Its sales are expected to increase by 15% in each of the next two years. The enhanced model sells for $1,850 and sold 24,345 units last year. Its sales are expected to decrease by 5% in each subsequent year. The luxury model which sold 15,575 units last year is expected to sell 25% more units in each of the next two years. The price of the luxury model is $2,200. The worksheet described below presents one projection of the company's income based on sales projections that use all three factors (units sold + expected increase x price). Recreate this worksheet. When you copy formulas, remember that some references to cells should not be adjusted.

```
SOFTWARE SALES

1987 SALES BY PACKAGE TYPE
    WORD PROCESSOR       1,770
    WORKSHEETOR          2,541
    COMMUNICATOR           980
EXPECTED CHANGES (NEXT TWO YEARS)
    WORD PROCESSOR       -0.12
    WORKSHEETOR           0.15
    COMMUNICATOR          0.33
COST PER UNIT
    WORD PROCESSOR      $89.50
    WORKSHEETOR         $49.50
    COMMUNICATOR        $32.50

PROJECTED SALES INCOME
===============================
                          1989        1990        1991        1993
    WORD PROCESSOR    $158,415    $139,405    $122,677    $107,955
    WORKSHEETOR       $125,779    $144,646    $166,343    $191,295
    COMMUNICATOR       $31,850     $42,360     $56,339     $74,931
                     -------------------------------------------
                      $316,044    $326,412    $345,359    $374,182
```

Check the effect on income of a price rise of $150 per model. For a price rise of $75.

C. A software production firm produces three pieces of software under the imaginative names, Word Processor, Worksheetor, and Communicator. The firm has prepared the following worksheet displaying the sales for each software package in 1987, the cost of each package, and the expected increase or decrease in sales in each of the next several years. The first column of the projected income is composed of formulas that compute the actual income realized in 1987. Recreate this worksheet by producing the formulas for the 1987 income and by producing one column of formulas for computing the sales income for 1987. Then copy the column of formulas in the final two columns.

```
                            SALES INCOME FORECAST
PARAMETERS
=================
MOTOR BIKE SALES (THIS YEAR)
  BASIC                 20,150
  ENHANCED              24,345
  LUXURY                15,575
EXPECTED CHANGES (NEXT TWO YEARS)
  BASIC                   0.15
  ENHANCED               -0.05
  LUXURY                  0.25
COST PER UNIT
  BASIC                 $1,500
  ENHANCED              $1,850
  LUXURY                $2,200
```

PROJECTED SALES INCOME
==============================

	LAST YR.	THIS YEAR	YR. AFTER
BASIC	$30,225,000	$34,758,750	$39,972,562
ENHANCED	$45,038,250	$42,786,337	$40,647,021
LUXURY	$34,265,000	$42,831,250	$53,539,062
	$109,528,250	$120,376,337	$134,158,646

What is the effect on income if Word Processor is repriced at $79.50 and Communicator is repriced at $35.50?

D. A manufacturer of electric mixers is attempting to estimate the amount of money that would be earned if either of two factors are varied. The sale price of a mixer is currently at $30 and will be varied by $2 per unit. The current level of sales is 5,000 per year and will be varied in increments of $250. The worksheet results are shown below:

ELECTRIC MIXER INCOME SCENARIOS

# UNITS SOLD	CURRENT UNIT COST
5,000	$30

	$30	$32	$34	$36	$38
5,000	$150,000	$160,000	$170,000	$180,000	$190,000
5,250	$157,500	$168,000	$178,500	$189,000	$199,500
5,500	$165,000	$176,000	$187,000	$198,000	$209,000
5,750	$172,500	$184,000	$195,500	$207,000	$218,500
6,000	$180,000	$192,000	$204,000	$216,000	$228,000
6,250	$187,500	$200,000	$212,500	$225,000	$237,500
6,500	$195,000	$208,000	$221,000	$234,000	$247,000
6,750	$202,500	$216,000	$229,500	$243,000	$256,500
7,000	$210,000	$224,000	$238,000	$252,000	$266,000
7,250	$217,500	$232,000	$246,500	$261,000	$275,500
7,500	$225,000	$240,000	$255,000	$270,000	$285,000
7,750	$232,500	$248,000	$263,500	$279,000	$294,500
8,000	$240,000	$256,000	$272,000	$288,000	$304,000
8,250	$247,500	$264,000	$280,500	$297,000	$313,500

Except for the initial statement of the number of mixers sold and of the initial cost, the numbers, including the column headers and row headers, are created by formulas. Recreate the worksheet. When you create the initial income formula ($30 x 5,000 = $150,000), this formula can be copied in several steps to fill the table. Do not create a new formula in each cell.

The product manager for electric toasters asks to see the results produced by this worksheet when the number of toasters sold is 8,950 and the starting price is $12.50 per unit. The $2 difference between columns can remain.

Part IV

Database Management with PC-FILE+

Chapter 14

Database Management: Using PC-FILE+

CHAPTER OUTLINE

What are Databases?
An Example of a Database
Making a Working Copy of PC-FILE+
Invoking PC-FILE+
    Help Screens
    Field Names
    Field Lengths
    Numeric Fields
    More About Fields
The Master Menu
    Teach Mode
Adding Records
    Duplicating Data Commands
Printing the Database
Job Database
Printing to the Screen
Adding Records
Finding and Deleting Records
Printing Records
Finding and Editing Records
    The Record Pointer
    Searching by the Key Fields
    Searching by Record Number
    First and Last Record
    Next and Prior Record
    Browse
    Exiting Find
Printing the Database
Exiting PC-FILE+
Backing Up Your Files
Exercises

In addition to word processors and spreadsheets, database management programs are the third type of program commonly found on microcomputers. This chapter will introduce you to the basic techniques for creating, organizing, and utilizing a database manager. Specifically, you will:

1. Define a database structure with which to capture data,
2. Input records to the database,
3. Explore the features of PC-FILE+ available from the Master Menu,
4. Create a simple listing of the records contained in the database and print the listing,

5. Edit the contents of selected records using four methods of selecting records to edit,
6. Examine the database using the browse technique,
7. Delete selected records.

WHAT ARE DATABASES?

A database is a collection of records that contains comparable types of data about people, events, or objects. A telephone directory, for instance, is a database that provides a name, an address, and a telephone number for each person listed. The directory entries follow some rules, even though variations are accepted. There must always be a name, even though a company name and an individual's name may be treated as being equal. Similarly, there must always be a telephone number listed. It would not make sense to show either a name or a telephone number, but not both. To make the directory useful, the names must appear in the same column each time and the telephone numbers must appear in their own column, otherwise searching for an entry would be difficult. Addresses, on the other hand, are optional.

Databases are useful for many purposes. Other examples of databases include:

1. Inventories of stock, supplies, or equipment,
2. Records on employee hirings, salaries, and training,
3. Facilities and vehicle records related to maintenance and repair,
4. Mailing list records,
5. Sales history and billing databases,
6. School and voter registration lists,
7. Airplane reservation and seating assignments, and
8. Library book catalogs.

Many databases are kept by hand, not on a computer. Computerized databases are easier to manipulate and to keep up to date, however.

In a telephone directory, a single entry is called a record. A record consists of three elements (a name, an address, and a number) called fields. Each record has the same elements. The collection of records is called a database.

Often the term *database manager* is given a restricted, technical meaning. This restricted definition is a program that can work with several data files simultaneously. Also, generally, a database manager stores data in well-defined computer structures. A file manager works with one file at a time and uses a simple method of storing its records. PC-FILE+ is, properly speaking, a file manager. For this book, however, it will be described as a database manager, a more popularly understood term.

AN EXAMPLE OF A DATABASE

Computer Software Associates is a company that employs part-time programmers to take on software projects that the company has contracted to produce for its client companies. The part-time programmers are paid from reports filed with the company manager. Each report requires:

1. The programmer's identification number,
2. The programmer's proficiency level, a company assigned number that is used to calculate the charge-back cost to the client, and the pay rate for the programmer,
3. A client identification number,
4. A job identification number. Any client may have several projects in process,
5. A job title,
6. The hours of progamming time used on the project.

Computer Software Associates has been increasingly successful in locating clients and is finding that it should computerize the reports filed by its employees. To this point, work file record reports (*see* Figure 14–1) have been handwritten and look like,

Billing No.	104
Programmer ID	10
Rank	2
Client ID	127
Job ID	1502
Job Title	Accts Payable
Hours Spent	7.5

Figure 14–1. Work File Record Report.

Since the reports are filed on cards, the manager sorts the cards in order of programmer identification at the end of each pay period as the basis for computing the programmer's pay. At the end of each billing cycle, the cards are sorted by client identification and job identification number to determine the cost per job per client. As the number of jobs has increased, so has the number of programmers. Keeping accurate records has become a problem. Consequently, the manager of the programming group has asked that a computerized database be developed that could be used to facilitate the preparation of these reports and to aid in other analyses.

MAKING A WORKING COPY OF PC-FILE+

Before proceeding you will need four diskettes. Two diskettes will be used to hold PC-FILE+ programs and PC-FILE+ utilities. The other two disks, if you need them, will be used to hold your original files and your backup files. Boot up your computer with DOS. With your DOS diskette in drive A and with the DOS prompt "A>" showing, place a blank diskette in drive B and enter the following commands, waiting for the completion of one command before entering the next,

Format b

You will be instructed to insert a blank diskette in drive B. Since the diskette is already there, hit any key to begin the formatting. After the formatting is completed, you will be asked if you wish to format another disk. Answer "Y" if you need to format more disks and "N" if you do not.

Place the PC-FILE+ Program diskette in drive A and a formatted disk in drive B and enter,

```
copy a:pcf.exe b:
copy a:pcf.hlp b:
copy a:pcfile.pro b:
```

which will copy the PC-FILE+ program files to your working copy. The diskette in drive B is your working copy of PC-FILE+. Label it "PC-FILE+ WORKING PROGRAM." Then place the PC-FILE+ Utility diskette in drive A and a formatted disk in drive B and enter,

```
copy *.* b:
```

Label the diskette in drive B, "PC-FILE+ WORKING UTILITIES."

INVOKING PC-FILE+

With the DOS prompt "A>" visible, place a formatted diskette in drive B and your working copy of PC-FILE+ in drive A and type,

pcf The command for starting PC-FILE+.

If you have to exit PC-FILE+ before this exercise is completed, you can generally return to the Master Menu by pressing **Enter** or **Esc.** When you see the Master Menu, press Q to quit, then Q again. Retrieve your database file by typing **"A>pcf"** and, when the list of databases appears, highlighting **JOBSDB** and pressing **F10.** Then continue with the Master Menu command you were using when you exited.

Shortly you will see the PC-FILE+ copyright screen with the prompt,

```
 (Alt)-H - HELP (at any time)
 Please reply  ^v
Which drive for the database (A-Z) >A<
```

B Enter "B" to select drive B as the default drive on which files will be created. You will then see the prompt,

```
 Please reply  ^v
  What path for the data? >_                                <
```

↵ Enter key. The default path will be used. Paths are used to identify directories that are typically used on hard disk microcomputers. You will then see the prompt,

```
You will need to define a database. Please give it a name.
Type a name
><
```

This prompt will change slightly when you have databases on the disk. This is the way it appears when the diskette in use has no PC-FILE+ files on it. You are going to build a database of records on completion of programming assignments. Respond by entering,

jobsdb The name of the database to be defined: an abbreviated form of "JOBS DATABASE."
↵ Enter key

PC-FILE+ will then display that "JOBSDB is a new file," and will prompt,

```
B:\jobsdb is a new file.
```

```
 Please reply ^v
Do you want to define it? Y/N >Y<
```

This prompt allows you to exit PC-FILE+ by typing "N" if you saw that the filename had been typed incorrectly.

↵ Enter key, to begin to create the new database. PC-FILE+ offers two methods of describing the contents of a database file: the "fast" method and the "paint" method.

↵ Enter key, since the end results are the same, the examples in this book will use the fast method. When you are prompted for a choice, choose "fast".

The database definition screen appears next as in Figure 14–2. This screen enables you to describe the "structure" of the JOBSDB database records. The structure of a record consists of a complete list of the field names composing each record within the database and the length of those fields. A field is a specific piece of information you want included in each record. A programmer's identification number and a programmer's name are examples of two fields. As the fields are filled with data, a complete record is created. The records that are stored together in one file are called a database.

```
Enter the field NAMES in their relative positions.
You can place the names anywhere on the screen.
=========================================================================
 >          <      [       ]     [       ]      [       ]
[           ]      [       ]     [       ]      [       ]
[           ]      [       ]     [       ]      [       ]
[           ]      [       ]     [       ]      [       ]
[           ]      [       ]     [       ]      [       ]
[           ]      [       ]     [       ]      [       ]
[           ]      [       ]     [       ]      [       ]
[           ]      [       ]     [       ]
[           ]      [       ]     [       ]
[           ]      [       ]     [       ]
[           ]      [       ]     [       ]
[           ]      [       ]     [       ]
[           ]      [       ]     [       ]
[           ]      [       ]     [       ]
[           ]      [       ]     [       ]
[           ]      [       ]     [       ]
[           ]      [       ]     [       ]
[           ]      [       ]     [       ]
[           ]      [       ]     [       ]
[           ]      [       ]     [       ]
[           ]      [       ]     [       ]

Please respond. (F10) when complete. (Alt)H for help.
```

Figure 14–2. Database Definition Screen.

PC-FILE+ uses several steps to define the structure of a record. Using the database field name definition screen, you do two things. You name the fields to be included in each record in your JOBSDB database, and you can indicate where each field will be displayed on the screen. This allows you to place information on the screen in a way that makes sense to you and, hopefully, has a pleasing appearance. When you are done naming the fields, PC-FILE+ presents the field length definition screen as in Figure 14–6 to allow you to set the length of each of the fields. Figure 14–3 illustrates how the structure of the database being constructed here can be visualized and how the data from three records would relate to this structure.

```
                              FIELDS

BILL_NUM  PRG_ID  RANK CLT_ID  JOB_ID  JOB TITLE         HRS#

103       12      2     115  1436 PROPERTY MANAGMNT  7.6 <record one
104       12      2     115  1436 PROPERTY MANAGMNT  7.3 <record two
105       13      3     142  1601 INCOME STATEMENT   3.5 <record three
```

Figure 14–3. Sample Database Structure and Three Records

Help Screens

PC-File+ has an extensive set of context sensitive help screens. The help screens "pop up" when called with the Alternate and H keys. The screens are said to be context sensitive because the help screen changes based upon where you are in the program. That is, as you execute commands and the menus on your screen change, the help you need changes. Therefore the help screens are adapted to the most likely points of assistance that are required in a particular setting. Before proceeding, experiment with the help option. Enter,

`Alt-H` Alternate and H keys pressed simultaneously. To call up a help screen that looks like,

```
Help field names into the
locations on the screen where you'd
like them to appear.

The columns are important. As you
use more columns in any row, the
maximum data width of any field in
that row becomes less.

Also, access to the fields for data
entry purposes will be from top to
bottom down the first column, then
down the second column, etc.
```

Figure 14–4. Sample Help Screen.

The arrow keys can relocate the help window to a new location. The placement of the help screen is used for all future help windows that are called up. In a similar fashion, the Up and Down arrow keys are used to change the place of the "Please reply" windows at the user's convenience. Press,

`F10` Function key F10, to exit the help window.

Field Names

Field names are selected by the user. A field name can be up to twelve (alphabetic, numeric, or other) characters. Later, when you produce reports based on this structure, you will find that the field name will be truncated to the width of the field. Thus, a field name like PROGRAMMERID with a field length of four, will be printed in reports as PROG. Therefore, try to make the field name as descriptive as you can with no more than the number of characters selected for the field length.

Usually it is best to avoid the use of characters such as "*" and """ that may be confusing at best and may cause unwanted effects at worst.

PC-FILE+ normally left-justifies data being entered. Numbers on which computations may be carried out should be right-justified. By terminating a field name with a "#" sign, the entries will be right-justified. When reports are generated, field names that are followed by the number sign will automatically be totaled and averaged.

Caps Lock Put caps lock on.

Field names are entered by typing the data between the brackets and pressing the Enter key. Corrections can be made by moving the cursor with the Arrow keys and using the Del key to delete letters. Letters typed will be entered in overtype mode unless you first press the Ins key. Pressing Ins will cause the cursor to change to a bright block and letters typed will be inserted at the location of the cursor between characters already present. You can exit from insert mode by pressing the Ins key a second time.

Notice that the first field contains the cursor and is framed by solid triangles rather than by brackets. This is the active field for definition. **Type, and with the Return key** (or the Tab key), enter the following field names, so that the screen looks like Figure 14–5.

```
Enter the field NAMES in their relative positions.
You can place the names anywhere on the screen.
```

```
[BILL_NUM          ]  [         ]  [         ]  [         ]
[PRG_ID            ]  [         ]  [         ]  [         ]
[RANK              ]  [         ]  [         ]  [         ]
[CLT_ID            ]  [         ]  [         ]  [         ]
[JOB_ID            ]  [         ]  [         ]  [         ]
[JOB_TITLE         ]  [         ]  [         ]  [         ]
[HRS#              ]  [         ]  [         ]  [         ]
                      [         ]  [         ]

[                  ]
```

Figure 14–5. Completed Field Name Definition Screen.

Examine your entries. If there are any corrections to be made, make them now. You can move the cursor among field names with the Arrow keys. The Delete key can delete unneeded characters. The Ins key can be used to change from overwrite mode to insert mode. When the Ins key is pressed, the cursor changes to a block to signify the change. The "#" sign following HRS signifies that data entered in this field will be right-justified and treated as a number. Remember that you are not only indicating the name of the field, but also the position on the screen PC-FILE+ will display the contents of the field. When you are satisfied that the field names are entered as in the example above, press

F10 Function key F10, to complete the definition of the database structure and to place the field names on the data entry screen. You will then see the field length definition screen shown in Figure 14–6.

Field Lengths

Field lengths specify how many characters or digits can be entered into a field. Field lengths should be defined carefully. If a field is declared to be too short, all of your data cannot be stored. For instance, a last name field length of eight could not hold all of the characters in names like "Brownstone," or "Quackenstein."

Numeric Fields

Numeric fields will be totaled and averaged automatically by PC-FILE+. The results of each of these operations will be printed at the end of each listing of records. The space allotted for the printing of the total and the average will be limited to the length assigned to the numeric fields even though the complete values require the use of extra characters. The truncated values will be inaccurate *and there is no warning that truncation has occurred.* Therefore, if you need to print 10 characters to see an accurate total, you must define the field length as 10 even though any one record will need only 3 characters to display the amount for that record. For example, assume that you have a file with 100 records, each of which has an amount field of length 3 (999 maximum). If you total this field, you could have a sum of 99,900 (100 × 999), which takes up 6 print columns including the comma. Because the field is defined as length 3, all you would see is 900!

```
Enter the display length (1-65) for each field
The 'superfield' maximum size for this database is 1185
```

```
BILL_NUM      >_  <
PRG_ID        [   ]
RANK          [   ]
CLT_ID        [   ]
JOB_ID        [   ]
JOB_TITLE     [   ]
HRS#          [   ]
```

Figure 14–6. Field Length Definition Screen.

More About Fields

Although you should generally make field lengths large enough to hold the largest entries you expect to make, don't be extravagant with the length. During printing, columns will be made as wide as the field length. Thus, a last name field length of 20 will use up about one fourth of your paper's width even though there are no names that long. Also, as records are created and stored on the diskette, each record will store the full field length even though a shorter length is adequate. In a large database, this can be significant. For example, if the name "Doe" is stored within a field of length 20, there are 17 blanks stored in addition to the 3 necessary letters. In a database of 1,000 records, if there are 5 extra letters in each last name field, 5,000 blank characters will be stored. If there were 10 fields, each of which stored 5 extra characters, the excess storage would be a minimum of 50,000 characters.

By default, when records are printed there will be one space between columns. You should not leave spaces in the fields of a record to format report columns.

```
Enter the display length (1-65) for each field
The "superfield" maximum size for this database is 1185
```

```
BILL_NUM      [3  ]
PRG_ID        [6  ]
RANK          [4  ]
CLT_ID        [6  ]
JOB_ID        [6  ]
JOB_TITLE     [18 ]
HRS#          >3  <
```

Figure 14–7. Completed Field Length Definition Screen.

When you have entered the field lengths as in Figure 14–7, press

F10 Function key F10, to complete the specification of field lengths.

```
There are two types of fields:

  Regular fields:
      The entire length of the field is displayed
      on the screen at one time.

  Window fields:
      The field is longer than the number of characters
      displayed on the screen. You can scroll left and
      right to display the data.

      Please reply  ^v
    Are any of the fields Window fields?  Y/N >N<
```

Figure 14–8. Field Type Identification Screen.

All of the fields in this data base are regular fields. If any of the fields you define are Window fields, the screen will explain that a Window field is displayed differently from a Regular field.

N No, there are no window fields. The next screen displays,

The fields will be accessed from left to right, and top to bottom as you draw them on the screen.

```
 BILL_NUM     Please reply  ^v
   PRG_ID    Would you like to change this sequence?  Y/N >N<
     RANK
   CLT_ID
   JOB_ID
JOB_TITLE
     HRS#
```

This screen is asking whether you wish to change the sequence in which PC-FILE+ prompts for data when appending records to the database.

N No, to accept the sequence and placement suggested by PC-FILE+.

THE MASTER MENU

After PC-FILE+ creates the database JOBSDB, you will see the Master Menu that looks like Figure 14–9.

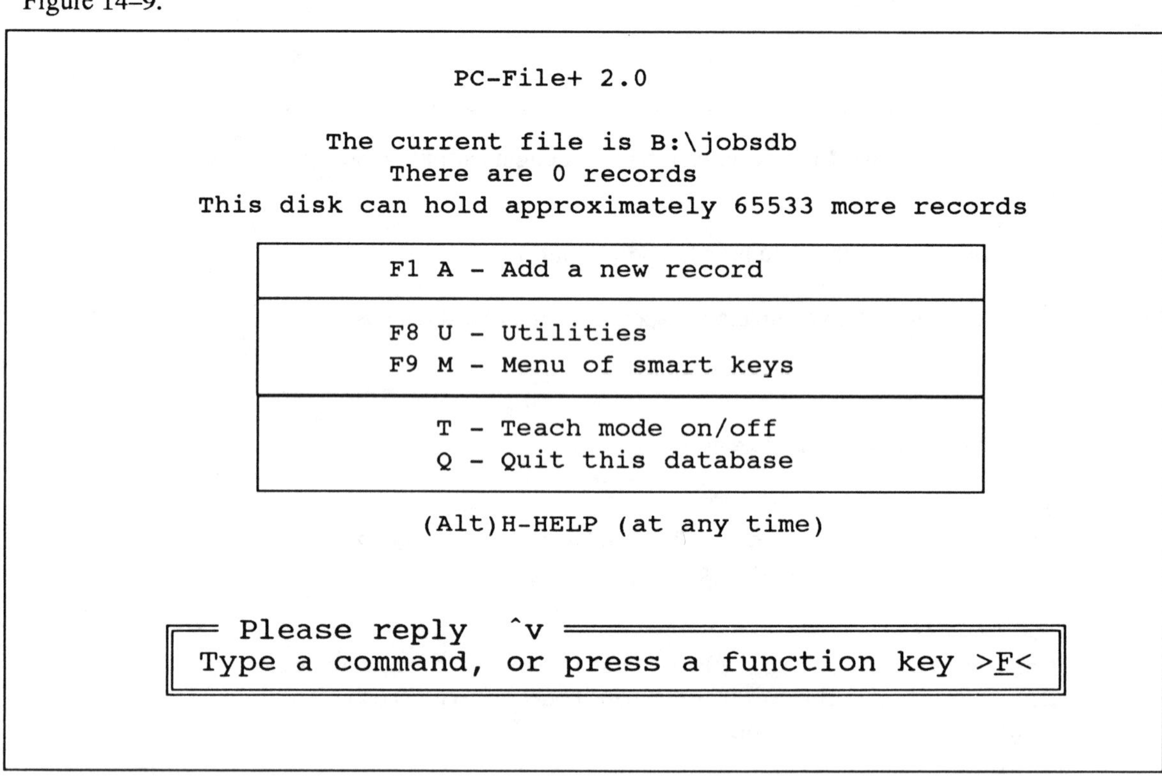

Figure 14–9. Master Menu for PC-FILE+.

The number 65533 shown as the number of additional records that can be added may vary depending on the amount of unused space on your diskette.

Choices from the Master Menu can be entered by pressing the correct function key or letter key. Generally, you must return to the Master Menu screen to select one of the functions listed. Once you have selected a choice from the menu, for instance to add a new record, you can continue within that procedure, until you are finished. If you have engaged in one of these operations and you wish to return to the Master Menu you can often do so by pressing the Escape key or, if the correct menu is present, the letter "Q" to return to the Master Menu.

Teach Mode

Notice the choice "T" for "Teach mode." Selection of this choice will automatically call up help screens each time a new screen is displayed. Help does not have to be called for with the Alt-H keys.

This chapter will show you how to add, delete, and list records, as well as how to exit from PC-FILE+.

ADDING RECORDS

The first database operation you will select is that for adding records. PC-FILE+ will prompt you with a blank form with which you can enter data into records, and records into the database. Press

F1 Function key F1, the ADD key. You will see a screen,

```
Record number 1                                              A

BILL_NUM        >   <
PRG_ID          [   ]
RANK            [   ]
CLT_ID          [   ]
JOB_ID          [   ]
JOB_TITLE       [   ]
HRS#            [   ]

Please respond. (F10) when complete. (Alt)H for help.
```

Figure 14–10. The Add Screen.

Text and numbers can now be typed and entered. Notice the cursor in the first field. Enter the following record,

```
BILL_NUM        >101<
PRG_ID          [10      ]
RANK            [2  ]
CLT_ID#         [127     ]
JOB_ID          [1502    ]
JOB_TITLE       [ACCOUNTS PAYABLE   ]
HRS#            [7.5]
```

Figure 14–11. First Completed Record.

remembering to press the Enter key after each field entry. The Arrow, Ins, and Del keys can be used to move the cursor and to edit the fields if necessary. After you press the Enter key for the number of hours, the cursor will move back to the field named BILL_NUM. You may move through the fields editing your entry until it is as shown. When the record is complete and correct, press F10. You will be prompted to confirm that the data is correct with the prompt,

F10 Function key F10, to center the record

```
 Please reply  ^v
O.K. to ADD? Y,N,or X(stop asking) >Y<
```

If you press either the Enter key or "Y", the data will be accepted. If you press "X", then PC-FILE+ will no longer ask you to review your entries before it enters the records into the database. Press

↵ Enter key, to accept the data. The record will be added to the database, and a second blank form will appear. A prompt,

```
Record number 2
```

at the top of the screen shows that you are adding the second record. Enter the second record,

```
BILL_NUM     >102<
PRG_ID       [10]
RANK         [2]
CLT_ID#      [127]
JOB_ID       [1502]
JOBTITLE     [ACCOUNTS. PAYABLE]
HRS#         [8.0]
```

F10 Function key F10. Once the F10 key has been pressed after the hours worked have been entered, the prompt appears again to check your data. Assume that you need to make some changes.

N No, to modify the entry. Alter the PRG_ID to 12 and the JOB_TITLE to "ACCOUNTS PAYABLE."

F10 Function key F10, to accept the changed entry.

Y Yes, to continue to have PC-FILE+ ask about the correctness of the data. The third blank form appears.

Whenever you have finished a record and do not wish to re-examine the contents of future records, press "X" to suppress the display of the prompt. The data for the next six records is displayed in a tabular form, not as a screen form. Remember to press the F10 key when each record is completed. Each row of data contains the entries for a complete record. Make the following field entries:

BILL_NUM	PRG_ID	RANK	CLT_ID#	JOB_ID	JOB TITLE	HR#
103	12	2	115	1436	PROPERTY MANAGMNT	7.6
104	12	2	115	1436	PROPERTY MANAGMNT	7.3
105	13	3	142	1601	INCOME STATEMENT	3.5
106	14	1	131	1575	SOFTWARE INSTALL	6.8
107	11	2	135	1575	SOFTWARE INSTALL	3.2
108	13	3	118	1440	LEASE MANAGMNT	5.7

Stop entering data when you see the blank entry form for record number 9. PC-FILE+ retains knowledge of the last field entries you make.

Duplicating Data Commands

When you are entering a record in which a field entry is the same as that entered in the same field of the previous record, you can type the Control and "F" keys simultaneously in the field. PC-FILE+ will enter the previous entry for that field in the current record. To illustrate, make the following entry using Control-F in the fields displaying ^F:

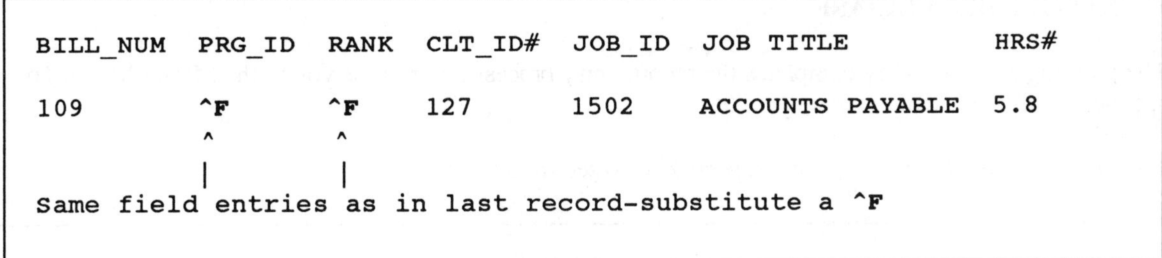

BILL_NUM	PRG_ID	RANK	CLT_ID#	JOB_ID	JOB TITLE	HRS#
109	^F	^F	127	1502	ACCOUNTS PAYABLE	5.8

Same field entries as in last record-substitute a ^F

Figure 14–12. Copy Previous Field Command.

Enter the fields except for the PRG_ID and RANK fields. In these fields **enter a control-F in the PRG_ID field and press Return. Enter a control-F in the RANK field and press Return.** The values in the previous record's PRG_ID and RANK fields are inserted. Now complete the remaining fields of the record.

Similarly, the Control-D(uplicate) key combination will fill in the entire record with data that duplicates the previous record. Again, you may choose to use Control-D when the previous record is very similar to the record you are currently entering even though some fields have to be changed.

PC-FILE+ also provides you with the capability to read the data from one field into memory with the Control-R(ead) key sequence. In any field, if you press Control-R, the data is saved in memory ready to be recalled whenever it is needed. The data is recalled when you press Control-W(rite). Only one piece of data can be stored at a time, but it can be written out as often as necessary.

Remember to take advantage of these duplicate-the-previous-data characters as you enter the following records. The field entries with a control-F are the same as the previous record's entries. Entries with Control-D that display a minus sign are left alone.

BILL_NUM	PRG_ID	RANK	CLT_ID	JOB_ID	JOB TITLE	HRS#
110	10	2	135	1585	LABELS PROGRAM	3.5
111	^F	^F	142	1595	DEPRECIATION PRGM	2.3
112	12	^F	127	1502	ACCOUNTS PAYABLE^R	3.6
^D113	-	-	-	1503	ACCOUNTS RECEIV.	8.0
114	^F	^F	118	1440	LEASE MANAGMNT	4.7
115	14	1	131	1575	SOFTWARE INSTALL	5.2
116	13	3	127	1502	^W	5.8
117	^F	^F	142	1596	EMPLOYEE DATABASE	8.0
118	14	1	115	1435	MAINTENANCE D.B.	^F
^D119	-	-	-	-	-	3.8
120	12	2	^F	1436	PROPERTY MANAGMNT	7.0
121	10	^F	135	1586	AMORTIZATION SCHED	5.3

You can see that the use of Control characters can save you considerable amounts of typing when entering some types of data in which there is a frequent repetition of data between records. When the last record is completed and you have pressed the F10 key, you will receive another blank form to fill in. PC-FILE+ knows you are finished entering data when you press the F10 key *before you enter any characters, including spaces,* into the blank form.

F10 Function key F10, to complete data entry and to return to the Master Menu.

PRINTING THE DATABASE

The pressing of the F10 key completes the record entry process and returns you to the Master Menu. To see the records you have entered, type,

F6 Function key F6, or "R," the Reports key, to see the screen,

```
Which type of report would you like to produce?

Page format    One record on each page. Field
               names are shown beside the data.

Row format     One record prints on each line.
               The fields line up in columns.

Free format    You'll "paint" each section of
               the report. This is very flexible
               but more work than the above.

Commands       You use the report command language
               to define every aspect. This is
               very flexible and powerful, but
               requires considerable planning.

               ╔═ Please reply  ^v ═══════╗
               ║ Enter  P, R, F, or C >R< ║
               ╚══════════════════════════╝
```

Figure 14–13. Report Format Selection Screen.

R Row format, the default format for reports. The next screen appears as,

```
              Number of columns to print from left to right

 Record No. > <
      BILL_NUM     [    ]
      PRG_ID       [    ]
      RANK         [    ]
      CLT_ID#      [    ]
      JOB_ID       [    ]
      JOBTITLE     [    ]
      HRS#         [    ]
```

Enter the numbers 1 through 8 in the entry blocks. These numbers designate the order in which the fields will be printed in the report.

F10 Function key F10, to complete the designation of field columns. You will see the screen,

```
You may now enter a permanent TITLE LINE for this report.
 The title only prints on the first page of the report.
      (If you enter nothing, then a title will be
       requested every time the report is printed.)
```

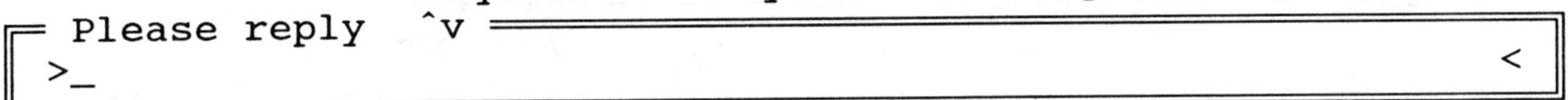

```
Please reply  ^v
>_                                                              <
```

JOB DATABASE

The title to appear at the top of the report.

↵ Enter key. A message, "Creating Report Work File," appears. This is followed by the prompt,

```
Please reply  ^v
Would you like to save this report format?  Y/N >N<
```

Y Yes, save the report format so it could be reused again in the future. Saving a report format avoids your having to reestablish the order of the fields and the report title.

REPORT1 The report format filename.

↵ Enter key. The report menu now appears as shown in Figure 14–4. Check to see that your printer is on.

```
                          REPORT MENU

Output to Printer, Screen, Disk      P/S/D         >P<
Number of copies                      1-99         [1]
Do Detail lines?                       Y/N         [Y]
Do Subtotals?                          Y/N         [N]
Left margin (extra spaces)            0-99         [0]
Page length (in "lines")                        [ 66]
Pause after each page?                 Y/N         [N]
Start at which page number?         1-9999         [1]
Type size (Normal/Condensed)           N/C         [N]
Remove blank lines and spaces          Y/N         [N]
Flip/cy/data active?                   Y/N         [Y]
Print All or Selected records          A/S         [A]

Press (Esc) to return to PC-File+ menu
```

Figure 14–14. Report Menu Screen.

F10 Function key F10, accepts all default values of the Report Menu.

X Print all records without asking for confirmation. The report is printed with the report title, the date and time, the page number, and the first seventeen records now displayed in the order that you entered them. The report appears as,

```
                         JOB DATABASE
     01-01-80 AT 0:42 a.m.                              Page 1
Recrd  BIL  PRG_ID  RANK  CLT_ID  JOB_ID   JOB_TITLE            HRS
====================================================================
    1  101  10      2     127     1502     ACCOUNTS PAYABLE     7.5
    2  102  12      2     127     1502     ACCOUNTS PAYABLE     8.0
    3  103  12      2     115     1436     PROPERTY MANAGMNT    7.6
    4  104  12      2     115     1437     TENANT LIST          7.3
    5  105  13      3     142     1601     INCOME STATEMENT     3.5
    6  106  14      1     131     1575     SOFTWARE INSTALL     6.8
    7  107  11      2     135     1575     SOFTWARE INSTALL     3.2
    8  108  13      3     118     1440     LEASE MANAGEMENT     5.7
    9  109  13      3     127     1502     ACCOUNTS PAYABLE     5.8
   10  110  10      2     135     1585     LABELING PROGRAM     3.5
   12  112  12      2     127     1502     ACCOUNTS PAYABLE     3.6
   13  113  12      2     127     1503     ACCOUNTS RECEIV.     8.0
   14  114  12      2     118     1440     LEASE MANAGMNT       4.7
   15  115  14      1     131     1575     SOFTWARE INSTALL     5.2
   16  116  13      3     127     1502     ACCOUNTS PAYABLE     5.8
   17  117  13      3     142     1596     EMPLOYEE DATABASE    8.0
   18  118  14      1     115     1435     MAINTENANCE D.B.     8.0
   19  119  14      1     115     1435     MAINTENANCE D.B.     3.8
   20  120  12      2     115     1436     PROPERTY MANAGMNT    7.0
   21  121  10      2     131     1586     AMORTIZATION SCHED   5.3
--------------------------------------------------------------------
   TOTALS:          HRS                                      120.60
Printed 21 of the 21 records.
     PRIMARY SORT FIELD: unsorted
     SELECTION CRITERIA:
     All records
```

Figure 14–15. Printed Jobs List.

The total for the HRS field is given because the field name was typed as HRS#. The "#" identified this field as numeric, so this field was automatically summed.

If your total is not the same as that shown because the values for one or more records are incorrect, don't worry. In the section "Editing Records," you will have a chance to fix entries that had incorrect values in the HRS field.

After the report is printed a report status screen will appear.

↲ Press Enter key, the Master Menu will return.

PRINTING TO THE SCREEN

There are times when you will want to print a report to the screen rather than to the printer. This is desirable because you can check the format of the report heading, the arrangement of the columns and the organization of the database. If any of these are incorrect, you can correct them before wasting paper unnecessarily. Print the report to the screen by entering,

F6 Function key F6, the Report key.
1 Select report format [1] the identifier for REPORT1 which has already been defined.
F10 Function key F10, to complete the selection.

S Select screen output from the print menu screen for the "Output to Printer, Screen, or Disk," query.

F10 Function key F10, to initiate the printing to the screen. The headings and the detail lines for the first seventeen records will print to the screen and you receive the prompt,

```
Please reply  ^v
More...  Press (Enter) >_<
```

↵ Enter key, to see the detail lines for the remaining four records and to see the prompt,

```
Please reply  ^v
Ready for Final Totals.  Press (Enter) >_<
```

↵ Enter key, to see the total line as it was originally printed and to see the prompt,

```
Please reply  ^v
Completed.  Press (Enter) >_<
```

↵ Enter key, the Master Menu returns.

ADDING RECORDS

If you did miss one or more records, they can be added to records you currently have in the database by selecting F1 from the Master Menu. By pressing this function key you will receive the same blank entry form you received before. Add records by filling in the form and pressing F10. Exit the appending of records operation by pressing F10 before entering any information into the form.

FINDING AND DELETING RECORDS

At this point we will delete record number 7 from the database. If your database has any other records that should be deleted, delete them now also. Enter,

F2 Function key F2, or "F" to find a record. Before a record can be deleted it must be "found." The following prompt will appear,

```
How shall we locate the record?

B. Beginning of file (first record)
E. End of file (last record)
N. Next sequential record in file
P. Previous record in file
R. Relative record number
+. Browse forwards in file (PgDn)
-. Browse backwards in file (PgUp)
Q. Quit the Find. Return to main Menu.
```

Figure 14–16. Search Menu.

```
Please reply  ^v
Choose from the menu >S<
```

R Relative record number search. Examine your printed database listing and identify the record number maintained by PC-FILE+. Enter this number in response to the prompt,

```
Please reply  ^v
What record number to find: >_<
```

7 Enter the record number for the record to be found prior to being deleted.
↵ Enter key, to see the prompt,

```
Q<
D Delete
M Modify
S new Search
E End of file
B Beginning "
N Next record
P Prior record
R get by Rcd#
+ browse down
- browse up
Q Quit finding
```

Figure 14–17. Find Menu.

D Delete, to delete the record.
Y Okay to delete. If you have any additional records to delete, "find" them first and then delete them. When the last record to be deleted has been deleted, proceed to the next step.
Q Quit the find menu. The Master Menu returns.

PRINTING RECORDS

Print the records in your database again. Since you have already defined a report format, REPORT1, you can reuse this format, thereby altering the procedure described earlier in the chapter. Record 7 should not appear or be included in the total for the HRS# field. If you appended records the new records may not appear in the location shown earlier. Do not be concerned by this. PC-FILE+ adds records in the "blank" record spaces left by deleted records and at the end of the database. New records cannot be inserted at any other locations. To reprint the database enter,

F6 Function key F6, or "R," the Reports key, to see the report-type screen,
↓ Down arrow as necessary to highlight the REPORT1 format.
F10 Function key F10 to use the REPORT1 format that is highlighted.
P Print the report at the printer.
F10 Function key F10, to accept the other default values in the Report Menu.
X To print entire report. The report appears as,

```
                         JOB DATABASE
   01-01-80 AT 0:42 a.m.                             Page 1
Recrd  BIL  PRG_ID  RANK  CLT_ID  JOB_ID   JOB_TITLE           HRS
=================================================================
    1  101  10       2    127     1502     ACCOUNTS PAYABLE    7.5
    2  102  12       2    127     1502     ACCOUNTS PAYABLE    8.0
    3  103  12       2    115     1436     PROPERTY MANAGMNT   7.6
    4  104  12       2    115     1437     TENANT LIST         7.3
    5  105  13       3    142     1601     INCOME STATEMENT    3.5
    6  106  14       1    131     1575     SOFTWARE INSTALL    6.8
    8  108  13       3    118     1440     LEASE MANAGEMENT    5.7
    9  109  13       3    127     1502     ACCOUNTS PAYABLE    5.8
   10  110  10       2    135     1585     LABELING PROGRAM    3.5
   12  112  12       2    127     1502     ACCOUNTS PAYABLE    3.6
   13  113  12       2    127     1503     ACCOUNTS RECEIV.    8.0
   14  114  12       2    118     1440     LEASE MANAGMNT      4.7
   15  115  14       1    131     1575     SOFTWARE INSTALL    5.2
   16  116  13       3    127     1502     ACCOUNTS PAYABLE    5.8
   17  117  13       3    142     1596     EMPLOYEE DATABASE   8.0
   18  118  14       1    115     1435     MAINTENANCE D.B.    8.0
   19  119  14       1    115     1435     MAINTENANCE D.B.    3.8
   20  120  12       2    115     1436     PROPERTY MANAGMNT   7.0
   21  121  10       2    131     1586     AMORTIZATION SCHED  5.3
-----------------------------------------------------------------
   TOTALS:        HRS                                      117.40
Printed 20 of the 21 records.
      PRIMARY SORT FIELD: unsorted
      SELECTION CRITERIA:
      All records
```

Figure 14–18. Report Number 2.

↵ To return to Master Menu.

FINDING AND EDITING RECORDS

Frequently, it is necessary to change the data in individual records after they have been entered. Changes may be required because field entries were entered incorrectly and because the information they contain may change over time. For instance, an account balance field might change as payments are made.

You will change some of the data in the records you have entered to illustrate how to edit the contents of record fields. If you have made any mistakes in entering the records, you can edit the contents of those fields also. To edit the records, you must first have the Master Menu on your screen.

The Record Pointer

PC-FILE+ maintains a record "pointer" into the database. This pointer addresses one specific record. As various find commands are issued below, the record pointer is altered to point to the location of the found record.

Searching by the Key Field

To edit records, you must first locate them. There are several ways by which you can find the correct record. If you know the contents of any field in a record, you can search for it. In your database, the first field, BILL_NUM, is a field designed to contain a unique number for each record in the database. If records are deleted, you will lose records with certain BILL_NUM numbers. PC-FILE+ also keeps track of record numbers for all of the records. The record numbers maintained by PC-FILE+ do not necessarily correspond with BILL_NUM numbers in any way.

To initiate the search-by-key process enter,

F2 Function key F2, or "F," the Find key, to modify database entries. You will see the search menu again.

In your database, the first field is called BILL_NUM, a field designed to contain a unique number for each billing record. You can find any billing if you know the BILL_NUM number. Assume that record number 104 is incorrect in displaying the JOB_ID as 1436 and the JOB_TITLE as "PROPERTY MANAGMNT." To locate the record, enter

S Search for data in the find menu. You will see the screen:

```
  Simple search:
      you fill in the blanks
  Complex search:
      you type in a formula

 Please reply  ^v
 S(Simple search), C(Complex search), Q(Quit)  S/C/Q >S<
```

Figure 14–19. Search Type Menu.

S Simple search. Choosing a simple search brings up another screen:

```
Please supply the search data below F

  BILL_NUM >***<
    PRG_ID [******]
      RANK [****]
    CLT_ID [******]
    JOB_ID [******]
 JOB_TITLE [*****************]
      HRS# [***]
```

Figure 14–20. Search Criteria Screen.

This screen is requesting that you enter a value to be searched for in one of the fields.

104 The BILL_NUM for record number 4.
F10 Function key F10. The record will appear:

```
Record number 4                                          F

  BILL_NUM [104]
    PRG_ID [12          ]
      RANK [2     ]
    CLT_ID [115         ]
    JOB_ID [1436        ]
 JOB_TITLE [PROPERTY MANAGMNT ]
      HRS# [7.3]

  =>F<== <^>v ==
   D Delete
   M Modify
   F Find (cont.)
   S new Search
   E End of file
   B Beginning "
   N Next record
   P Prior record
   R get by Rcd#
   - browse down
   - browse up
   Q Quit finding
```

Figure 14–21.

Type the following to change the record:

M Modify
↲ Enter key four times to place the cursor in the JOB_ID field.
1437 A new JOB_ID.
↲ Enter key

TENANT LIST

A new JOB_TITLE.

Del Delete key six times to remove "NAGMNT."
F10 Function key F10, to complete the change and update the record. The search submenu reappears.

Searching by Record Number

The previous record search was based on the contents of a field. PC-FILE+ can find any record if you know the contents of any field in that record. If two records have the same field with the same contents, PC-FILE+ will find and display the one which was entered first. Pressing "F" when the find menu is visible will continue a search, and the next record meeting the search criteria will be presented if it exists. You can also move to a record based on the record number maintained by PC-FILE+. The record number is the record's place in the file, i.e., the first record typed in is record one, etc. If any record is deleted, all the records typed after it are renumbered. Edit record 10 (BILL_NUM = 110) by entering

R	Get by Record number.
10	The record number maintained by PC-FILE+.
↵	Enter.
M	Modify, to initiate editing.
↵	Enter key, five times to place the cursor in the JOB_TITLE field.
→	Right arrow, five times to place the cursor under the "S" in "LABELS."
Del	Delete the "S."
Ins	Insert on. Notice the cursor changes to a block to show that Insert is toggled on.
ING	The letters to be inserted to have the entry read, "LABELING PROGRAM."
F10	To complete the change and update the record.

First and Last Record

PC-FILE+ allows you to move quickly to the first and last records in the database. To edit the last record in the database, enter,

E	End, to move to the last record.
M	Modify it.
↵	Enter key, three times to place the cursor in the CLT_ID field.
131	An altered client identification number.
F10	To complete the change and update the record.

In a similar fashion you can move to the first record in the database by selecting "B" from the search submenu.

Next and Prior Record

Recall that PC-FILE+ maintains a pointer into the database that identifies the currently active record. You can move back and forth in the database by pressing the "N and P" keys to move to the next and prior records, respectively. Pressing the "N" key will advance the record pointer once toward the "bottom" of the database. Similarly, "P" will decrease the record pointer by one and move you back one record at a time toward the "beginning" of the file.

Experiment with these two movements.

N	Next. Advance one record. The prompt "Not found. Press (Enter) >_<" occurs because you were at the last record.
↵	Enter key, the find menu appears.
E	To return to the last record.
P	Prior. Move back one record.

Browse

The four search techniques discussed so far are record-oriented. You find a record and change it, find the next record and change it, and so on. These techniques are satisfactory when you know precisely what records you need to edit. Sometimes you need to see large groups of records so you can locate errors. The browse approach to editing can be used to see many records at a time. Type,

+	To enter browse

Browse produces a listing of twenty records beginning at the last record at which the cursor was located. The listing also shows the PC-FILE+-maintained record numbers in the first column alongside the user-maintained BILL_NUM numbers. Browse is useful for locating incorrect entries. By noting the record numbers, you can return to locating the records by record number or key contents.

Many databases contain too many fields to display all of the columns (fields) on a single screen. PC-FILE+ displays seventy-five characters on a line in browse. In large databases, to see fields that are not in view, press the Tab key to move the view of the screen one field at a time. Return to the fields to the left by pressing Shift and Tab once for each field move.

Typing a minus instead of a plus will also put PC-FILE+ into browse. When you have entered browse, you can press either the plus or the minus sign to scan groups of records in any pertinent direction. The PgDn and PgUp keys correspond to the plus and minus keys in their effect on entering browse and scanning records.

Exiting Find

Return to the Master Menu by entering,

Q Quit.

PRINTING THE DATABASE

Print the database as described earlier in the chapter. Your listing will appear as shown in Figure 14–22.

```
                              JOB DATABASE
     01-01-80 AT 0:42 a.m.                                 Page 1
Recrd  BIL  PRG_ID  RANK  CLT_ID  JOB_ID  JOB_TITLE              HRS
================================================================
    1  101  10       2    127     1502    ACCOUNTS PAYABLE       7.5
    2  102  12       2    127     1502    ACCOUNTS PAYABLE       8.0
    3  103  12       2    115     1436    PROPERTY MANAGMNT      7.6
    4  104  12       2    115     1437    TENANT LIST            7.3
    5  105  13       3    142     1601    INCOME STATEMENT       3.5
    6  106  14       1    131     1575    SOFTWARE INSTALL       6.8
    8  108  13       3    118     1440    LEASE MANAGEMENT       5.7
    9  109  13       3    127     1502    ACCOUNTS PAYABLE       5.8
   10  110  10       2    135     1585    LABELING PROGRAM       3.5
   11  111  10       2    142     1595    DEPRECIATION PRGM      2.3
   12  112  12       2    127     1502    ACCOUNTS PAYABLE       3.6
   13  113  12       2    127     1503    ACCOUNTS RECEIV.       8.0
   14  114  12       2    118     1440    LEASE MANAGMNT         4.7
   15  115  14       1    131     1575    SOFTWARE INSTALL       5.2
   16  116  13       3    127     1502    ACCOUNTS PAYABLE       5.8
   17  117  13       3    142     1596    EMPLOYEE DATABASE      8.0
   18  118  14       1    115     1435    MAINTENANCE D.B.       8.0
   19  119  14       1    115     1435    MAINTENANCE D.B.       3.8
   20  120  12       2    115     1436    PROPERTY MANAGMNT      7.0
   21  121  10       2    131     1586    AMORTIZATION SCHED     5.3
----------------------------------------------------------------
  TOTALS:         HRS                                         117.40
Printed 20 of the 21 records.
     PRIMARY SORT FIELD: unsorted
     SELECTION CRITERIA:
     All records
```

Figure 14–22.

EXITING PC-FILE+

To leave PC-FILE+, you must first have the Master Menu in view. Then press,

Q Quit the Master Menu.
Q Quit processing with PC-FILE+. The other alternatives are to change databases and not exit PC-FILE+ with "D," or to return to the Master Menu and to continue working with the same database with "R."

BACKING UP YOUR FILES

Backup your PC-FILE+ files by using the DOS copy command. Place the PC-FILE+ files diskette in drive A and the backup files diskette in drive B. Then enter,

```
copy a:jobsdb.* b:
```

↵ Enter key,

This action saves the database, but does not save other files created by PC-FILE+ such as report format or index files. To copy all files from drive A to drive B (but be sure that you want all of the files from A to overwrite those on B) enter,

```
copy a:*.* b:
```

EXERCISES

A. A central services department for a small corporation is responsible for carrying out services that are charged back to departments. These services are putting postage on mail, distributing the telephone charges that are sent on the monthly bill, duplicating charges for printing, xeroxing, mimeographing, etc., and distributing supplies of varying types. Create a database called SERVICES and enter the following records:

length of 4	length of 3	length of 4	length of 17	length of 7, numeric (#)
INVO	DEP	CODE	DESCRIPTION	CHARGE
1940	101	1100	POSTAGE	55.39
1941	102	1100	POSTAGE	27.80
1942	103	1100	POSTAGE	32.70
1943	104	1100	POSTAGE	19.75
1944	104	1200	TELEPHONE (BASE)	278.23
1945	102	1200	TELEPHONE (BASE)	125.19
1946	103	1200	TELEPHONE (BASE)	99.56
1947	104	1200	TELEPHONE (BASE)	156.27
1948	101	1400	DUPLICATING	23.19
1949	101	1400	DUPLICATING	19.80
1950	102	1400	DUPLICATING	17.90
1951	103	1400	DUPLICATING	89.95
1952	101	1400	DUPLICATING	27.80
1953	102	1400	DUPLICATING	95.45
1954	102	1400	DUPLICATING	52.00
1955	101	1300	TELEPHONE (LD)	79.34

INVO	DEP	CODE	DESCRIPTION	CHARGE
1956	102	1300	TELEPHONE (LD)	377.10
1957	103	1300	TELEPHONE (LD)	95.45
1958	104	1300	TELEPHONE (LD)	47.01
1959	104	1500	SUPPLIES	55.55
1960	104	1500	SUPPLIES	98.50
1961	101	1500	SUPPLIES	67.77
1962	102	1500	SUPPLIES	34.56
1963	101	1500	SUPPLIES	33.45
1964	103	1500	SUPPLIES	145.66
1965	103	1500	SUPPLIES	90.30

After you have created the database, print it out. Return to the Master Menu. Add the following records:

INVO	DEP	CODE	DESCRIPTION	CHARGE
1966	101	1400	DUPLICATING	27.80
1967	102	1500	SUPPLIES	113.45
1968	104	1300	TELEPHONE (LD)	54.55

Modify record number 5 by changing the department to 101. Modify record number 10 to have a CODE of 1100 and a DESCRIPTION of "POSTAGE."

Delete record number 7 and the record with the INVO number of 1961. Print out the revised database.

The database will be used again in the exercises following chapters 11 through 13.

B. A principal of a small school has had a roster of the school's faculty typed up. After reviewing the roster, the principal decided to have the list put into a database so that the list could be analyzed and updated regularly. Create a database called ROSTER with the following records:

NAME (length of 25)	RANK (length of 10)	DEPARTMENT (length of 10)	S (length of 1)	SALARY (length of 10, numeric (#))
NABBORT, NATHAN	ASSOCIATE	HUMANITIES	M	35000
BARTONE, BARRY	PROFESSOR	HUMANITIES	M	36700
RASTER, RONALD	ASSOCIATE	HUMANITIES	M	31200
MARCH, MARCIA	ASSOCIATE	HUMANITIES	F	39800
YARROW, YANCY	ASSOCIATE	HUMANITIES	M	35600
FRANELLY, FRED	LECTURER	HUMANITIES	M	20050
ABELL, ANA	ASSOCIATE	HUMANITIES	F	38200
DYSON, DIANA	ASSOCIATE	MATH	F	36500
WILKE, WARREN	LECTURER	MATH	M	23450
JONESBURGHER, JACK	LECTURER	MATH	M	21400
QUARREN, QUINELLA	ASSOCIATE	MATH	F	35900
SMITTY, SAMUEL	ASSISTANT	PHYS. ED.	M	24550
LOCHNER, LOUISE	ASSOCIATE	PHYS. ED.	F	32500
ORRAN, OPHELIA	ASSISTANT	PHYS. ED.	F	28400
HARBERSON, HAROLD	PROFESSOR	SCIENCE	M	37120
CRANSMANN, CARLITA	ASSISTANT	SCIENCE	F	29500
ZARRONNE, ZELDA	PROFESSOR	SCIENCE	F	40200

NAME	RANK	DEPARTMENT	S	SALARY
PARSONS, PAUL	ASSISTANT	SCIENCE	M	23500
WALTERS, WILLIAM	ASSISTANT	SCIENCE	M	23200
ARBOR, ALAN	INSTRUCTOR	SOCIAL SCI	M	31250
MICHELSON, MARIA	INSTRUCTOR	SOCIAL SCI	F	27100
GARBER, GRETEL	PROFESSOR	SOCIAL SCI	F	41050
VALOUR, VALERIE	INSTRUCTOR	SOCIAL SCI	F	23400
TEATHER, TERRY	ASSISTANT	SOCIAL SCI	F	31500
KRISTIANNE, KATHERINE	PROFESSOR	SOCIAL SCI	F	40500

Print the database. Add the following records:

NAME	RANK	DEPARTMENT	S	SALARY
BEASLEY, BRENDA	ASSOCIATE	SOCIAL SCI	F	36500
TEFFORD, THOMAS	PROFESSOR	SCIENCE	M	37700
SEDGE, SAMANTHA	ASSOCIATE	HUMANITIES	F	33300

Modify Ronald Raster's record by increasing his salary to $32,600 and change Quinella Quarren's name to Quinella Harberson.
Delete record number 5 for Yarrow and record number 24 for Terry Teather.
Print out the revised database. This database will be reused in chapters 11 through 13.

C. A small distributor of software obtains its software from a variety of small companies. It sells this software to computer stores. It has a small inventory that is to be kept on a computer database. Using PC-FILE+, create the database with the name SOFTWARE with the following data:

PRODUCT	MFR	PURCH_PRICE	NUM_BOUGHT
MOUSER	XYZ SOFTWARE	18.75	41
SPACE FLIER	BARTON INC.	15.75	35
WORD DRILL	DAISY PRODUCTS	19.00	17
CROSS WORD	BARTON INC.	15.00	20
ACCOUNTS RECEIV.	QR BOOKKEEPING	49.00	20
MAIL LABELER	QR BOOKKEEPING	49.00	41
SPACE SQUAD	XYZ SOFTWARE	17.00	70
MY MONEY MGR.	DAISY PRODUCTS	22.50	22
FAST SPREADSHEET	CYBERNETICS	27.00	11
ACCOUNTS PAYABLE	QR BOOKKEEPING	52.00	49
ATOM SMASHER	FRANK ASSOC.	12.75	61
EXPERT FILE	MOUNTAIN INC.	75.00	12
TIME SCHEDULER	MOUNTAIN INC.	32.00	79
APPOINTMENT KEEPER	KEYBOARD INC.	30.50	15
WORD ANALYZER	WILD DAISY INC.	21.00	7
CAVES AND CAPTORS	XYZ SOFTWARE	16.25	16
SEA CAPTAIN	BARTON'S MFR.	15.60	20
REPORT WRITER III	QR BOOKKEEPING	58.50	19
FAST CODER	PROGRAMMER'S INC	78.00	51
WHALE HUNTER	XYZ SOFTWEAR	17.50	20
PROGRAM GENERATOR	PROGRAMMER'S COR	79.00	12
FONT STYLER	GRAFF MAKER	23.50	50
PICTURE BOOK	GRAPH MAKER	43.45	13
GRID DISPLAY	PHILLIPS LTD.	225.90	52

CARD FILER	H.D.T. SOFTWARE	122.50	93
MAXITEXT	THE ASSOCIATES	305.00	42
DATA WORKS	C & I ASSOCIATES	255.00	81

After the database has been created, print it out in its entirety.Add the following records.

MAXICALC	THE ASSOCIATES	196.78	20
THE PROJECTOR	S & S ASSOCIATES	225.00	56
TEXT EDITOR	JONY ASSOCIATES	98.99	19

Modify the spelling of "GRAFF" to "GRAPH." Change the price of Data Works to 225.00 and the manufacturer of Sea Captain to Garage Data Inc.

Delete the entry for record number 13. Delete the record for Caves and Captors.

Print out the revised database. This database will be reused in the exercises in chapters 11 through 13.

Chapter 15

More on Databases: A Client File

CHAPTER OUTLINE

In this chapter you will extend your knowledge of how to create and manipulate databases. The database you construct in this chapter will offer the opportunity for you to

1. Specify a ''mask'' that automatically inserts data in selected fields within a database,
2. Find records in the database quickly by using the contents of record fields. Five search techniques are used.

INTRODUCTION

Computer Software Associates needs to keep a master list of its client companies. It could then produce mailing lists and, eventually, integrate this database with the jobsdata database to produce billings for the clients. The new database is to include the data that is now kept on a telephone card file. The hand-kept forms look like,

```
Client Id 115
Client Name Acme Realty
Street Addr. 100 Elm Street
City Wellston
State NV
Zip Code 19870
```

Figure 15–1. Client Record.

Computer Software Associates currently has fifteen active clients, but the list has periodic additions and deletions.

CREATING THE DATABASE

After placing the working disk of PC-FILE+ in drive A and your formatted files diskette in drive B, you can begin creating a new database when you have the "A>" prompt from DOS.

Caps Lock Caps Lock put on.
PCF The PC-FILE+ program command.
↵ Enter key
B Use drive B as the default drive.
↵ Enter key, to keep the default data path.
CLIENTS The name of the new database. *Do not press the Enter key.*
F10 Function key F10, to begin to create the new database.
↵ Enter key, to accept "Y" as the answer to the prompt, "Do you want to define it? >Y<"
F Fast method of defining the database.

The field definition screen will appear. Define the following fields in the locations shown. By placing the field names on every other row, the entry form can be made to resemble a paper form or otherwise made more convenient for the user. Press the Enter key twice at the end of each entry. You can edit the entries with the use of the Arrow, Del, and Ins keys.

Enter the field NAMES in their relative positions.

You can place the names anywhere on the screen.

```
[CLT_ID        ]   [         ]   [         ]   [         ]
[              ]   [         ]   [         ]   [         ]
[CLT_NAME      ]   [         ]   [         ]   [         ]
[              ]   [         ]   [         ]   [         ]
[STREET        ]   [         ]   [         ]   [         ]
[              ]   [         ]   [         ]   [         ]
[CITY          ]   [         ]   [         ]   [         ]
[              ]   [         ]   [         ]
[ST            ]   [         ]   [         ]
[              ]   [         ]   [         ]
[ZIP           ]   [         ]   [         ]
[              ]   [         ]   [         ]
TELEPHONE      <   [         ]   [         ]
[              ]   [         ]   [         ]
[              ]   [         ]   [         ]
```

Figure 15–2. Database Definition Screen.

```
[              ]      [          ]      [          ]
[              ]      [          ]      [          ]
[              ]      [          ]      [          ]
[              ]      [          ]      [          ]
[              ]      [          ]      [          ]
[              ]      [          ]      [          ]
```

Figure 15–2—*Continued*

When all the fields have been properly defined type,

F10 Function key F10, to complete the creation of the database structure. Assign field lengths to the seven fields as follows:

Enter the display length (1–65) for each field
The "superfield" maximum size for this database is 1185

```
CLT_ID        >3  <
CLT_NAME      [20]
STREET        [15]
CITY          [10]
ST            [2 ]
ZIP           [5 ]
TELEPHONE     [9 ]
```

Figure 15–3. Field Length Definition Screen.

F10 Function key F10, to accept the field lengths as correct.
N No, only regular fields are in use.
N No, do not alter the method of accessing the fields.

AUTOMATIC FIELD ENTRIES

Constants

PC-FILE+ has the capacity for automatically entering the contents of specified fields. Many times, field contents are predominantly of one type even though other entries are possible. In a personal telephone directory, you may have some entries for friends, relatives, and business contacts whose telephone numbers begin with different area codes than your current area code. Most of the entries will be from within your current area code, however, since this area contains the people with which you are most frequently in contact. A database that can automatically insert entries in these fields can save you keystrokes. The automatic entries can be overridden if the automatic entry is not appropriate for a given record.

In the records to be entered (*see* "Adding Records" below), the CITY field is most often "Wellston," and the ST field is most often "NV." It would be helpful to have PC-FILE+ make these entries for you. Then you would only have to type in the entries that are different from these.

"Constants" allow PC-FILE+ to enter data into fields in this way. Put **Caps Lock off.** With the Master Menu in view, enter,

F8 Function key F8, or "U," the utilities key. To obtain the Utilities menu and prompt shown below,

```
PC-FILE+ UTILITIES MENU

C. Clone (Change the database definition)
D. Duplicate records (find and list)
E. Export the current database
G. Global operation-modify and delete
I. Import a PC-File+ database or other file
M. Maintenance-Copy, Delete, or Rename a PC-File+ file
N. Name of field, mask, constant, or calc (modify)
P. Profile files (set up configuration)
S. Smart keys (modify)
U. Undelete records

Q. Quit Utilities-Return to Master Menu

Please reply ^v
Enter your selection. >Q<
```

Figure 15–4. Utilities Menu.

N Name of field, mask, constant or calc selection. This will lead to the screen that displays,

```
< Which FIELD's Name, Mask, Constant, or Calcs to change
[1] CLT_ID
[2] CLT_NAME
[3] STREET
[4] CITY
[5] ST
[6] ZIP
[7] TELEPHONE
```

Figure 15–5.

CITY The first field name to be given a constant.
F10 Function key F10, the next prompt is

```
Please reply ^v
Change (N)Name (M)Mask (K)Constant or (C)Calcs >N<
```

K Constant, the selection that allows the user to pre-enter data in fields and to receive the prompt,

```
 Please reply  ^v
 New constant "xxx"  >_                <
```

"Wellston"*A

The constant to be entered. The quotation marks mean insert this entry in every new record. The "*A" indicates that the data is to be inserted only during the addition of records and not when they are recalled for modification. A "*M" would restrict automatic insertion of the constant to the modification procedure and the omission of either of these pairs of symbols would allow the constant to be inserted at both points, addition and modification.

↵	Enter key
ST	The second field name to be given a constant.
F10	Function key F10
K	Constant
"NV"A	The constant to be entered in the ST field.
↵	Enter key
ZIP	The third field to be given a constant.
F10	Function key F10
K	Constant
"19870"A	The constant
↵	Enter key
F10	Function key F10, to stop adding masks, the Utilities Menu returns.
Q	Quit, to return to the Master Menu.

Calculations and Masks

Constants are used to enter field contents automatically. Calcs, or calculations are used to calculate the contents of a field based on the contents of other fields. For instance, an annual salary field could be divided by 12 to automatically calculate and insert a monthly salary. A mask is used to limit the characters or numbers you are allowed to enter in the field. For instance, a person entering records can be forced to type only capital letters, or numbers in some fields. Constants, calculated fields, and masks can be added to a database field after it has been created (just as you have just done). You have used these features in chapter 14.

ADDING RECORDS

With the Master Menu in view, add records by entering

F1 Function key F1, or "A," the ADD key. After memory has been initialized, a record form appears that already has entries for the CITY, ST, and ZIP fields. These entries, in whole or in part, can be overtyped or deleted with the Del key if the field entries are not correct for a given record. If the field entries are correct, press Enter to accept the automatic entry and to move to the next field. Create the database with records that follow. Note that two records have the city "Newtown" and another "Newton." These are the proper entries. Also note that "Newtown" is one character smaller than "Wellston." You can type a new entry over a mask entry, but extra characters like the last "n" must be deleted before entry.

CLT_ID	CLT_NAME	STREET	CITY	ST	ZIP	TELEPHONE
115	Acme Realty	100 Elm Street	Wellston	NV	19870	765–4000
118	Riverside Properties	20 Oak Lane	Wellston	NV	19870	765–3580
127	Fast Accounting	77 Washington	Newtown	NV	19801	376–3010
131	Green Auto Sales	3583 Riverside	Paradise	UT	29875	885–9002
135	Direct Marketing Inc	12 First Ave.	Newtown	NV	19801	376–2756
136	Sheet Metal Works	101 Center St.	Paradise	UT	29875	885–9111
116	Tonal Music Co.	55 Center St.	Paradise	UT	29875	885–0101
101	Joe's Haberdashery	95 Madison Dr.	Wellston	NV	19871	675–3691
110	Quick Trucking	26 Circle Dr.	Wellston	NV	19870	675–3620
123	Alice's Restaurant	19 Star Lane	Paradise	UT	29875	885–1785
124	Hart's Breaker Motel	Paradise Road	Wellston	NV	19870	675–4120
133	Pat's Hair Styling	15 Veterans Ln	Wellston	NV	19870	675–4500
140	Druggist's Distrib.	191 Mill Rd.	Newton	NV	19801	376–1901
141	Eagle Markets	27 Liberty St.	Wellston	NV	19871	675–4700
142	Wellston Holding Co.	1 Lunar Lane	Wellston	NV	19871	675–2725

Figure 15–6.

When you have entered the telephone number for Wellston Holding Co., enter

F10 Function key F10, to complete this record.

F10 Function key F10, a second time to stop the addition of records to the client database and to return to the Master Menu. Even though constants were added to the record, PC-FILE+ did not enter the record into the database since no other characters were added to the record.

SEARCHING FOR RECORDS

From the Master Menu you may elect to search for records based on the contents of one or more of the records' fields. It is not reasonable to search for records visually when a database gets large. Using browse, you can only see twenty records at a time. This is not many when your database contains a thousand records. Searching for a last name that is common to many records may be equally awkward since you may have to locate many incorrect records before you find the correct one. You may not even be sure if you have a correct spelling to use in searching. You can use the record number to display or edit a record if you know what the record number is, but you may not know the number. The search procedure available in PC-FILE+ permits you to locate records with considerable flexibility. It also allows you to change the records if that is desired. Press,

F2 Function key F2, or "F," The Find key. The find menu appears.

S Search for data (not for record numbers as before). You will see the prompt,

```
Simple search:
  you 'fill in the blanks'
Complex search:
  you type in a formula

== Please reply ^v ==
S(Simple search), C(Complex search), Q(Quit)  S/C/Q >S<
```

Figure 15–7. Search Type Menu.

s Simple search, to obtain the search screen below.

Please supply the search data below F

```
CLT_ID        >***<
CLT_NAME     [********************]
STREET       [***************]
CITY         [**********]
ST           [**]
ZIP          [*****]
TELEPHONE    [********]
```

Figure 15–8. The Search Criteria Screen.

There are four types of searches that can be used. These are explained in the help screen which can be called up with

Alt-H Alternate and "H," the help key which displays,

```
Replace asterisks with data to look for
    Examples:
    JONES**** look for JONES
    ?SMITH*** sounds like SMITH
    ~QUE***** scan across for QUE
    _E_E***** wildcard search for E
    in location 2 and 4
    K******** Names starting with K
    --------------------------
    You can enter search data in more than
    one field. If you do, ALL that you
    enter will be compared before you
    record is considered "found."
```

Exact Match

The simplest type of search is the exact search. It is illustrated by the first example in the Help window. An exact search locates the records with the contents specified in a field within the search screen. The search screen field contents are compared with the contents of the same fields in the database's records. To use the exact search you must know exactly how to reproduce the entry in a field. If you wish to search your client database for the records with the zipcode of 19870 and not those with any other zipcode, including 19871, type,

↓ Down Arrow five times, to place the cursor in the ZIP field.
19870 The search string value that matches the contents of some of the ZIP fields.
F10 Function key F10, to initiate the search and to display the first record meeting that criterion
F Find, to see the next record with a ZIP of 19870, in response to the prompt block indicating the options available. Notice that the next record to appear also has the ZIP field value of 19870.
F Find, four times to see the remaining records with the zip code of 19870. On the last "F" you will see the message indicating that there are no more records that match the search value. You receive the prompt,

```
╔═ Please reply  ^v ═══════════╗
║ Not found. Press (ENTER) >_< ║
╚══════════════════════════════╝
```

↵	Enter key, to return to the type-of-search prompt.
S	Simple search. Notice that the old criterion has been removed.

The exact search can be used in any of the fields. You could search for "Eagle Markets" to find the only record with that string of characters in the CLT_NAME field. All Nevada records could be located with "NV" in the ST field.

You pressed "F" to continue the search when records were found. Had you pressed an "M" to modify, you could have edited the contents of the fields. Had you pressed "Q," the search would have been stopped. Had you pressed "D," the record would have been deleted.

Sounds Like (Soundex) Search

Soundex is a search based on the sound of a field's contents, rather than on the precise spelling of the name. For instance, if the criterion entered in a first name field of a telephone directory was "Carol," the search might pick up "Carole," "Carl" or "Caryle" as well as "Carol." Complete two soundex searches as follows:

↵	Enter key, to move the cursor to CLT_NAME.
?heart's	The question mark causes a soundex search for the string, "heart's."
F10	Function key F10, to begin the search and to find "Hart's" within the CLT_NAME field for one record.
S	To start a new search with a different search value.
S	Simple search
↵	Enter key three times, to place the cursor in the CITY field of the search criteria screen.
?Newtowne	The soundex search string.
F10	Function key F10, to start the search and to find "Newton," as well as "Newtown," in the CITY field.
F	Find three more times to see the entries in the CITY field that sound like "Newtown" and to receive the prompt that no more entries can be found.
↵	Enter key to return to the search-type menu.
Q	Quit the search and return to the Master Menu.

Scan Across Search

At times you may wish to search for a record for which you know part but not all of the entry. For instance, you may know that a last name ended in "man," but you did not know whether the name was "Silverman," "Brigmann" or some other name. The "tilde" serves as the scan across sign. By preceding a string of characters with the tilde, PC-FILE+ will search at the specified field for every record. It will locate records that contain the search string anywhere in the selected field. To see how this works, look for all client records in which there is an "ee" in the CLT_NAME by typing,

F2	Function key F2, or "F," the Find key.
S	Search for data.
S	Simple search
↵	Enter key once to move the cursor to the CLT_NAME field.
~ee	The scan across sign, the tilde, followed by "ee," which is the search string.
F10	Function key F10, to begin the search and to find the record for "Green Auto Sales."
F	Find, to continue to find "Sheet Metal Works."

F	Find and to receive the prompt that there are no more records which contain "ee."
↵	Enter key to return to the search-type screen.

Try it again looking for all STREET addresses with "St." in them by typing,

S	Simple search
↵	Enter key twice to move the cursor into the STREET field.
~St.	The scan across sign followed by "St."
F10	Function key F10, to start the search and to find the entry for "101 Center St."
F	Find three times to see the next two records with the entry "St." in the STREET field and to receive the prompt that no more records can be found that meet the search criterion.
↵	Enter key to return to the search-type screen.

Wildcard Search

In PC-FILE+, the underscore serves as a wildcard. A wildcard matches any single letter. A wildcard in a last name field of a telephone directory search criterion screen might be "_oe," which would match the last names of "Doe" or "Roe" where the underscore matches both the "D" and the "R." The criterion "_row_" would match "*B*row*n*" or "*T*row*e*." One does not have to specify whether the letters between the wildcards are upper- or lowercase. Find all the CLT_ID entries with a 3 as the second letter by entering,

S	Simple search
_3_	Wildcard followed by "3" followed by wildcard.
F10	To initiate the search.
F	Find key four times, to find the other records with "3" in the center of the CLT_ID field and to receive the prompt that no more records meeting the criterion can be found.
↵	Enter key to return to the search-type screen.

Identify all Wellston records by using the ZIP field. There are two zip codes for this city. Type,

S	Simple search
↵	Enter key five times to move the cursor to the ZIP criterion field.
1987_	Four numbers followed by the wildcard, which matches any number following the 1987
F10	Function key F10, to begin the search.
F	Find key eight times to locate the appropriate records and to exhaust the search.
↵	Enter key to return to the search-type screen.

Multiple Criteria

In each of the searches above, one criterion was used to select records for display. Often more than one criterion is needed. A political analyst might ask, "Display the voting records for married women with two or more children." A marketing analyst may wish to identify all businesses in San Francisco that have purchased a particular product in the last year. In the current database, identify all records with "ea" anywhere in the CLT_NAME and "Wellston" in the CITY field by typing,

S	Simple search
↵	Enter key to move the cursor into the CLT_NAME criterion field.
~ea	The scan across sign followed by the search string "ea."
↵	Enter key twice to move the cursor into the CITY criterion field.
?Wellstown	The soundex sign followed by the entry "Wellstown" to catch spellings such as, "Wellston," and "Wellstown" in the CITY entries (though there are none of the latter).
F10	Function key F10, to initiate the search.

F Find three times to find the remaining records and to end the search.
↵ Enter key to return to the search-type screen.
Q Quit and return to the Master Menu.

PRINTING RECORDS

In the previous chapter you printed the entire database, including the record numbers. In this chapter you will again print all of the records but not the record numbers. The procedure for doing this illustrates how you can be selective in the printing of all of the fields in the database. With the Master Menu present enter,

F6 Function key F6, or "R," the Reports key, to see the report-type screen.
F10 Function key F10 with the top line of the report format screen highlighted. This allows you to create a new report format.
R Row format, the default format for reports. The next screen displays the field names and a bracketed column to designate the order of the fields on the printed page. You do not have to select every field. Fill in the numbers 1 through 7 as shown below, noticing that there is no number in the Record No. space.

Number of columns to print from left to right

```
Record No.  > <
CLT_ID      [1]
CLT_NAME    [2]
STREET      [3]
CITY        [4]
ST          [5]
ZIP         [6]
TELEPHONE   [7]
```

F10 Function key F10, to complete the designation of field columns. You will see the screen requesting a title.

CLIENT DATABASE

The title to appear at the top of the report.

↵ Enter key. A message, "Creating Report Work File," appears. This is followed by the prompt,

```
Please reply  ^v
Would you like to save this report format?  Y/N >N<
```

Y Yes, save the report format so it could be reused again in the future. Saving a report format avoids your having to reestablish the order of the fields and the report title.
REPORT2 The report format filename.
↵ Enter key. The report menu now appears as shown below:

F10 Function key F10, accepts all default values of the Report Menu. The screen displays the first record in the database. At this point you have the option of printing each record individually (Y), of not printing the record (N), of quitting the report (Q), or of printing the entire database without being prompted at each record (X).

X Do not prompt for individual records. The report is printed with the report title, the date and time, the page number, and the first seventeen records are now displayed in the order that you entered them. The report appears as,

```
                              CLIENT DATABASE

April 28, 1989 at 12:37 p.m.                                Page 1

CLT        CLT_NAME               STREET             CITY       ST  ZIP    TELEPHONE
=====================================================================================
115   Acme Realty              100 Elm Street     Wellston   NV  19870  765-4000
118   Riverside Properties     20 Oak Lane        Wellston   NV  19870  765-3580
127   Fast Accounting          77 Washington      Newton     NV  19801  376-3010
131   Green Auto Sales         3583 Riverside     Paradise   UT  29875  885-9002
135   Direct Marketing Inc     12 First Ave.      Newtown    NV  19801  376-2756
136   Sheet Metal Works        101 Center St.     Paradise   UT  29875  885-9111
116   Tonal Music Co.          55 Center St.      Paradise   UT  29875  885-0101
101   Joe's Haberdashery       95 Madison Dr.     Wellston   NV  19871  675-3691
110   Quick Trucking           26 Circle Dr.      Wellston   NV  19870  675-3620
123   Alice's Restaurant       19 Star Lane       Paradise   UT  29875  885-1785
124   Hart's Breaker Motel     Paradise Road      Wellston   NV  19870  675-4120
133   Pat's Hair Styling       15 Veteran's Ln    Wellston   NV  19870  675-4500
140   Druggists Distrib.       191 Mill Rd.       Newton     NV  19801  376-1901
141   Eagle Markets            27 Liberty St.     Wellston   NV  19871  675-4700
142   Wellston Holding Co.     1 Lunar Lane       Wellston   NV  19871  675-2725
-------------------------------------------------------------------------------------
TOTALS:
Printed 15 of 15 records.
PRIMART SORT FIELD: unsorted
SELECTION CRITERIA:
All records
```

Figure 15–9. Completed Report.

↵ Enter key. Upon notification that the report is completed to return to the Master Menu.

EXITING PC-FILE+

To leave PC-FILE+, you must first have the Master Menu in view. Then press,

Q Quit the PC-FILE+ Master Menu.
Q Quit processing with PC-FILE+.

BACKING UP YOUR FILES

Backup your PC-FILE+ files by using the DOS copy command. Place the PC-FILE+ files diskette in drive A and the backup files diskette in drive B. Then type

```
copy a:clients.* b:
```

↲ Enter key

This operation saves the file, CLIENTS, but not files related to the database.

EXERCISES

A. Retrieve the central services' charges database, SERVICES, used in the exercises in chapter 14. Add 10 records to the database, remembering to use the control characters to aid you in the typing, as follows:

1970 101 1400 DUPLICATING	13.11
1971 101 1400 DUPLICATING	22.80
1972 102 1400 DUPLICATING	10.50
1973 102 1400 DUPLICATING	13.45
1974 102 1400 DUPLICATING	7.77
1975 102 1400 DUPLICATING	50.45
1976 103 1400 DUPLICATING	12.00
1977 101 1300 TELEPHONE (LD)	88.24
1978 102 1300 TELEPHONE (LD)	100.05
1979 103 1300 TELEPHONE (LD)	42.55

Experiment with the FINd techniques of search, scan across, and wildcard. Locate, for instance, all records that have a 5 in the invoice field and all records for department 101.

B. Retrieve the school roster database, ROSTER, used in the exercises in chapter 14 and add 9 records to the database, remembering to use the control characters to aid you in the typing, as follows:

NAME	RANK	DEPARTMENT	S	SALARY
PASQUALE, PETER	ASSOCIATE	SCIENCE	M	33300
HARPSNER, HILDEGARD	PROFESSOR	SCIENCE	F	37700
TUCKER, TRISCA	ASSISTANT	PHYS. ED	F	24200
EARDMAN, ELIZA	ASSOCIATE	HUMANITIES	F	36800
BARRISTON, BOB	LECTURER	HUMANITIES	M	35600
DIESON, DAVID	ASSISTANT	HUMANITIES	M	22150
ABUHL, ABRAHAM	ASSOCIATE	HUMANITIES	M	32200
PASCAL, PARKER	INSTRUCTOR	MATH	F	31500
BARITONE, BART	INSTRUCTOR	SOCIAL SCI	F	24950

Practice the FINd searching techniques on this database. Identify any faculty who have the letters "AR" in their names. Find the faculty who have a double "r" in their names.
Locate all associate professors. Identify all humanities assistant professors.

C. Retrieve the file SOFTWARE. Add the following 6 records:

PRODUCT	MFR	PURCH PRICE	NUM BOUGHT
MAXITEXT	THE ASSOCIATES	305.00	42
DATA WORKS	C & I ASSOCIATES	255.00	80
TWO-D PLAN	C & I ASSOCIATES	55.50	34
CHART-IT!	SANE SCREENS	122.50	50
FILE CONTROLLER	S & S SOFTWEAR	59.59	27
MAP DESIGNER	QXR INC.	234.00	15

Using the FINd technique, locate all entries with a "Q" in them. Locate all entries with the word "Associates" in the MFR field.

Identify all the product names with "WORD," in them. FINd all records for entries with the word "software" in the manufacturer field. Try a soundex search.

Chapter 16
Advanced Database Manipulations

CHAPTER OUTLINE

Databases are used frequently because the data they contain can be recognized quickly and printed out selectively. In this chapter you will

1. Learn how to sort a file into a new order based upon one or more of the fields in the records,
2. List only selected fields in the records,
3. Delete and add records to the database.

RETRIEVING EXISTING FILES

In the chapters 14 and 15 on databases in this manual, you created new databases each time. For this chapter, you will use the database CLIENTS again. With the DOS prompt ''A>'' showing, place the PC-FILE+ diskette in drive A. To retrieve the database type,

pcf

↵	Enter key
B	To specify which drive for the database.
↵	Enter key, to accept the default pathway.
↓	Down arrow key once (may vary) to place the cursor in the entry ''CLIENTS.''
F10	To begin using the CLIENTS database.

The Master Menu appears with the header line,

```
The current file B:\CLIENTS
    There are 15 records
This disk can hold approximately 4220 more records.
```

The number of additional records that can be added is related to the amount of free space on your diskette. The space remaining is divided by the record size to arrive at this estimate. Since the amount of space varies with each person's diskette, the estimate of 4,220 shown here will be different for many persons.

PRINTING THE DATABASE

Shortly, you will be sorting the records in the client database in different ways. To see how the sorted lists compare with one another and with the original database, print out the database as it now exists. Do this by entering,

F6	Function key F6, or "R," the Reports key, to see the report-type screen,
↓	Down arrow as necessary to highlight the REPORT2 format.
F10	Function key F10 to use the REPORT2 format that is highlighted.
P	Print the report at the printer.
F10	Function key F10, to accept the other default values in the Report Menu.
X	Do not prompt to print individual records. Print them all. The report appears as,

```
                              CLIENT DATABASE

April 28, 1989 at 12:37 p.m.                                Page 1
CLT       CLT_NAME              STREET              CITY      ST  ZIP    TELEPHONE
==================================================================================
115  Acme Realty             100 Elm Street      Wellston  NV  19870  765-4000
118  Riverside Properties    20 Oak Lane         Wellston  NV  19870  765-3580
127  Fast Accounting         77 Washington       Newton    NV  19801  376-3010
131  Green Auto Sales        3583 Riverside      Paradise  UT  29875  885-9002
135  Direct Marketing Inc    12 First Ave.       Newtown   NV  19801  376-2756
136  Sheet Metal Works       101 Center St.      Paradise  UT  29875  885-9111
116  Tonal Music Co.         55 Center St.       Paradise  UT  29875  885-0101
101  Joe's Haberdashery      95 Madison Dr.      Wellston  NV  19871  675-3691
110  Quick Trucking          26 Circle Dr.       Wellston  NV  19870  675-3620
123  Alice's Restaurant      19 Star Lane        Paradise  UT  29875  885-1785
124  Hart's Breaker Motel    Paradise Road       Wellston  NV  19870  675-4120
133  Pat's Hair Styling      15 Veteran's Ln     Wellston  NV  19870  675-4500
140  Druggists Distrib.      191 Mill Rd.        Newton    NV  19801  376-1901
141  Eagle Markets           27 Liberty St.      Wellston  NV  19871  675-4700
142  Wellston Holding Co.    1 Lunar Lane        Wellston  NV  19871  675-2725
----------------------------------------------------------------------------------
TOTALS:
Printed 15 of 15 records.
PRIMART SORT FIELD: unsorted
SELECTION CRITERIA:
All records
```

Figure 16–1. Report Number 2.

↵ Enter key to return to the Master Menu after the report is printed.

REDUCING COLUMN NUMBERS AND ALTERING THEIR ORDER

Past listings have shown the database fields in the order in which they appear in the record structure. At times, you may wish to change the order of the fields, or to avoid printing some of the fields at all. This can be done. You will print the list so that it contains only the CLT_NAME, TELEPHONE, and CLT_ID fields in that order. This will eliminate some fields and print the fields in an order that is different from the order of the fields in the data structure. Enter,

F6 Function key F6, or ''R,'' the Reports key.
F10 Function key F10, to start a new report format.
R Row format. the column identification screen appears. Enter a 1, 2, and 3 in the three fields which are to be printed as shown below.

Number of columns to print from left to right

```
Record No.           > <
CLT_ID               [3]
CLT_NAME             [1]
STREET               [ ]
CITY                 [ ]
ST                   [ ]
ZIP                  [ ]
TELEPHONE            [2]
```

Figure 16–2.

F10 Function key F10

TELEPHONE LIST

The name of the new report format.

↵ Enter key
Y Yes, save the report format.
REPORT3 The report format name.
↵ Enter key
F10 Send the report to the printer.
X Do not request confirmation. The report is printed and appears as Figure 16–2. The

```
                        TELEPHONE LIST
April 28, 1989                          Page 1
CLT_NAME                  TELEPHONE       CLT
==============================================
Acme Realty               765-4000        115
Riverside Properties      765-3580        118
Fast Accounting           376-3010        127
Green Auto Sales          885-9002        131
```

Figure 16–3. Abbreviated Record.

```
Direct Marketing Inc        376-2756        135
Sheet Metal Works           885-9111        136
Tonal Music Co.             885-0101        116
Joe's Haberdashery          675-3691        101
Quick Trucking              675-3620        110
Alice's Restaurant          885-1785        123
Hart's Breaker Motel        675-4120        124
Pat's Hair Styling          675-4500        133
Druggist's Distrib.         376-1901        140
Eagle Markets               675-4700        141
Wellston Holding Co.        675-2725        142
---------------------------------------------
TOTALS:
Printed 15 of the 15 records.
PRIMARY SORT FIELD: unsorted
SELECTION CRITERIA:
All records
```

Figure 16–3—*Continued*

Master Menu returns.

↵ Enter key, to return to the Master Menu.

SORTING

The client database was created without using any particular order. A major reason for using computerized databases is the ability they provide to sort the records rapidly. Sorted lists are generally much more useful than unsorted lists. A telephone directory would be useless if the names were randomly arranged. A business office would have a difficult time issuing bills if, as in the jobs database constructed in chapter 14, the individual bills could not be sorted by client and job identification numbers.

Put the client list into a sorted order of the CLT_ID by typing,

F7 Function key F7, or "S," the Sort key which produces a list of the record's fieldnames and the prompt,

```
SORT FIELD # 1 > <
```

This prompt is asking identification of the field on which the reorganized list will be sorted first. You will sort on the CLT_ID, so respond,

1 The sort field will be field # 1, CLT_ID. You could also type in the name of the field but typing the number is faster.

F10 Function key F10

A Ascending order which will place the records in the report with the CLT_ID beginning at the lowest numbers and ascending to the highest.

F10 Function key F10, to complete the selection of sort fields. Additional sort fields could be used if there was a possibility that CLT_IDs might duplicate themselves.

B The work area disk drive to be used is drive B. This drive must have room on it for the sorted file. A status screen keeps you informed about the progress of the sort When the sort has been completed, the main menu returns.

Using the instructions in "Printing the Database," print the database again with report format REPORT2 to see the effect of the sort. Your report should look like the one pictured in Figure 16–3.

```
                 CLIENT DATABASE
April 28, 1989                     Page 1

CLT_NAME                 TELEPHONE   CLT
=========================================
Joe's Haberdashery       675-3691    101
Quick Trucking           675-3620    110
Acme Realty              755-4000    115
Tonal Music Co.          885-0101    116
Riverside Properties     765-3580    118
Alice's Restaurant       885-1785    123
Hart's Breaker Motel     675-4120    124
Fast Accounting          376-3010    127
Green Auto Sales         885-9002    131
Pat's Hair Styling       675-4500    133
Direct Marketing Inc     376-2756    135
Sheet Metal Works        885-9111    136
Druggist's Distrib.      376-1901    140
Eagle Markets            675-4700    141
Wellston Holding Co.     675-2725    142
-----------------------------------------
TOTALS
Printed 15 of the 15 records.
PRIMARY SORT FIELD: CLT_ID
SELECTION CRITERIA:
All records
```

Figure 16–4. Sorted Database Report.

Return to the Master Menu

RESORTING THE DATABASE

The sorting of the database on the CLT_ID field presumably implies the order in which clients first contracted for jobs with Computer Software Associates. A date field could, of course, have been used to show the same order. The current sort order, by identification number, is no more useful than the original order for some other purposes such as producing an alphabetical listing of client names.

The Post Office gives a discount on postage for mailings that are bundled according to city and zipcode since presorting saves the postal workers a considerable amount of time. Sort the list by zipcode, but within that sorted list, arrange the companies by their identification number by typing,

F7 Function key F7, or "S," the Sort key which produces a list of the record's fieldnames and the prompt,

```
SORT FIELD #1 > <
```

This prompt is asking identification of the field on which the reorganized list will be sorted first. You will sort on the ZIP and CLT_ID, so respond,

6	The first sort field will be field # 6, ZIP. You could also type in the name of the field but typing the number is faster.
F10	Function key F10
A	Ascending, notice the "A" next to the field name, ZIP.
1	The second sort field will be field # 1, CLT_ID. Since there are ties within the ZIP fields, records with the same ZIP will be sorted by CLT_ID.
F10	Function key F10
A	Ascending, notice the "A" next to the field name, CLT_ID.
F10	Function key F10, to complete the selection of sort fields. Additional sort fields could be used if there was a possibility that CLT_NAMEs might duplicate themselves.
B	The work area disk drive to be used is drive B. This drive must have room on it for the sorted file. A status screen keeps you informed about the progress of the sort. When the sort has been completed, the main menu returns.

PRINTING THE DATABASE

Create a new report format to print this database. Shortly, you will be sorting the records in the client database in different ways. To see how the sorted lists compare with one another and with the original database, print out the database as it now exists. Do this by entering,

F6	Function key F6, or "R," the Reports key, to see the report-type screen.
↓	Down arrow as necessary to highlight the REPORT2 format.
F10	Function key F10 to use the REPORT2 format that is highlighted.
P	Print the report at the printer.
F10	Function key F10, to accept the other default values in the Report Menu.
X	Print the entire database. The report appears as,

```
                              CLIENT DATABASE
April 28, 1989 at 12:57 p.m.                                  Page 1

CLT CLT_NAME                STREET              CITY        ST   ZIP    TELEPHONE
=====================================================================================
127 Fast Accounting         77 Washington       Newtown     NV  19801    376-3010
135 Direct Marketing Inc    12 First Ave.       Newtown     NV  19801    376-2756
140 Druggist's Distrib.     191 Mill Rd.        Newton      NV  19801    376-1091
110 Quick Trucking          26 Circle Dr.       Wellston    NV  19870    675-3620
115 Acme Realty             100 Elm Street      Wellston    NV  19870    765-4000
118 Riverside Properties    20 Oak Lane         Wellston    NV  19870    765-3580
124 Hart's Breaker Motel    Paradise Road       Wellston    NV  19870    675-4120
133 Pat's Hair Styling      15 Veteran's Ln.    Wellston    NV  19870    675-4500
101 Joe's Haberdashery      95 Madison Dr.      Wellston    NV  19871    675-3691
141 Eagle Markets           27 Liberty St.      Wellston    NV  19871    675-4700
142 Wellston Holding Co.    1 Lunar Lane        Wellston    NV  19871    675-2725
116 Tonal Music Co.         55 Center St.       Paradise    UT  29875    885-0101
123 Alice's Restaurant      19 Star Lane        Paradise    UT  29875    885-1785
```

Figure 16–5. Resorted Report.

```
131 Green Auto Sales       3583 Riverside   Paradise  UT  29875   885-9002
136 Sheet Metal Works      101 Center St.   Paradise  UT  29875   885-9111
---------------------------------------------------------------------------
TOTALS:
Printed 15 of the 15 records.
PRIMARY SORT FIELD: ZIP
SELECTION CRITERIA:
All records
```

Figure 16–5—*Continued*

↵ Enter key, to return to the Master Menu.

DELETING RECORDS

Assume that two clients no longer have contracts with Computer Software Associates. Their records are to be deleted from the client list. The two records to be deleted are for Wellston Holding Company and Quick Trucking. Determine their record numbers by using the browse facility. Type,

F2 Function key F2, or "F" to find a record. Before a record can be deleted it must be "found." The following prompt will appear,

```
How shall we locate the record?
```

```
S. Search for data (find)
B. Beginning of file (first record)
E. End of file (last record)
N. Next sequential record in file
P. Previous record in file
R. Relative record number
+. Browse forwards in file (PgDn)
-. Browse backwards in file (PgUp)

Q. Quit the Find. Return to main Menu.

   Please reply  ^v
 Choose from the menu >S<
```

Figure 16–6.

Find Menu

+ Browse. Examine the database listing and identify the record numbers for the Wellston Holding Company and for Quick Trucking which are maintained by PC-FILE+.

R Get the record by using record number.

11 The number for Wellston Holding Company in response to the prompt,

```
Please reply ^v
What record number to find: >_<
```

↲ Enter key, to see the prompt,

Figure 16–7. Search Menu.

D Delete, to delete the record.
Y Yes, it is okay to delete the record.
R Get the second record by record number.
4 The record number for Quick Trucking.
↲ Enter key
D Delete the record.
Y Yes, it is okay to delete the record.

LOOKING AT THE RECORDS

You will now look at the records in your database again using the browse procedure. The records for Quick Trucking and Wellston Holding should not appear or be included in the total for the HRS# field. PC-FILE+ adds records in the ''blank'' record spaces left by deleted records and at the end of the database. New records cannot be inserted at any other locations.

PgUp Page Up key (or +), to enter browse. Observe the absence of records with the PC-FILE+ maintained record numbers of 4 and 11.
Q Quit the Find menu. The Master Menu returns.

UNDELETING RECORDS

Records may be deleted inadvertently or may need to be recalled. PC-FILE+ provides an ''undelete'' capability that puts a record back into active status. To undelete a record PC-FILE+ utilities are used. You will undelete the two ''deleted'' records by entering,

F8 Function key F8, or ''U,'' the Utilities key.
U Undelete records. The first ''deleted'' record is displayed with a ''/'' in the first position of the first field. The slash is a deletion marker.

1 A 1 to replace the slash in the first field, thereby converting the number to 110 and undeleting the record. PC-FILE+ searches for the next record that has been marked as deleted, finds and presents record number 11.
1 A 1 to convert the first field to 142 and undeleting record number 11. A screen indicates that two records were undeleted.
↵ Enter key, to return to the Utilities Menu.
↵ Enter key, to return to the Master Menu.

Use the F2 and + keys to look at the database. Note that the two deleted records have been restored. The capacity to undelete a record is only possible if it is undeleted before new records are created. The new records may be written into the positions of the deleted records which become unaccessible at that point. Similarly, there is a command PCFIX which will repair corrupted databases. This command will remove any deleted records and prevent their recapture.

IMPORTING AND EXPORTING FILES

In chapter 10, you printed a file to the disk with As-Easy-As in order to create a file that could be imported by a word processor such as PC-WRITE. In this chapter, you will create a similar file from within PC-FILE+. PC-WRITE is unable to integrate a PC-FILE+ database file directly. By printing a file to disk, you create a series of lines of text that can be imported. Do this from the Master Menu by typing,

F8 Function key F8, or "U," the Utilities key which brings up the Utilities Menu.
E Export the current database. "Exporting" is the term used by PC-FILE+ and many other programs to designate procedures that reformat the data in files that can be read by other programs.
B Drive B will receive the export file.
↵ Enter key, the default data path need not be changed.
↵ Enter key, to accept "CLIENTS" as the filename of the exported file and to see the prompt screen,

```
                    EXPORT A DATABASE

              Database exported: B:\CLIENTS

     B.  dBASE .DBF files
     C.  PC-Calc                         (by ButtonWare)
     D.  DIF                             (i.e. Visicalc, etc.)
     F.  Fixed length                    (i.e. random files)
     L.  Lotus PRN
     M.  Mail-merge                      (comma-delimited)
     P.  Peachtext                       (i.e. 1 field per line)
     S.  Sylk                            (Microsoft Multiplan)
     T.  Text editor (SDF)               (i.e. fixed length, c/r)
     U.  User-defined delimiters
     V.  Visicalc
     W.  Word Perfect
     X.  Compressed                      (by PC-File export)

      Please reply  ^v
   Which format do you want to export to? >X<
```

Figure 16–8. Export Files Menu.

This screen illustrates some of the file transfer formats that are available. For instance, option W would print out the file's records in a form that could be read easily by WordPerfect. The option to be used here is T for a text editor. The records will eventually be read into a document prepared with PC-Write, which uses text files. Continue by entering,

T Text editor (SDF) format. SDF is an abbreviation for ''Standard Data Format.'' As with most commands that write a file to disk, if there is an existing file by the same name a confirmation of permission to overwrite the old version of the file will have to be responded to. Since this is the first time this file is being saved, no permission is required.

Y Yes, flip data if contained in a field with a tilde. There are no tildes in any of the records so the response here is not currently important.

A All fields are to be exported.

A All records are to be exported. If you responded ''N'' you would be asked to determine how records to be exported are to be identified. Despite this somewhat misleading prompt and rèsponse, PC-FILE+ will ask for confirmation that each record is to be written to the new file, CLIENTS.SDF The following prompt appears to request confirmation of the export of each record,

```
 Please reply  ^v
Export?  Y, N, X or Q >_<
```

X Export all records without asking for confirmation. After the last record has been exported you will receive the prompt,

```
 Please reply  ^v
Export completed.  Press (Enter) >Y<
```

↵ Enter key, to return to the Utilities Menu.

Q Quit the Utilities Menu and return to the Master Menu.

This book will not utilize PC-FILE+ import file capabilities. Execution of the import command is, essentially, the reverse of exporting a file. You would have to have a file in a format the PC-FILE+ recognizes on your disk. The import command would convert the data from its original form into a form that PC-FILE+ operates on.

EXITING PC-FILE+

To leave PC-FILE+, you must first have the Master Menu in view. Then press,

Q Quit using the Master Menu.

Q Quit processing with PC-FILE+. The other alternatives are to change to a different database and not exit PC-FILE+ with ''D,'' or to return to the Master Menu and to continue working with the same database with ''R.''

BACKING UP YOUR FILES

Back up your PC-FILE+ files by using the DOS files copy command. Place the PC-FILE+ files diskette in drive A and the backup files diskette in drive B. Enter,

```
copy a:clients.* b:
```

Additional Methods of Back Up

The DOS commands for copying files offers a fast method of backing up files. It should be noted, however, that the Utilities Menu also offers a copy files command that can be used to back up files. This procedure while slower than backups with the DOS copy command, allows the user to remain in PC-FILE+ in case more work needs to be completed in PC-FILE+.

DOS also provides a backup command that is described in the chapter on hard disk management which can back up files in a different format.

EXERCISES

A. Retrieve the central services database, SERVICES, used in chapters 14 and 15. Print out the records in order of department. Sort the database by department and code. Print this list. Print this list to disk with the filename SERVLIST. This file will be used as an exercise in chapter 18.

B. Retrieve the school roster database, ROSTER, used in chapters 14 and 15. Print out the records sorted by sex. Sort the database by department and rank. Print this list. Print this list to disk with the filename FACLIST. This file will be used as an exercise in chapter 18.

C. Retrieve the database, SOFTWARE, used in chapters 14 and 15. Print out a list sorted by the manufacturer. Print out a list sorted in order of product name. Print this list to disk with the filename PRODLIST. This file will be used as an exercise in chapter 18.

Chapter 17
Additional Features of PC-FILE+

CHAPTER OUTLINE

Databases are not static. They change frequently through the addition, deletion, and modifications. Sometimes more substantive changes are required. Fields must be added or deleted. For example, a new governmental regulation may require that a piece of data never collected before must be added. New databases similar to older ones must be created. A departmental inventory, for instance, can be used for more than one department even though the records are different. Changes of the same kind must be made to large numbers of records. For instance, a telephone area code may change when the telephone company divides up an existing code into two area codes. In this chapter you will,

1. Learn how an existing database structure can be used as the template for a second database.
2. Create calculated and masked fields which extend the kinds of automatic data entry available in PC-FILE+,
3. Structure a field so that PC-FILE+ looks up the data it needs in another database,
4. Use a global modify command that rapidly changes the contents of fields in a PC-FILE+ database,
5. Learn about several useful commands and utilities that ease the task of using PC-FILE+,
6. Make a file more secure by restricting its usage to persons who know the password into the file.

RETRIEVING AN EXISTING FILE

Run the PC-FILE+ program and retrieve your file JOBSDB. Refer to the beginning of chapter 13 if you need help in this respect.

COPYING A DATABASE

You will begin this chapter by "copying" the database JOBSDB. In this process you duplicate the database structure and the records in a database with a different name. A large university may have a department that develops a database that keeps selected records on its graduate students' progress through their degree program. A different department learns of the database and wishes to install an identical database on their computer. The cloning process of PC-FILE+ facilitates this by letting the second department replicate the structure quickly and accurately. Begin the copy process by entering,

F8	Function key F8, or "U," the Utilities key, to obtain the Utilities Menu.
M	Maintenance (Copy, Delete, or Rename).
C	Copy the file.
D	Database file.
B	The file is on drive B.
↵	Enter key, to accept the path.
↓	Down arrow as necessary to highlight the file, JOBSDB.
F10	Function key F10, to complete the selection of JOBSDB.
B	The duplicate file will be on drive B.
↵	Enter key, to accept the path.
NUJOBS	The filename for the duplicate file.
↵	Enter key. You may notice that three files NUJOBS.DTA (the data file), NUJOBS.NDX (an index file that keeps the records in the original or last sort order) and NUJOBS.HDR (a file that keeps track of the record structure, field lengths, and field masks) are listed at the top of your screen as they are copied. The Utilities Menu returns.
Q	Quit and return to the Master Menu. Notice that at the top of the Master Menu the filename, JOBSDB, is still present. NUJOBS has been created but is not yet in use.

SWITCHING TO A NEW DATABASE

NUJOBS has been created as our test file. Switch to using this file by entering,

Q	Quit the Master Menu.
D	Different file to be put into use.
B	The file is on drive B.
↵	Enter key.
↓	Down arrow as necessary to highlight the file, NUJOBS.
F10	Function key F10, to complete the selection of NUJOBS. The file is selected and put into use. At the top of the Master Menu you will see that there are 21 (this may be different for your file) records in the new database. They are replicas of those found in the file, JOBS.

CLONING THE DATABASE

"Cloning" is a term that PC-FILE+ uses to identify the process of altering the basic structure of the database. One modifies a record when changing it, but clones a database when altering the structure. You will:

1. Add a field, GROSSPAY# to the structure. This field will contain a number that is calculated by PC-FILE+ based on an hourly rate and the number of hours spent on the job.

2. Add a field, CUST_NAME to the structure. This field will correspond to the field, CLT_NAME, in the CLIENTS database. CUST_NAME will be "looked" up in the CLIENTS database. In a corporate setting it would be desirable to keep the two field names identical since they name comparable data. In this tutorial, however, the use of distinctive names will facilitate your understanding of how the look up procedure in a field is organized.
3. Delete the fields BILL_NUM and PRG_ID.
4. Change the width of JOB_TITLE to 20 from 18.

Proceed by entering,

F8 Function key F8, or "U," the Utilities key.
C Clone the database and to receive the screen,

```
Field names: 12 letters or less.  Data locations: [ ]
  Example:   CITY [NEW YORK      ]              Press (Alt)H for help
  Please make changes to your data-entry screen  21:80
   BILL_NUM [     ]
     PRG_ID [        ]
       RANK [      ]
     CLT_ID [        ]
     JOB_ID [        ]
  JOB_TITLE [                  ]
       HRS# [     ]
```

Figure 17–1. Cloning Screen.

Notice that the cursor is on the top line with BILL_NUM.

Deleting Fields

F5 Function key F5 which deletes the entire line, thereby deleting the field BILL_NUM. If there had been other fields on the line, as might be true in a large database or in a database which you choose to place other fields on this line, all of the fields on the line would have been deleted, not just the first. The Delete key will delete one field and leave those to the right alone. The F6 will delete the last field on a line.

Del Delete key 21 times to delete the PRG_ID field. In this database, since there is only one field per line, the effect of F5 once and of the multiple use of the Delete key are the same in so far as they both delete the field, but the Delete key leaves the line; a line that will be used to hold a new field.

F5 Function key F5 to delete the entire line.

Adding Fields and Changing Field Widths

Add the fields CUST_NAME (length 20) and GROSSPAY # (length 8). Also expand the width of JOB_TITLE to 20, an increase of 2. Use the Enter key to open new lines, the F5 key to delete vacant lines, the arrow, Home, and End keys to move the cursor, and the normal alphabetic characters to redesign the format of the screen so it looks as follows:

```
Field names: 12 letters or less.  Data locations: [ ]
 Example:  CITY [NEW YORK      ]           Press (Alt)H for help
 Please make changes to your data-entry screen  21:80
      RANK [  ]
    CLT_ID [      ]
    JOB_ID [      ]
 JOB_TITLE [                    ]
 CUST_NAME [                    ]
      HRS# [   ]
 GRSS_PAY# [        ]
```

Figure 17–2. Modified Database Structure.

F10	Function key F10, to complete the modifications.
N	No, there are no window fields.
Y	Yes, change the order of the fields. The modifications shown above did not place the fields in the correct location. If new fields had been placed correctly you might choose "N" to avoid reorganizing the order. When the request to reorder the fields appears, change the numbers to look like,

```
          Please number the fields in the order desired
======================================================================
      RANK >1 <
    CLT_ID [4 ]
    JOB_ID [2 ]
 JOB_TITLE [3 ]
 CUST_NAME [5 ]
      HRS# [6 ]
 GRSS_PAY# [7 ]
```

Figure 17–3. Reordered Fields.

F10	Function key F10, to complete the reordering. The next screen identifies the fields from the current database, NUJOBS, that can be used as possible equivalents for the still new database you are structuring. GRSS_PAY # does not appear since the current database has only one numeric field.
F10	Function key F10 seven times to accept the default correspondences suggested by PC-FILE+.
B	Place the new file on drive B.
↵	Enter key.
NUJOBS2	The revised database structure and filename.
↵	Enter key.
A	All records are to be cloned (added) to the new database. You could be selective with the "S" option if you wished.
X	Do not ask for confirmations. Clone all records.
Y	Yes, switch to the new database.

The field JOB_TITLE was adjusted to width 20 in this process. By the deleting spaces instead of inserting them between the brackets, the width could be narrowed. The reduction of spaces should be made carefully since some of the records may have entries that are at the maximum width. Some data will be lost if the space is reduced.

Browse

Examine the contents of the new database by entering,

F2 Function key F2, the Search key.
PgUp The Page Up key to enter Browse. You will see a screen full of records in which the data has been correctly placed in all of the fields except for the CUST_NAME and GRSS_PAY # fields which are empty. There was no way by which PC-FILE+ could create this data.
Q Quit to return to the Master Menu.

RENAMING, EDITING, MASKING, AND CALCULATING FIELDS

The next set of changes will be made in a manner in which data is entered into records. In chapter 11 a constant was used in several fields of the CLIENTS database to automatically enter the most common values for each field. These entries could be overridden by the person entering the data. In the current database you will

1. Change the name of the JOB_ID field to ID_NUM,
2. Add an edit ''mask'' to restrict entries in the field, RANK, to the numbers 1 through 4,
3. Calculate the value for GRSS_PAY #,
4. Look up the CLIENT_NAME.

Begin the process by entering,

F2 Function key F2, the Search key.
N ''Name of field, mask, constant, or calc (modify).''
2 The number for the JOB_ID field.
F10 Function key F10.
N Name. Change the name of this field.
ID_NUM The new field name.
F10 Function key F10. The name is changed on the screen and is marked with a triangle.
7 The number for the GRSS_PAY field.
F10 Function key F10.
C Calculate the field value. The following prompt appears,

```
Please reply  ^v
New calcs (a + b)  >________________________________<
```

(HRS *14.50).2

This formula can be constructed with any valid field names, numeric constants, and mathematical operators (+, –, /, *). The .2 determines how many decimal points will be displayed. In this example, the value of HRS # for a given record will be multiplied by a pay rate of $14.50 per hour. The answer will be displayed with two decimal places.

↵ Enter key.
1 The next field, RANK, which will be given an editing mask. ''Editing,'' in this context has a different connotation than simply changing data being entered. In data processing, ''editing,'' is often used to refer to procedures that guarantee that a data entry operator is entering correct data (a number in the range of 1 to 1,000, for instance) and not incorrect data.
F10 Function key F10.
M Mask entries to the RANK field.
:*14: This mask will permit the user to enter the numbers in the series 1, 2, 3, 4, but no other numbers. This is one mask among many that could be constructed. The PC-FILE+ manual has other illustrations. Other masks, for instance, include,

:AZ Permits only capital letters to be entered.
:az Permits only lower case letters to be entered.
:YYMMDD* Enters the date.
F10 Function key F10.
5 The CUST_NAME field. This field is to be made into a relational field. A relational field is a field that receives its value from another database. In this case, we wish the name to be obtained from the CLIENTS database. How can PC-FILE+ do this? Both this database and the CLIENTS database contain the field CLT_ID. CLT_ID is a "key," into the CLIENTS database. The formula to be used follows the syntax,

```
(@key,database2,matching_field,field_name)
```

in which

@ is a required symbol to identify the start of a relational field,
key is the field name in the current database which can be found in the other database,
database2 is the name of the database from which a value is being sought,
matching_field is the field name in database1 that corresponds to the key field in the current database,
field_name is the name of the field in database2 that holds the value sought for the field in which this calculation is being entered.

F10 Function key F10.
C Calculation.

CLIENTS, CLI_ID, (CLT_ID,CLT_NAME)

A calculation that says, "Take the value found in the CLT_ID of the current record, look at the database CLIENTS, find the value of CLT_ID of this database in the CLT_ID field of CLIENTS, return to this record's CUST_NAME field the value of CLT_NAME; a field in the CLIENTS database." This formula can also be looked at in this way:

```
(@CLT_ID,CLIENTS,CLT_ID,CLT_NAME)
 |  |       |       |     |
 |  |       |       |        The value sent back from CLIENTS to the field with this calculation
 |  |       |       |
 |  |       |          The field whose value must match the value of the 1st CLT_ID
 |  |          Find the database by this name. It holds the value sought
 |   Take the value in this field of the current record
The @ sign is a required identifier
```

F10 Function key F10, to complete the relational calculation
F10 Function key F10, to complete the changing of the fields in this database.
Q Quit the Utilities Menu and to return to the Master Menu.

Seeing and Using the Masks, Edits, and Calculations

Enter browse to see the records by entering,

F2 Function key F2, or "F," the Find key.
B Get the first record.

M	Modify the record.
F10	Function key F10. No changes will be made now. The record will stay on the screen briefly but long enough for you to see relational data, the name "Fast Accounting," looked up for the CUST_NAME field, and the GRSS_PAY will also be calculated to be 108.75.
2	Get the next record
M	Modify the record.
5	Attempt to change the RANK to 5. A beep is heard and the number is not accepted since it is not in the range of valid numbers (0–4).
F10	Function key F10 and stop making changes to the record.
F10	Function key F10, to return to the Master Menu.

Continue by recalling all of the records one at time and having the empty fields calculated when the F10 key is pressed. Try changing some of the RANK values to numbers larger than 4. If it occurs that the CLT_ID field contains a number that is not found in the CLIENTS database, the message, "?NOT FOUND" will be displayed. Correct the CLT_ID value.

Adding Records

The calculations and masks created and used in modifying records will continue to function in the process of adding records. Add two records with data of your own choosing and notice how the order in which the data is requested for the fields is different from the order in which the fields appear on the screen. Try entering an incorrect CLT_ID (155 for instance) or a RANK of 8. What happens when you enter a value for CUST_NAME?

GLOBAL MODIFY OR DELETE

Sometimes it is necessary to make the same changes to a large number of records. For example, if a customer database contained a field for the sales contact person there will be a need to change the name of the salesperson periodically. If "Walker, T." was replaced by "Sun, Y." then the change might affect 50 records. Similarly, there may be a need to purge a large number of records from a database simultaneously. A mailing list manager might, for instance, wish to delete all records for customers who have never placed an order, or who have not placed an order since some date. The global modify and global delete commands are used for this purpose. Assume that the client with the CLT_ID of 115 has merged with the client whose CLT_ID is 127. The CLT_ID of 127 is to be used for both organizations. Use the global modify capability of PC-FILE+ by entering,

F8	Function key F8, or "U," the Utilities key.
G	Global operations– "modify or delete"
M	Modify.
S	Selected records will be changed.
S	Simple search. A search screen is presented.
↓	Down arrow as necessary to place the cursor in the CLT_ID field.
115	The CLT_ID to be changed.
F10	Function key F10.
↓	Down arrow as necessary to place the cursor in the CLT_ID field.
127	The value to replace 115.
F10	Function key F10.
X	Do not ask for confirmations. The changes are made to your records on the screen and you are notified how many records were changed.
↵	Enter key
Q	Quit the Utilities Menu.

The global deletion command sequence is essentially the same as the global modify command sequence illustrated here. But be careful! Deleting records is always a serious operation when real data is involved. The global deletion of records, and the global modification of records, is even more serious.

Return to the master menu and print the modified database.

PASSWORDS AND SECURITY

Many databases contain data that is confidential. PC-FILE+ provides several levels of password protection that restrict usage by persons who do not have permission to do so. While these techniques are not highly secure, they do provide a reasonable level of security. Passwords can be applied to control:

1. Access to the **Master Menu.** This prevents intruders from accessing, viewing, or changing any files on the system.
2. Access to databases through the use of a **file password.** This access can be controlled to permit or prohibit the addition, deletion, modification, or sorting of records.
3. Access to **system activities** such as defining reports, adding editing masks, and cloning databases.
4. The ability to **override passwords.** This facility allows you to bypass other passwords and to prevent other persons from having any access to many PC-FILE+ commands.

In this section you will use one type of password, that for restricting access to a single file. Passwords are from 1 to 3 characters in length. Any printable character on the keyboard is permissible. Possible passwords are:

CAT
Y6#
990
(!)

When you assign a password, don't forget it! Otherwise you will not be able to access the file yourself. Add a password to the file CLIENTS by entering,

F8	Function key F8, or "U," the Utilities key.
P	Profile, to change the set up configuration.
E	Edit an existing profile.
A	The profile is on drive A.
↲	Enter key.
↓	Down arrow once to select PCFILE(.PRO).
F10	Function key F10. The following screen appears,

```
SCREEN COLORS:             Background    (0-7)   >_<
                           Foreground   (0-15)   [ ]
Foreground color for field names        (0-15)   [ ]
DATABASE DEFAULTS:              Drive    (A-Z)   [ ]
                                          Path   [ ]
                              Database name      [              ]
OPTIONS:          Case sensitive finds   (Y/N)   [N]
                  Case sensitive sorts   (Y/N)   [N]
 Skip to next field when field full      (Y/N)   [N]
```

Figure 17–4. Profile Screen.

```
                    Fast view     (Y/N)    [N]
                    Fast write    (Y/N)    [N]
                  Expert menus    (Y/N)    [N]
PRINTER DEFAULTS:  Define/Modify  (Y/N)    [N]
MENU PASSWORDS:    Define/Modify  (Y/N)    [N]
KEVIN MACRO:       Define/Modify  (Y/N)    [N]
SNAPSHOT LABEL:    Define/Modify  (Y/N)    [N]
```

Figure 17–4—*Continued*

↓	Down arrow to place the cursor in the choice "MENU PASSWORDS:." Notice that this screen allows you to change many features of PC-FILE+ including the use of color if you have a color monitor.
Y	Yes, change passwords.
F10	Function key F10, to receive the following prompt,

```
                         PC-File+ Passwords

         Enter any combination of three letters and/or numbers.
    If you do not want a particular menu item to have a password,
                  just leave the password field blank.

             PC-FILE+ MASTER MENU PASSWORD >_   <
                             ADD PASSWORD [     ]
                          MODIFY PASSWORD [     ]
                          DELETE PASSWORD [     ]
                            SORT PASSWORD [     ]
                          SYSTEM PASSWORD [     ]
                     XXX OVERRIDE PASSWORD [     ]
```

Figure 17–5. Passwords Screen.

pcf	The initials of PC-File+ will be used as a password to the Master Menu. No other passwords will be entered at this point. You may enter some if you wish to experiment with the password capability. You can print the screen with PrtSc to keep track of the passwords for now. Obviously, passwords are less secure if there are printed passwords around for people to find.
F10	Function key F10.
Y	Yes, save the file.
Y	Yes, it is okay to replace PCFILE.PRO.
Q	Quit the Utilities Menu. The Master Menu appears and requests that you enter the password at the bottom of the screen. This request (demand?) will appear each time you use PC-FILE+.
pcf	The password.
↵	Enter key, full access to the Master Menu is now returned to you.

THE CALCULATOR HOT KEY

An additional feature of PC-FILE+ is the ability to call up a simple calculator for quick calculations. This feature may be used if you were entering prices for items sold and for some of the customers you needed to include a discount before the sale price is entered.

Alt-C The Alternate and C keys pressed simultaneously that produces the calculator screen,

Figure 17–6. Calculator Screen.

125 * .85 Give the customer a discount rate of 85% on a sale of $125.
↵ Enter key, to compute the answer, 106.25.
↵ Enter key, to exit the calculator.

The calculator can be called at any time from within PC-FILE+.

EXITING PC-FILE+

To leave PC-FILE+, you must first have the Master Menu in view. Then press,

Q Quit using the Master Menu.
Q Quit processing with PC-FILE+. The other alternatives are to change to a different database and not exit PC-FILE+ with "D," or to return to the Master Menu and to continue working with the same database with "R."

BACKING UP YOUR FILES

Back up your PC-FILE+ files by using the DOS files copy command. Place the PC-FILE+ files diskette in drive A and the backup files diskette in drive B. Enter,

```
copy a:clients.* b:
```

EXERCISES

A. Retrieve the database, SERVICES. Clone the database to a file called CLONE1 and make the DEP field 10 character wide. Use the global modify command to change 101 to "Marketing," 102 to "OPERATIONS," 103 to "Sales," and 104 to "FINANCE." Print the database.

B. Retrieve the database, ROSTER. Clone the database to a file called CLONE2 and make the SEX field 6 characters wide. Use the global modify command to change the "M" to "Male" and the "F" to "Female." Print the database.

Part V

Advanced Topics

Chapter 18
Integrating Files

CHAPTER OUTLINE

PC-Write, As-Easy-As, and PC-File+ are excellent stand alone systems for solving the types of problems that they are designed to address. They were developed, however, by different companies to meet what they perceived to be the user's needs. The three packages were not especially designed to relate to any other products except those that might be produced by the same company. This is no different than it is for most software packages.

The sharing of data between programs is important, however. If you wish to write a report that refers to a subgroup within a database, you may wish to actually include the records for that subgroup in your document. Within the same report you may want to include a spreadsheet projection. In neither case do you want to have to retype all of the data over again if it already exists in either your database or in your spreadsheet.

In this chapter, you will prepare a memorandum that uses the data from a database and from a spreadsheet saved in earlier chapters. This is the most typical form of interprogram communication required of software packages. You will

1. Load PC-Write and prepare a business memorandum,
2. Retrieve a spreadsheet that was printed to disk,
3. Retrieve a database report that was printed to disk,
4. Edit the appearance of both of the retrieved files to conform with the margins of the letter.

Before beginning this chapter, use the DOS DIR command to be sure that you have the files SALES.PRN and CLIENTS.SDF on your files diskette. You will need both files to carry out this chapter.

LOADING PC-Write

Boot your computer with the working disk for PC-Write (or if the computer is already running, set the default drive to A and place the PC-Write diskette in drive A). When you have the "A>" prompt from DOS, type

ed b:memo3
↲

and press the Return key. This will cause the word processing program to be loaded into DOS and a check will be made to see whether the file MEMO3 already exists on drive B. You will see the Copyright/Registration screen and the prompt,

```
File not found; Esc to retype or F9 to create "b:memo3"
```

to which you should press the F9 key to enter the editor. When the PC-Write text entry screen appears, the area for text will take up almost all of the screen. Immediately above the screen appears the status line,

```
Esc:Menu Push Reform-. 99% Free.0% Thru.Read "b:memo3"
```

Check the ruler you are using by pressing the F2 key. The ruler displayed should appear as,

```
L----P----T----T----T----T----T----T----T----T----T----T----T----R
^    ^                                                           ^
|    |                                                          65
|    5
0
```

the default ruler that places the left hand margin at the tenth print column. Whenever you press the Return key, a new paragraph is begun in print column 15. A right margin is located at the seventy-fifth column.

ENTERING DATA AND RETRIEVING TEXT FILES

The first four lines of the memorandum are to appear at the left-hand margin as,

To: J. K. Sweeney, Manager, Southwest
Fr: T. M. Ouster, National Accounts Director
Date: April 23, 1987
Re: Sales Picture

When you enter the editor, the cursor is automatically placed at the left margin setting. Whenever you press Return, however, the cursor will return to the paragraph marker. If you want to type at the left margin, you must move the cursor to that location with either the left Arrow or Backspace key. After you enter the first line, use the left Arrow five times to place the cursor at the left margin in order to enter the second line. After each pressing of the Return key, you will have to use the left Arrow key to move the cursor back to the margin.

Press the Return key an extra time after the final heading line to leave a blank line before beginning the body of the memorandum. Enter the first paragraph which is,

```
I wanted to share the year-end summary of sales data with you
J. K. Although your region's sales for the second half of the
year have not been as good as they were for the first half, I
think that as the economy improves, our sales should increase
significantly in all regions. The overall sales picture for the
company is as follows:
```

Press the Enter key twice at the end of the paragraph to leave a blank line. Place the diskette with the file SALES.PRN in drive B. Retrieve the file SALES.PRN by pressing, the Control and F3 key simultaneously. This will bring up the prompt,

```
File to insert (Esc:cancel F8:dir): "b:*.*"
```

Change the filename to ''b:sales.prt'' on the spreadsheet that was printed to disk in chapter 7. Press Return. The file is retrieved and is outlined because the editor is ''Marking,'' as you will note from the status line about the text entry area. The cursor is in the lower left-hand side of the imported text block. Use the Backspace and Del keys to remove the extraneous arrows and the symbol -, behind and in front of the cursor from the screen. Leave your cursor under the ''A'' in ''AVERAGE.'' Then press the F5 key to remove the ''Marking'' indicator.

Use the Backspace and Del keys to remove the extraneous spaces at the left margin. Also use these keys to remove the unneeded blank lines between the first paragraph and the retrieved spreadsheet.

When the spreadsheet has been correctly placed in the memorandum, place the cursor behind the number 19,281 that represents the average yearly total of sales for all regions. Press the Enter key twice and enter the paragraph,

```
As you know J. K., we have been attempting to diversify our
corporate offerings by expanding our training and custom software
development activities. I'm sure that you will be pleased to know
that we have recently acquired a software company, Software
Associates, that is in the southwest. F. Johnson, the founder of
Software Associates is remaining with the firm. He is going to
contact you shortly to develop a coordinated approach to
encouraging our combined customer base to consider us for solving
their total computer needs. The present customer base for
Software Associates is,
```

pressing Return twice to leave a blank line after the paragraph.

Place the diskette with the file CLIENTS.SDF in drive B. Retrieve the client database that was printed to disk in chapter 16 by pressing. Again, use the Backspace and Delete keys to remove extraneous lines and spaces. Since the printing of the report included the unneeded database client numbers (CLT), use the Del key to remove the three numbers for each record.

When the database has been aligned with the left-hand margin that defines the rest of the memorandum, delete the report header and the total lines that are automatically produced by PC-File+, but that are not needed now.

Enter the closing paragraph by moving the cursor to the line beneath the client list and pressing the Enter key. This indents the cursor to the paragraph marker. Then type,

```
At least six of these companies will be in the market for
multi-user, computer networks in the next 3 months. Let's get
together at the next sales meeting to map out a firm strategy for
providing needs-based solutions to these new customers.
```

CAUTION ABOUT RETRIEVING FILES

In this exercise, you retrieved two files that were written to disk by PC-File+ and by As-Easy-As. Writing or printing a file to disk produces a text file that only contains spaces and characters. The file does not contain control characters that have special meanings to the software packages that created them. You cannot read a database file or a spreadsheet file into a word processor directly. These files must be printed to disk first.

SAVING AND PRINTING THE FILE

The memorandum is complete. Print it by pressing the F1 key to bring up the system/help menu F7, to start the printing process. The file MEMO3 is first written to the disk. You will see the prompt,

```
File to print (Esc:cancel F8:dir): "b:memo3"
```

↲ Enter key. If you elected to have several print rulers on the PC-Write diskette, you see the prompt screen,

```
Print control filename (Esc:exit Enter:none): "_"
```

to which you enter the filename for the printer you are currently using. Press Return. If you have only the default printer file you will not see this prompt..

The next prompt will be,

```
Esc:Exit F9:Print to a file F10:Printer is ready
```

Press the F10 key if the printer is turned on and if it is connected to your computer. You will see a menu of choices that you can make while the printing is in process. The top lines of the menu are:

```
Waiting. Print from "b:resume.res" to "PRN," ready to begin.
F1:Help-screen F3:Finished F5:Input-end F7:Repeat-pages
   F9:Page-Stop
F2:Exit-to-DOS F4:Dos-command F6:User-Input F8:Skip-pages
F10:Continuous

Show help screen, giving dot commands and other information

Press F10 if your printer is using continuous paper, or press F9
if the printer uses a single sheet feeder.
```

BACKING UP THE FILE AND EXITING THE EDITOR

When you are returned to the editor, save your file again (it was saved for you during printing) to your backup diskette by removing the diskette from drive B and replacing it with your backup diskette. Save the file on the backup diskette by pressing F1, followed by the pressing of F3.

Stop working on your document by pressing F2 to exit to DOS. The DOS prompt will be the next line placed on your screen.

INTEGRATED SOFTWARE PACKAGES

Commercial software is now available that combines the features of a word processor, a spreadsheet, and a database manager in one package. Some packages include additional capabilities for communications and graphics. Software that combines these different kinds of processing into one environment is often easy to learn, and the transfer of data between the several types of processing software is generally made easy.

Integrated software often has the disadvantage of being unable to provide a high degree of excellence in all facets of the processing provided. Because a microcomputer's memory is limited, and the whole integrated software package is large, many documents and spreadsheets cannot be made too big. Limitations on the size of the software cause the developer to omit some features.

EXERCISES

A. In the exercises for chapter 10, you printed a spreadsheet file to disk that was titled, GRADES.PRN. Using PC-Write compose a letter from a Professor R.O. DuLac of the Physics Department to the Dean of the College. In the letter explain how you have been experimenting with some unique, audiovisual course materials. A sample of students who have been restricted from using standard class materials compose the group whose grades make up the spreadsheet. Use the GRADES.PRN file in the letter to display the students' grades. The grades as an average are 10% above the average for the traditionally taught course. Dr. DuLac would like the Dean to consider a grant of $25,000 to the Physics Department to offer the audiovisual course to 100 students in the next semester.

B. In the exercises for chapter 10, you printed a spreadsheet file to disk that was titled, INCOME.PRN. Using PC-Write, compose a letter to the regional manager for car distribution to local dealers that explains that your dealership is receiving too many vans and not enough trucks. Use INCOME.PRN in your letter to provide evidence that the sales at your dealership support your request.

C. In the exercises for chapter 16, you printed a spreadsheet file to disk that was titled, SERVLIST.SDF. Using PC-Write, compose a memorandum to the department heads that explains that you are experimenting with a new computer billing and tracking system. Incorporate the results displayed in SERVLIST.SDF in your memorandum and ask them to review their records to see whether there are any inaccuracies. If there are any inaccuracies, they should notify you.

D. In the exercises for chapter 16, you printed a spreadsheet file to disk that was titled, MFRATIO.PRN. Using PC-Write, compose a memorandum for the principal, G.K. Washington, to the Board of Trustees of the school. The memorandum should explain that special efforts have been made over the past three years to improve upon the proportion of female to male teachers employed at the school. Incorporate the contents of FACLIST.SDF in the memorandum as evidence of the number of females at the current time. Prior proportions were lower.

E. In the exercises for chapter 16, you printed a spreadsheet file to disk that was titled, PRODLIST.SDF. Using PC-Write, compose a memorandum from the director of the purchasing department explaining that a reconciliation of the current inventory list needs to be made with the actual software held in the warehouse by the shipping department. Incorporate the PRODLIST.SDF information in the letter that is sent to the shipping department.

Chapter 19

Hard Disk Management

CHAPTER OUTLINE

ADVANTAGES OF USING HARD DISKS

As the purchase price of microcomputers has dropped, the number of persons and organizations that have acquired microcomputers with hard disks has increased noticeably. In chapter 2 you were introduced to the Disk Operating System (DOS) and to some of the commands that DOS provides. All of the commands described in that chapter assumed that you were using a two disk drive microcomputer system. In this chapter you will be introduced to new commands and options of commands that you already know, which will enable you to work effectively on another common type of computer: a computer with both a floppy disk system and a hard disk system. There are many reasons why hard disk systems are preferable to floppy disk systems, including:

1. ***To avoid handling floppy disks.*** There are literally thousands of computer programs available to the computer user. The average user obtains three or four programs that will be used regularly and perhaps another ten or twenty that will be used only occasionally. In addition to these, most programs expect the user to create files that will be saved. In a very short period of time the typical computer user will have a significant number of diskettes with which to deal. Keeping track of where needed files reside, what the files are called, and whose files are whose can become an onerous task. A hard disk replaces many floppy disks, something on the order of thirty floppies to one ten-megabyte hard disk. This consolidation reduces the necessity for physically handling, and possibly damaging, the floppy disks.
2. ***To increase access speed.*** Hard disks spin rapidly, so the speed with which programs can be loaded into memory is faster than is true of programs that reside on floppy disks. Data, documents, and worksheets can also be obtained more quickly.
3. ***Some programs require a hard disk or are made more convenient with one.*** A program like WordPerfect has important components like the Speller and the Thesaurus that come on several diskettes. It is possible to use these by switching the diskettes while you are creating a document, but when all of the programs have been installed on a hard drive, the access to these subprograms is greatly facilitated. There are some programs that are so large that they simply will not work without all of the diskettes having been loaded onto a hard drive.
4. ***To organize files.*** Generally, one organizes files on floppy disks by storing those that belong together on the same diskettes. On a hard drive, files can be organized in hierarchical manner (similar to a family tree), so files that belong together, are together logically.

DISADVANTAGES OF USING HARD DISKS

As the price of hard disks has decreased, the number of people acquiring them has increased substantially. The hard disk, desirable as it is, has drawbacks.

1. ***Cost.*** The addition of a hard disk will increase the cost of a microcomputer $300 or more, depending on the size of the disk.
2. ***Effects of failure or damage.*** A ten megabyte hard disk will hold the equivalent of thirty floppy diskettes. Damage to the hard disk or unintentional formatting of the hard disk will lead to a total loss of data on that disk—a situation too painful to think about. If you have not been conscientious about keeping backup files, your panic will be justified, even if the cause is excusable.
3. ***Complexity even with organization.*** Hard disks can store large numbers of files. In this chapter you will learn about hard disk directories, which can help to organize your programs, documents, worksheets, databases, and other files. Even with a good method of organization, however, you can find it confusing to deal with the obstacles that a hard disk presents.
4. ***Organizing information hierarchically.*** Directories that are used to organize hard disk files cannot be dealt with effectively without a change in the way you conceptualize what a disk is like. You cannot see anything but the outside case of the hard disk, yet you must think about files being organized in an upside down tree, and about yourself moving up and down on the tree to locate files. You will have to use some commands that are unnecessary on a floppy drive system. Similarly, other commands will require you to use options that you would not otherwise need.
5. ***Sharing your disk.*** With a computer that uses floppy diskettes, sharing is seldom a problem. Several people might use the same program disk, but generally they will use their own files disks. Whose file is whose is rarely debated. A hard disk computer is typically a shared machine. This means that the people sharing the computer must adopt certain conventions and courtesies, otherwise each person can significantly affect the other users. The security on a personal computer is often so limited that you must assume that someone else can read, copy, destroy, or alter your files. Don't rely on the microcomputer to be more reliable than it is.

A SAMPLE HIERARCHY OF FILES AND DIRECTORIES

When using a microcomputer with two floppy drives, you implicitly organized your files by diskette. Your files are on your diskettes and other people stored their files on their own diskettes. Further, most active computer users will store logically related groups of files on the same diskettes: document files on one diskette, spreadsheet files on another, and so on. If you are especially active, you might subdivide your diskettes so that all of the files related to one activity, such as a course or an organization, are stored on one diskette and those related to other activities on other diskettes. Retrieval of a file involves physical location of the appropriate diskette.

This method of organization would be inappropriate for a hard drive. You cannot install and un-install hard drives like you can insert and remove floppy diskettes. Also, if you don't arrange your files effectively, you have a morass of filenames to deal with when you try to locate or retrieve files. The **dir** command, for instance, might list hundreds of filenames. Programs using the same filenames for different files would interfere with one another. Actually, since a filename can only be used once in a directory, the last file entered would replace the previous file.

Consequently, the method of organization on a hard disk is substantially different. It is comparable to organizing information in a large company. Different offices maintain their own files so that the president's correspondence is in the president's office, financial records are in the controller's office, and so forth. If a person named Jack Jones wanted to inquire about a bill he had received, he might look up the address of the company in a telephone directory, which was arranged alphabetically. He would go to that location, which is numerically organized on a street, and, assuming that more than one company was located in the building, he would check the building directory to locate the floor on which the company was on. The building directory is based on physical location. Upon arrival at the correct floor, he would check the floor directory to see where the billing office was located. When he arrived at that office, the clerk would know that billings were found in a particular set of file cabinets. The clerk would go to the room that those file cabinets were found in, locate the cabinet that had bills for people whose last names began with the letters "H" through "K," find the drawer for persons whose names were "James" through "Jyzk," open the drawer and find the area where the "Jones" files were, and finally, find the folder for "Jack Jones." The billing should be one of the entries in the folder, that is then retrieved for discussion.

On hard disks, a network of directories that parallels the distribution of pointers to the bill of Jack Jones can, and should, be used. Figure 19–1 describes the organization of a hypothetical hard disk. The

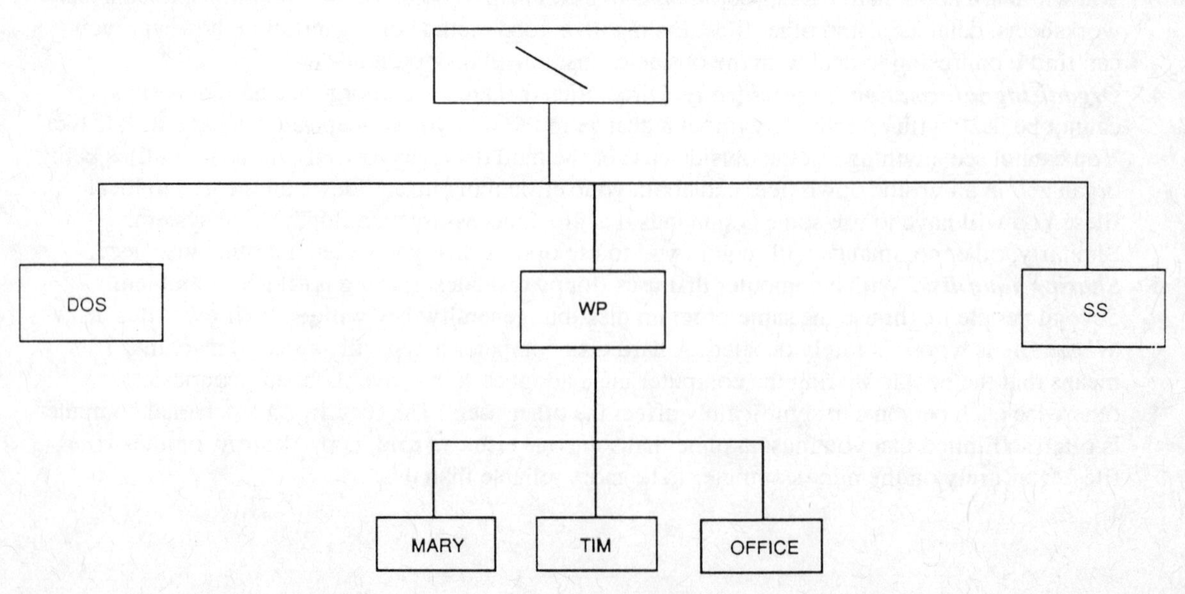

Figure 19–1. A Hypothetical Directory Structure.

tree, upside down—don't ask why, that's just the way computer types like to display them—begins with the location called "root." "Root" is represented in DOS commands as the backslash, "\." "Root" is a directory, and like all directories, it can "point" to files or it can point to other directories. Directories that are beneath other directories can be referred to as subdirectories.

When a disk is formatted, it has only one directory, the root directory. Other directories are created, and destroyed, by the users. It is up to them to decide how the disk is best organized. In the hypothetical directory structure displayed, the root directory points to three directories, represented by rectangles, which have the names DOS, WP, and SS, acronyms for Disk Operating System, word processor, and spreadsheet. Unlike the directories DOS and SS, which are empty, WP itself has subdirectories called MARY, TIM, and OFFICE. Figure 19–1 displays only the names of the directories in the hypothetical tree. Each directory can also point to files that contain programs, data, documents, or spreadsheets. Unlike directories, files do not point to anything. They are referred to as "leaves" of the tree. Figure 19–2 shows the same directory structure with files. The files are represented by ovals. In this structure, the directory DOS points to three files —COMMAND.COM, PRINT.COM, AND DISKCOPY.COM— but does not have any subdirectories. WP points to three subdirectories as well as two files, perhaps those that contain the word processing program. SS is an empty directory: it has no files and does not point to any directories.

If the user entered this directory structure at the level of root, as is normal when a hard drive system is booted, the **dir** command might display

Notice that **dir** would not display the names of directories and files that are pointed to by the subdirectories. It only "sees" the names of files and directories immediately below the root. The notations, . and . . will be discussed below. If you were to enter the command **cd**, the resulting response from DOS would be "\," to indicate that the directory currently active is the root.

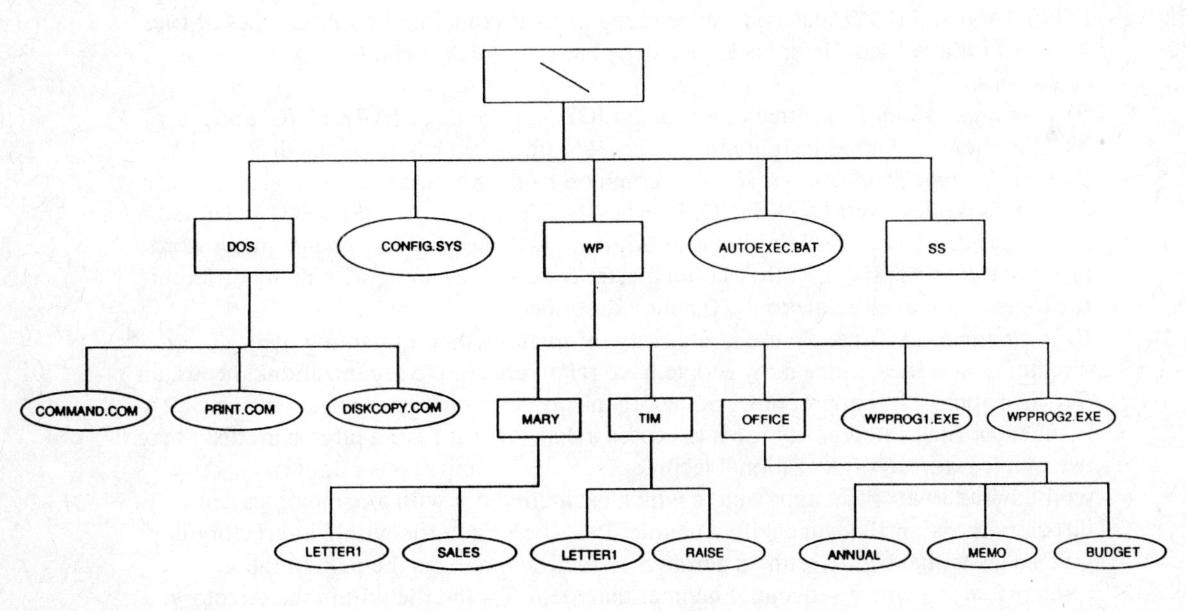

Figure 19–2.

If the currently active directory was SS, the response to the **dir** command would only be "." and ". .", then the C> prompt would return. This is because SS does not contain any files. If WP was the active directory the response by DOS would be

```
.  <DIR>
. . <DIR>
MARY     <DIR>      4-25-89    9:00a
WPPROG1 EXE 126988  1-12-89    11:20a
WPPROG2 EXE 23228   1-12-89    11:30a
TIM <DIR>           4-25-89    9:14p
OFFICE   <DIR>      4-25-89    9:23a
```

The DOS response to **cd** would be, ''\WP,'' which indicates that the pathway to the active directory is from root, through to WP. Look at Figure 19–2. What would the responses to **dir** and **cd** be if the active directory was MARY? DOS?

Directory Rationales

The use of directories is preferred over ''flat'' file methods of displaying filenames because files that logically belong together can be grouped together. There is little point in creating directories in which the files bore no relationship to one another, and there was no way of using directory names to determine where needed files could be located. There are several common bases on which to consider building and naming directories to make them useful.

1. ***By language or package.*** Directories named PASCAL, WP (*W*ord *P*rocessor), FORTRAN, and DB (*D*ata*b*ase) can be recognized as containing specific types of files. A search for a needed file or package can be reduced quickly to a few likely candidates.
2. ***By user name.*** Similarly, directories named JOHN, CAROL, MARKTING, and STAFF offer substantial insight into whose files are stored where on the disk.
3. ***By topic or applications area.*** Another common naming convention is to give directories names like MARKTING, PLANNING, TRAVEL, or PROJECT1. These directories could each contain files that originate with a common package like a word processor or spreadsheet, or they could cluster files that originate with many different packages, but that all relate to the function described.
4. ***By path name.*** Most people use a relatively informal method of naming their directories and files. Since most people have relatively simple organizational needs, an informal approach is appropriate. Some organizations, which produce extensive numbers of files, allow many users to access a disk, or that have a large hard disk, may need more rigorous organizational techniques. Such organizations might be well-advised to adopt an approach in which each directory with a common parent directory is assigned a name with a unique first letter. Each file within a directory is given a name that begins with an acronym, which summarizes the path to the directory, along with a sequential number that identifies the file within the directory.

   For instance, a filename such as WMP011 might signify that the file is located along the pathway that starts with *W*P and moves through *M*ARKTING and *P*ROJECTS, and among the files, it was the eleventh file created. If the filename is included at the base of the document, its retrieval location is determined rapidly.
5. ***By using a combination of techniques.*** As the above example illustrates, the naming of subdirectories will rarely have a single organizing theme. Unless one restricts the tree to one level, it is virtually impossible to use a single organizing principle to set up the hierarchy. A combination of organizing techniques will be appropriate at different branches of the tree.

Path Names

You will notice that there are two files in the hypothetical tree structure named LETTER1. Within the root or any single subdirectory, DOS will not permit the creation of two files with the same name. DOS does permit reuse of a filename if the files are created in different subdirectories. By default, DOS considers a filename to be prefaced by the path of subdirectories that lead up to the file. Therefore, the file that is designated with the path name \WP\MARY\LETTER1 can be distinguished from the file with the path name \WP\TIM\LETTER1. The latter path name is understood to mean, ''Find the file LETTER1 by beginning at root, proceed through the sub-directory WP, and find the file in the subdirectory TIM.

Filenames that are used without path names are assumed by DOS to be in the active directory. Path names can be used to unambiguously specify where a file is to be found, or as in the case of the **copy** command, where a file is to be placed.

Path names can include reference to the disk drive on which a file is to be found. The path name C:\WP\TIM\LETTER1 specifies that the file is to be found on drive C, as well as the subdirectories that must be traversed in order to locate the file.

Some examples of commands using path names include the following:

```
type c:\letters\mary\march\mr15
```

This will display the contents of the file MR15 (it must be a file for the command to execute successfully since the **type** command operates only on files, not on directories), which is found by successively traversing the directories on drive C from root, to LETTERS, to MARY, to MARCH. The command

```
del b:\doc\*.*
```

will delete all of the files in the subdirectory DOC under the root directory of drive B. The command

```
cd wp\frank
```

changes the active directory from the currently active directory to WP and then to FRANK. In this example, it is only known that the directory WP is beneath the currently active directory. It is not known where that directory, or the currently active directory are located in the hierarchy. The command

```
cd \wp\helen
```

is, because the path name begins with a backslash, known to start at root with WP immediately beneath root, and HELEN immediately below WP.

When constructing path names, keep the following rules in mind:

1. Path names cannot exceed 63 characters in length.
2. Directory names are separated from one another by backslashes. If a file is named at the end of the path name, it is separated from the preceding directory by a backslash.
3. A drive name may precede a path name.
4. When a path name begins with a backslash, it begins at the root of the tree's hierarchy.
5. When no leading backslash is present, the path name will begin at the currently active directory.

Default Path Names in Memory

The disk operating system retains knowledge of the currently active directory even though the active drive has been changed. For instance, suppose that the active drive was C, and the active directory was \WP\TOM. At the C> prompt, if you entered ''a:'' the prompt would be changed to A>. DOS retains the knowledge of the active directory on drive C. If you switched back to C with ''c:,'' you would be returned to \WP\TOM, not to root. Similarly, if you entered the command

```
A>copy *.* c:
```

all of the files on drive A would be copied to the currently active directory, \WP\TOM, and not to the root directory.

HARD DISK-RELATED COMMANDS AND OPTIONS

DOS possesses many commands and options. This chapter is designed to offer you some insight into the commands and command options that are most commonly used with hard disk drives. It is not a compendium of all of the important and useful commands available. Consult the DOS manual for more detailed information.

The cd (Change Directory) Command

The **cd** command is used to make another directory the active directory. Only one directory is active at a time. If the active directory was root and you typed

```
cd wp
```

the active directory would become \WP.

By typing

```
cd
```

DOS responds with the pathway to the active directory. DOS might respond with a pathway as long as

```
\wp\tim\personal\secret
```

which would show the active directory to be SECRET, which can be located by starting at root and progressing through TIM and PERSONAL before arriving at SECRET.

The **cd** command can be used to make a directory other than one below the current directory active. The command

```
cd wp\tim
```

would find the directory WP and make its subdirectory TIM the active directory. In this example, the pair of directories must be immediately beneath the currently active directory. As applied to Figure 19–2, the active directory would have had to have been root.

You can also issue the command

```
cd \wp\tim
```

which forces the search for the new active directory to begin at the root and continue until the desired directory is made active. This command can be issued anywhere in the hierarchy since DOS will always begin with the root of the tree.

The command

```
cd \
```

will make the root the active directory, regardless of where in the hierarchy the command is issued.

When the **dir** command is issued, the notations . and . . always appear. The . symbolizes the current directory pathway, while . . symbolizes the directory that is the pathway to the parent of the currently active directory. Assume that the currently active directory is MARY. Typing the command

```
cd ..
```

will make the parent directory of MARY active. This is the directory WP. A subdirectory can have only one parent. Root is its own parent. The command

```
cd .
```

means keep the current directory active. Although this command is legal, it is seldom used, for an obvious reason.

The command **cd** is the abbreviated form of **chdir,** which is also an acceptable DOS command.

The md (Make Directory) Command

Both hard and floppy disks have a root directory created as part of the formatting process. Other directories must be created by the user with the **md** command. Typically, you should be in the directory under which the new subdirectory is to be placed. Again, referring to Figure 19–2, if the active directory was OFFICE and the commands

```
md personnl
```

and

```
md personnl\policies
```

were issued, the first command would create a directory PERSONNL which was a subdirectory of OFFICE. The second command would indicate that from OFFICE a subdirectory PERSONNL could be found and that a new subdirectory, POLICIES, should be created under it. If these commands were issued, the hierarchy resulting would look like Figure 19–3.

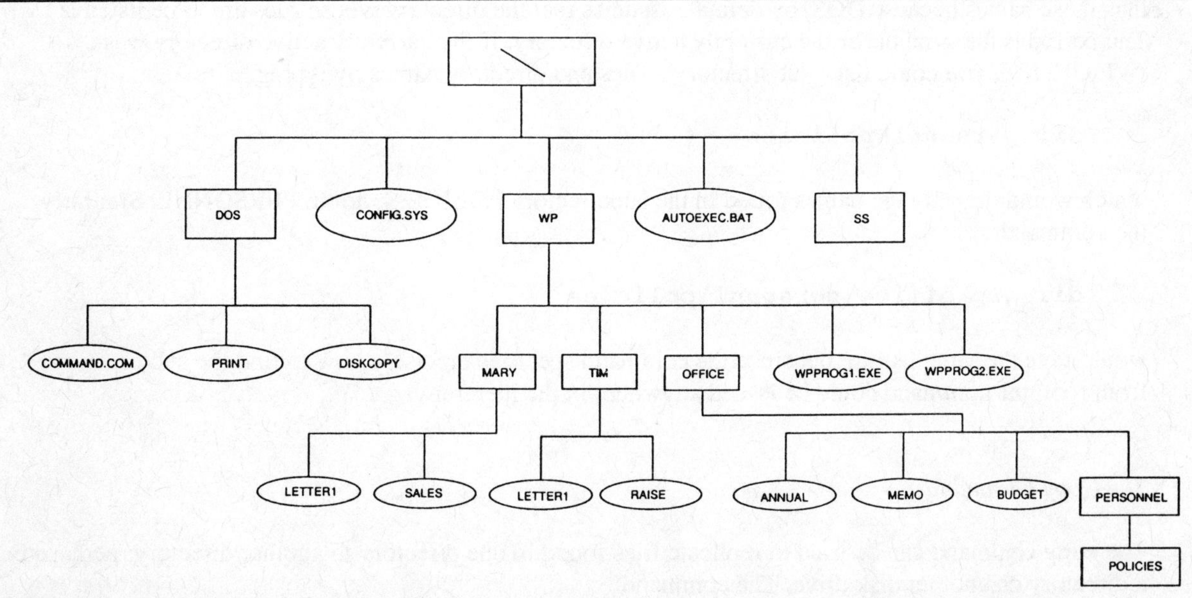

Figure 19–3. Sample Hierarchy.

The command **md** is an abbreviated form of the command **mkdir,** which will also work, although it is longer to type.

The rd (Remove Directory) Command

Once created, a directory need not be saved forever. It can be removed with the **rd** command. Before the **rd** command can be issued successfully, however, the directory being removed must be empty. Any files that are pointed to by the directory to be removed must be erased first. Any directories that are pointed to by the directory to be removed must be removed first. To determine whether a directory is empty, type the **dir** command. If the response shows any filenames, or any directory names other than

```
.  <DIR>
. . <DIR>
```

the directory is not empty. Be aware that there is a significant difference between the **erase** (or delete) command and the **rd** command.

```
rd policies
```

removes a directory, POLICIES, which must be empty.

```
erase policies
```

will give you the warning, "Are you sure (Y/N) " because erase deletes files. Even though you named a directory, the command will delete all of the files immediately beneath the directory POLICIES. POLICIES will not be removed by the erase command.

The dir (Directory) Command

The **dir** command has already been used to illustrate how it can be used to display the names of files and directories that are pointed to by the currently active directory. The command

```
dir
```

lists these names because DOS, by default, assumes that the directory whose files are to be listed is **.** The period is the symbol for the currently active directory. If the currently active directory was \WP\OFFICE, you could list a subdirectory's files and directory names by typing

```
dir personnl\policies
```

which would list only the names found in the subdirectory POLICIES, not in PERSONNL. Similarly, the command

```
dir \wp\office\personnl\policies
```

would give the same listing, but since the command specifies precisely how to find the subdirectory from root, the command could be issued anywhere in the hierarchy.

The Copy Command

The **copy** command can be used to replicate files found in one directory to another directory, perhaps in a directory on another disk drive. The command

```
A>copy b:\doc\*.* c:\wp
```

causes DOS to override the default path name **.** which would be used to locate the files to be copied with the disk drive designation of B. Although *.* indicates that all files are to be copied, the path name

\DOC specifies that only the files found in the DOC subdirectory are to be copied. Any files found at the root directory level or in any subdirectory will not be copied. The files that are copied from B:\DOC will be placed in the WP subdirectory of root on drive C. Similarly

```
A>copy b:*.* c:\wp
```

will copy any files found on drive B at the root directory level. It will not replicate any files that are found in subdirectories on drive B.

Unless otherwise specified by a drive designation and a path name, DOS uses the default of **.** as the active directory for both the source file, the file being copied, and the destination file, the second copy of the file. The command

```
C>copy a:myfile.doc
```

will cause DOS to assume that the copy of the file MYFILE.DOC, which is to be created, will be placed in the currently active directory. The destination is assumed to be **.** . In this example, since an adequate designation for the drive and filename were given, DOS assumed that this file was the source file.

The Format Command

The **format** command is a command you should always be cautious about using. It destroys all data on the disk when it is being used to reformat a disk, as opposed to formatting it for the first time. Most hard drive microcomputers have only one floppy drive, so the only legitimate **format** command that should be issued 99.999% of the time is

```
format a:
```

The command

```
C>format
```

would cause DOS to assume that you wished to format **.**, the currently active drive/directory. The format command cannot be restricted to the current directory, so the entire hard disk is formatted, wiping out all of the files, programs, subdirectories, documents, and worksheets stored on that drive. Some programs that are formally "installed" on the hard drive use hidden files, which, when destroyed, cannot be recaptured in any way. The only way to obtain these files is to buy a replacement disk from the software manufacturer.

The **format** command does issue a warning that data will be destroyed. Consider this warning seriously.

It is a rare occasion that should require the formatting of the hard disk! Never do so unless you are absolutely certain that this is required. If the microcomputer you are working on is not your computer, you have no right to format the hard disk.

The Backup Command

The **copy** command and the normal file saving procedures of applications programs that save files to disks other than the hard drive are generally adequate for ensuring users that their files can be recovered if the hard disk is damaged. Persons who are responsible for ensuring the security of data on a hard disk, as well as many users with extensive numbers of files, should consider using the **backup** command also, because of the limitations of the **copy** command. **Copy** is awkward to use since a directory may contain more files than the floppy disk can hold. In fact, a single large file may be too big to fit on one floppy disk. **Copy** does not allow a single file to overlap diskettes.

The **backup** command saves files in a different form than does the **copy** command. **Backup** can overlap files to different diskettes. It does, however, require that all of the backup diskettes must be kept in the same sequential order that the files are backed up. An error in the labeling of the diskettes can cause data that is backed up to become inaccessible. An example of the use of the **backup** command is

```
backup c:\ a:
```

which will back up all files at the root level, and only at the root level, of drive C. The backup files will be sent to the diskettes on drive A. The /s option used in

```
backup c:\ a: /s
```

will back up all of the subdirectories under the root of the drive C.

```
backup c:\wp\*.doc a:
```

will only backup the files with the extension .DOC in the WP subdirectory of the C drive. No other files are saved. Selective backups are desirable since a complete backup will take a long period of time and will require a substantial number of diskettes. Also, many files, such as your word processor and your spreadsheet program files, do not change, as opposed to your document and worksheet files. You should have the original program diskettes in a secure location, so there is no reason to back them up.

Backup has options that allow you to selectively back up only those files that have been changed since the last backup was made, or only those files that changed after a specific date. In addition, many hard disk owners have acquired tape backup units that speed up and simplify the process. Owners of such devices may use other commands and options.

The Restore Command

Files that have been created with the **backup** command can be retrieved with the **restore** command. It can restore one file, an entire disk drive, or all of the files in specific subdirectories.

```
restore a: c:\ /s
```

will restore from drive A all files that were backed up from drive C. All subdirectories will also be backed up, since the \s option was used. If this option was not used, only the files immediately under root would be backed up.

```
restore a: c:\ /p
```

uses the \p option. This option prompts the user before each file is backed up to determine whether the file is to be restored.

```
restore a: c:\wp\*.txt
```

will restore from drive A only the files that belong under subdirectory WP that have the extension .TXT.

Commercial programs that are copy protected will create hidden files on the hard disk that cannot be backed up. If a hard disk is damaged, it may not be possible to completely restore the program since these files cannot be restored. In these circumstances, the manufacturer of the program will have to be contacted for replacement disks.

The Prompt Command

The usual DOS prompt identifies the default drive and that is all. The prompt, ‘‘C>,’’ for instance, designates drive C as the default drive. This prompt does not fully reflect the default value held by DOS, however, since DOS keeps track of the default directory as well as the default drive. If you were using the subdirectory WP, the prompt would not display this assumed default directory. DOS provides users with some control over the display of the prompt to make the prompt more informative. Two options are of particular value. The command

```
prompt $p$g
```

uses the $p option to display the pathway to the current directory, while the $g option displays the greater than sign. After executing the command, you would see prompts that looked like

```
PROMPT              DEFAULT
C:\>                Drive: C, Directory: root
C:\WP>              Drive: C, Directory: WP, a subdirectory of root
C:\WP\PERSONAL>     Drive: C, Directory: PERSONAL, a subdirectory of
                    WP, which is a subdirectory of root
```

Figure 19–4. Sample Prompts With PG Option.

By using the $p option you receive a reminder about the current drive and directory with the completion of each DOS operation. Remember which defaults are in use when you switch drives because DOS doesn't forget even though you may switch default drives. Suppose you were using the default prompt and DOS simply displayed, "C>," but you were in the subdirectory WP. If you issue the DOS commands

```
C>a:
A>copy myfile c:
```

where would the copy of MYFILE be sent? To the root level of drive C? To the subdirectory WP? To somewhere else? Actually, the copy is placed in the subdirectory WP because DOS remembers the default directory you were in when you switched drives. Similarly, if you were to issue these commands and then entered

```
A>c:
```

you would be returned to the WP subdirectory. Use of the $p option helps you to keep track of where you are at any point. You would be made instantly aware of your default directory by the prompt that would display the drive and directories that compose your current pathway. If you use this option, though, be ready for occasional prompts such as

```
C:\WP\COURSES\POLSCI\SMITH\PSC101>
```

The Tree Command

An effective use of directories on large disk drives can lead to a huge number of files and directories. It may be that you will have difficulty keeping track of what files are on the disk and in which directories the files are located in. The **tree** command is one of several DOS commands that can be of assistance. Simply entering "tree" will provide you with a listing of directories and subdirectories that will look like Figure 19–5.

```
Path: \$$
Subdirectories:    None

Path: \WP
Subdirectories:    WORKSHOPS
                   OFFICE
                   BOOK

Path: \WP\WORKSHOPS
Subdirectories:    NONE
```

Figure 19–5. Sample Output from the Tree Command.

Only the directory names are displayed. The **tree** command can be issued with a /f option to display the names of files also. A sample display from the command, **tree /f,** is shown in Figure 19–6.

```
Path: \WP
Subdirectories:    WORKSHOPS
                   OFFICE
                   BOOK

Path: \WP\WORKSHOPS
Subdirectories:    NONE

Files:          ANNOUNCE
                REGISTER.LST
                HANDOUT.01
                HANDOUT.02
```

Figure 19–6. Sample Output from the Tree /F Command.

TWO SPECIAL FILES

When a computer running under MS-DOS is booted, the system will look to find out whether either or both of two files are present. These files, CONFIG.SYS and AUTOEXEC.BAT, contain instructions for the computer about how the system should be configured when control is turned over to the user. If these files exist, the commands they contain will be executed. If the files do not exist default values will be used. Both files are created by the user. Once created, the files are seldom altered, although the addition of new programs and peripherals to your system may require changes in both files.

CONFIG.SYS

CONFIG.SYS is the first file to be examined and executed by DOS. This file contains instructions that are used to adapt the operating system to the hardware. Some computers may have a mouse, two printers, a modem, or a digitizing tablet that make special demands on the operating system. CONFIG.SYS is read as the booting process is nearing completion in order for DOS to recognize and utilize the presence of these devices. A sample CONFIG.SYS file might contain the following lines:

```
FILES=15
BUFFERS=24
DEVICE=MOUSE
DEVICE=ANSI.SYS
```

Figure 19–7. Sample CONFIG.SYS File.

These lines are interpreted by DOS. Line 1 sets aside 15 locations in RAM, where information can be kept on up to 15 files that may be in use simultaneously. This may seem excessive but there are "files" that may not seem like files to you. The keyboard, or other "standard input" device, and the monitor, or other "standard output" device, are special files that are the origin of, and the destination of, characters being transmitted within the computer, in much the same fashion that a file on the disk is both the source and destination for characters.

The second line allocates RAM space for 24 locations where data can be kept as it is read from and written to files and various computer devices such as disk drives, the screen, and the memory. The third line adapts the system to a hand-moved "mouse" that is used with graphics programs. The last line enables the system to load another device driver that will let the screen and keyboard act like a standard communications terminal. Other device drivers may also be loaded in this file.

CONFIG.SYS may contain commands other than these, yet these commands may be entirely correct and necessary. Do not alter the CONFIG.SYS file unless you are certain of the effect of the changes.

AUTOEXEC.BAT

The second file whose command lines will be executed, if the file exists, is the file AUTOEXEC.BAT. The AUTOEXEC.BAT file contains DOS commands that can, in many cases, be issued at the prompt line and be successfully executed. By placing the commands in this file, the user can have DOS set up the operating environment without the user having to enter the commands manually. Any file given the extension .BAT should be an executable file. That is, it should contain DOS commands and language statements that DOS can execute just as though they were executed by the user.

A sample AUTOEXEC.BAT file is shown in Figure 19–8.

```
ECHO OFF
DATE
TIME
PROMPT $P$G
PATH=C:\;C:\DOS;C:\WP
```

Figure 19–8. Sample AUTOEXEC.BAT File.

Line one causes DOS to execute the commands that follow as "silently" as possible to avoid extraneous information being sent to the screen. If an AUTOEXEC.BAT file exists, the system will no longer automatically ask for the date and time. Hence, lines two and three prompt the user for the date and time. These lines may not be used if the system has a battery operated clock/calendar that keeps the date current. The fourth line changes the prompt to one that will show the complete pathway and the greater than sign. This line is executed before the user has seen a prompt.

The Path Command

The final line is used to identify the directories for DOS to search when you enter a command at the DOS prompt. If this line was missing DOS would only search the current directory for the command file that contains the instructions on how the command is to be carried out. For instance, if you issued the **format** command DOS would need to know where this command was to be found on the disk. DOS would look for the command in the current directory. If the command file was found, the command would be executed. If the command file was not found, the search would stop if there was no PATH command in the AUTOEXEC.BAT file. If the command file was not found, but there was a PATH command in the AUTOEXEC.BAT file, DOS would use this information to continue searching.

The dir and copy commands are internal commands. Internal commands are loaded into RAM when the system is booted. These and other commands are found in the file COMMAND.COM, which must be located under the root directory. Internal commands are always found by DOS because they are always in memory. They do not have to be searched for.

A subdirectory named DOS is often used to provide a ''home'' for the numerous DOS commands that are available and that are the ''external'' or ''transient'' command. External commands are not loaded into memory. External commands like **format** and **diskcopy** must be acquired from the disk. Rather than leaving all of these commands under root, where they will always be seen when the **dir** command is issued, a separate subdirectory will put the commands (except COMMAND.COM, which must be in the root directory) into a location where they will be accessible through the path command. If COMMAND.COM is not placed in the root directory, the system will not boot properly.

Whenever commands like **format** and **diskcopy** are issued, DOS searches for them on the disk. Unless the PATH command is given, DOS will only look for the command in the currently active directory and no further. The error message, ''Bad command or file name'' will be displayed even though the command file exists in another directory. The PATH command forces DOS to look in all of the directories in which the command sought is likely to be found. The larger the number of directories that are included in the search path, the more likely it is that the command will be found. If the command is incorrectly named, the longer will be the time it takes for DOS to determine that the command file does not exist.

In the example shown in Figure 19–7, the PATH command tells DOS that in addition to searching the current directory, it should first search the root directory, then it should search the subdirectory DOS, and last it should search the subdirectory WP. No subdirectories will be searched other than those listed and the current subdirectory. New subdirectories can be added when necessary.

Smart Files

There are three file extensions that will identify files that can be executed: .COM, .EXE, and .BAT. The file AUTOEXEC.BAT is one of many files that can be given the .BAT extension. The .BAT files are the so-called ''smart'' files because they can be created and then executed by the user at any time by entering the filename. Smart files can be created with a word processor capable of creating text files and with EDLIN, the text editor provided with DOS (not discussed in this book). Short smart files can also be created with a variation of the copy command. Many smart files are created to execute several DOS commands quickly in order to save the user time and to enable untrained computer users to use the computer effectively without having to understand DOS. One example of the creation of a smart file will be described. You do not have to carry out these commands. If you do, make sure that the default directory is the root directory. One could create a smart file called WP.BAT by entering

```
copy con wp.bat
```

This copy command will ''copy'' the characters entered at the keyboard (the **con**sole) and place them in a file called WP.BAT. Upon the pressing of the Enter key, the cursor will return to the left margin and no prompt will be displayed. The computer is awaiting characters from the console. You could enter the lines

```
cd wp
wp
cd \
```

and then "close" the file by pressing

F6 Function key 6
↲ Enter, to close the file and to receive the prompt, "1 File(s) copied."

Errors in the file can be corrected by recreating the file with the copy command or by using another text editor.

The file would be executed by entering

```
wp
```

When the smart file WP.BAT executes, the lines would be executed in sequence. They would be instructing DOS to change directories to the word processing subdirectory (line one) and then to issue the command **wp** with which to load the word processor (line two). You would then proceed to use the word processor. Whenever you exit the word processor and control returns to DOS, the third line that changes the directory back to the root is issued. Since there are no more lines in the file, the smart file completes its execution. The command **wp** could be executed many times.

.BAT files can be very complex. DOS provides a wide set of command structures similar to those found in programming languages like BASIC and Pascal. The lines of a .BAT file must be legal DOS commands.

COMMERCIALLY AVAILABLE DOS-RELATED PROGRAMS AND UTILITIES

DOS has its origins as the operating system for very small microcomputers. Many of the original machines that it was designed to operate had main memories (RAM) of only 64 K or 124 K. If DOS took up too much room in memory, then the corresponding sizes of programs and files that had to be held in memory were also reduced. Disk sizes were smaller also, so DOS had to fit on a single disk. As a consequence, DOS was designed to be as small as possible. As microcomputers increased their RAM, as their disk drives increased in capacity, and as they took on increasingly more sophisticated assignments such as multitasking (running several programs simultaneously), network connections, and windowing (being able to see several programs on the screen simultaneously), DOS grew and diversified. This has led to the introduction of more commands and options.

As a consequence, understanding and managing DOS has become more difficult. At times there are commands that you would like to have that are not provided by DOS. A number of commercial programs have been introduced to be purchased separately that can help users adapt to DOS more effectively. Among these resources are:

1. ***DOS managers.*** These programs provide menus and screens that show you what commands are available, what files are present, and which directory you are in. They also introduce some commands that are not present in DOS, such as commands for renaming a directory or moving a file between directories. The visual interface to DOS lessens the need to memorize commands and options.
2. ***Windowing software.*** These programs allow you to run many programs simultaneously. Each program is visible in one of the windows on your monitor's screen. In one window you could be in DOS while in another you could be sorting a data base. A third window might be running spreadsheet software. It should be noted that the extent to which your microcomputer can actually run these programs concurrently while they are doing compute-intensive or I/O (input/output) -intensive tasks depends on the speed and power of your computer's processor. Newer, faster computers can make effective use of this software.

3. ***Disaster recovery software.*** These programs help you to recover data that has been accidentally destroyed. Some programs allow you to "unerase" files that were deleted, retrieve data from files that have become corrupted, and "unformat" hard disks that were formatted. The extent to which these packages are successful depends upon the condition of the medium in question, and upon your ceasing to use the disk with other files and programs before the damage has been repaired. If you need help, get it immediately. Don't imagine the damage will heal itself.

EXERCISES

A. Write out the DOS commands you would use to:

1. Create a subdirectory named BOOKFILE.
2. With the prompt "A>" displayed, delete all of the files on disk drive B in a subdirectory JUNK.
3. Copy a file named HIDDEN.DOC on drive C and in a subdirectory named SECRETS, to drive A and name the duplicate file FOUND.BAK. Assume that the prompt is C:\>.
4. Copy a file named MYFILE.TXT on drive A and in a subdirectory named PAPERS to drive B and to a subdirectory BUSINESS, giving the duplicate file the same filename that it had on drive A. Assume that the prompt displays "C:\>."
5. Assume that the prompt displays "A\>." Display the names of files on disk drive C under the subdirectory WP, without displaying any other information about the files.
6. Assume that the prompt displays "A\>." Display the names of files on disk drive C under the subdirectory WP that have the extension .TXT, pausing at each screen full of information.
7. Assume that the prompt displays "C\>." Delete all of the files on disk drive C under the subdirectory WP that have the characters "CH" at the beginning of their filename.
8. Assume that the prompt displays "C\>." a) Change directories to the subdirectory SS. b) Change to the subdirectory (of SS) WORK. c) What would the prompt display?
9. Assume that the prompt displays "C:\WP\WORK\MEMOS>. a) What command would bring you to the directory WORK? b) With the same prompt described, what command would return you to the root directory? c) With the same prompt described above, if you entered the command "cd," what path name would be returned?

B. With a blank diskette in drive A, execute the following commands. Use the **dir** command to confirm that the commands you issue are executed correctly.

1. Format the disk in drive A.
2. Change drives to obtain the prompt "A\>."
3. Make three directories called DIR1, JUNK, and MISC.
4. Change directories to JUNK. Make a subdirectory FILES. Change directories to FILES.
5. Copy the file COMMAND.COM from the root directory of drive C to FILES.
6. Locate the file SORT.COM on drive C. It may be at the root or in a subdirectory DOS. Copy the file to the root of drive A.
7. Return to the root. Traverse the hierarchy of subdirectories with the **cd** command.
8. Use the command **"copy con thanks.bat"** to create a one-line file. The one line is "ECHO YOU ARE WELCOME." Execute this file by entering "THANKS."
9. Return to the root. Issue the **tree** and the **tree /f** commands.
10. Delete all files (not subdirectories) on the disk in drive A.

11. Remove all subdirectories from drive A.
12. With the **type** command, list the contents of the files AUTOEXEC.BAT and CONFIG.SYS that are found at the root directory of drive C.

C. If you have access to the shareware diskette, Computer Tutorial (PC-SIG disk # 403), from Computer Knowledge, place this diskette in drive A and enter ''tutor'' to start the program. Work your way through the following modules:
   6. Advanced IBM-PC DOS (subdirectories).
   7. DOS batch files.

Chapter 20

You Are Not Alone: Communicating with Larger Computers

CHAPTER OUTLINE

Mastering the use of a microcomputer is a valuable skill. Increasingly though, microcomputer users find that there are many reasons that motivate them to communicate with larger multiuser systems. Among these reasons are:

1. Corporate computers hold data and programs that are unavailable anywhere else. Data bases are frequently too large to fit on a microcomputer. To access this information, the only option is for the user to gain entry to the larger computer. Also, there are

many software programs that are developed by a corporation's information resource management personnel. These programs are seldom rewritten for personal computers.

2. Some of the programs on larger computers are very efficient at summarizing data in large data bases and putting this data into a form that can be used in personal computer software packages. The microcomputer may have programs that are not available for the larger system. By "downloading" this data, the two systems can be used for applications that are best adapted to each.
3. Users can "upload" data from a microcomputer to a larger computer. By passing the data up to the larger computer, the user can do analyses that would not have been possible on the microcomputer.
4. The user may need to share data with other users. MS-DOS has evolved primarily as a single-user system. This is changing, but even the strongest advocates of DOS do not see the likelihood of evolving PC local area networks into means of tieing more than a few dozen persons together. Multiuser mainframe and super minicomputers are designed to support many users with a variety of demands and with common needs. Electronic mail, calendaring, and other office automation systems encourage centralization of software and hardware. Making use of these systems may require the user to employ the microcomputer in the same way that "dumb" terminals were employed in earlier years.
5. In many organizations there is no large, central computing facility with which to communicate. Some of these organizations may have a local area micro-network that provides the opportunity for the microcomputers to communicate with one another easily. For those organizations that do not have a hardware-based networking procedure, it may be necessary to have the microcomputers communicate with one another. Communications software on both computers allows for the exchange of data and for a user of one computer to control another.

This chapter will show you how to use one software package, Kermit, to communicate with several larger computers. Kermit is a public domain software package created at Columbia University. It is unusual in that it runs on both microcomputers and on larger systems. This system independence makes it possible for larger computers to talk with one another, as well as with small systems. Further, Kermit runs on an assortment of manufacturer's equipment. It runs on microcomputers that use MS-DOS, Apple, and CP/M operating systems. It runs on IBM mainframe, DEC super minicomputer, and Cray super computer systems. Users of Kermit will find it to be standardized on all of these systems. In this chapter you will use Kermit

1. As a terminal to gain entry to several larger computers;
2. To transfer a file from the microcomputer to the host computer;
3. To transfer a file from the host system to the microcomputer;
4. To take advantage of a program on the host computer;
5. To capture output from a host computer on the microcomputer's printer and into a file on the microcomputer's disk drive.

Kermit is a copyrighted communications package that is maintained at Columbia University. Columbia University has granted permission to any individual or institution to use, copy, or redistribute Kermit and its documentation as long as they are not sold for profit and the copyright notice is retained. It is updated regularly and is available through many computer clubs and computer centers. In case you are wondering, "Kermit" is named after the muppet.

TERMS YOU NEED TO KNOW

Host computer: In any Kermit session the computer you are using (typically your PC) is the "local" computer and the computer you connect to is the "remote" or host computer.

Terminal: A terminal is like a PC that can only be used to communicate with computers. Terminals generally do not have their own processors, local memory, or disk space. Kermit will enable your PC to act like a terminal.

Login, Log on: Logging on is the process of making your PC known to the host computer. Logging on usually involves the identification of your login name and your password.

Communications protocols: In order for computers to communicate they must use the same settings for data transmission and reception. Protocols are the generally agreed upon standards for these communications settings: settings such as stop bits, baud rate, word size, and parity.

Baud rate: The baud rate is the ''speed'' with which computers— your PC and the host computer—send and receive data.

Parity: Parity is part of the communication settings that computers may use for error checking. Parity settings may be even or odd, but the most common setting is none.

Stop bit: Stop bits are part of the communications settings that computers use to signal the end of a word. Stop bits may be set to one or two, but are usually set to one.

Word size: Word size is the part of the communication settings that computers use to indicate how many bits (zeros and ones) are needed to construct a character. Word size (or word length) may be set to eight, but it is usually set to seven.

Full duplex/half duplex: Duplex is part of the communication settings. It controls which computer is to echo the characters typed at the keyboard to the screen. Most computers use or can use full duplex settings in which the host echoes back the characters to the screen. A significant exception is a typical IBM large computer, which uses half duplex settings. This requires the PC to send the character to the screen, as well as to the host.

Flow control: The two communicating computers will sometimes have delays during data exchange. Flow control is used to temporarily halt data transfer.

Packets: The communicating computers often exchange data in groups of characters called packets. The use of packets facilitates error checking. Kermit uses packet transfers, but many communications packages do not. They send the data in a continuous **stream** of characters.

Direct connect modem: A direct connect modem plugs directly into the telephone line, usually with a modular telephone connector.

Acoustic modem: An acoustic modem has a microphone and speaker that are coupled to the telephone handset.

Terminal emulation: In most cases the remote computer will expect you to be using a terminal instead of a personal computer for communication. Kermit solves this problem by causing the PC to emulate or behave like a terminal. The version of Kermit distributed with this book emulates a Digital Equipment Corporation (DEC) VT 102 terminal, although it can also emulate a DEC VT 52 (vt52) and Heath 19 (h19-u) terminals.

Communications ports: Microcomputers generally have one or more ''serial'' communication ports. Kermit will use one of these ports, connected to a modem, to communicate with the host computer.

IMPORTANT FILES ON THE KERMIT DISKETTE

MSKERMIT.INI

Kermit is capable of being modified interactively to adjust to host computer requirements. It can also utilize a batch file named MSKERMIT.INI to automatically configure itself when Kermit is started. Upon startup, Kermit executes the commands in the MSKERMIT.INI file. This file can contain commands, macro definitions, and communications settings for one or more communications ports. One example of an MSKERMIT.INI file is the one provided with the Kermit distributed with this book. It contains the following lines (numbered here for convenience)

```
COMMENT Sample MS-DOS Kermit initialization file.
COMMENT Should be named MSKERMIT.INI, and
COMMENT stored in current disk/directory or in your PATH.
set terminal VT102; Emulate a DEC VT102 terminal
set baud 1200; at 1200 baud
set warning on; Don't overwrite existing files!
set send pack 1000; use extended packets
set rec pack 1000; for send and receive
set block 3; and do extended error checking
take vt100.key; define function keys in vt100'ish fashion
set key \2408 ATD1230000; define Alt-F1 as this telephone no.
set key \2409 ATD1235555 ; define Alt-F2 as this telephone no.
COMMENT - Macro to communicate with CompuServe
define comp set par even, set baud 300, do u2 ; Use defs for u2 below
COMMENT - Macro for communicating with full-duplex computers bs key → bs.
define unix set timer off,set par no,set flo x,set hand no, do unix2,
define unix2 set loc off, take vt100.key, set key \270 \8
COMMENT - as above but with bs key → del.
def u set timer off,set par no,set flo x,set hand no, do u2
def u2 set loc off, take vt100.key, set key \270 \127
COMMENT - End of MSKERMIT.INI
```

Figure 20–1. Distributed MSKERMIT.INI File.

There are two types of comments in this file. Lines that begin with the word "COMMENTS" are not executed. The text that follows is for your interpretation only. Also, the text following semicolons is not executed.

The various "SET" commands configure the PC to behave as though it was a Digital Equipment Corporation VT 102 terminal that is communicating at 1200 baud, transmitting files in packets of characters that are 1,000 characters long. The define unix, unix2, u, and u2 lines are "macros" that set other protocol characteristics that enable the PC to communicate with a UNIX host computer. The define comp line sets the protocols that will enable you to dial CompuServe; an on-line resources services heavily used in business (see exercise C). The define macros are executed on demand by entering "do <macroname>" at the Kermit prompt, "KERMIT-MS>."

If these characteristics do not function correctly with your PC, your modem or your host computer, you will have to obtain assistance from your local computer support staff.

MSKERMIT.DOC

This is the PC Kermit users manual in "printer" form. It can be printed from your PC with the command

```
print mskermit.doc
```

MSKERMIT.DOC is the most accurate documentation available on Kermit.

KERMIT.EXE

This is the executable command file that starts Kermit. Usually PC Kermit is distributed with the name MSKERMIT.EXE, but since it is usually renamed to be KERMIT.EXE, it has been renamed for you.

TERMINAL EMULATION

A key feature of Kermit is its ability to faithfully mimic or emulate an ordinary terminal (sometimes know as a ''dumb'' terminal). Kermit version 2.30 can, in fact, emulate a very ''dumb'' terminal, three well-known text terminals, and a Tektronics 4010 graphics terminal. The default emulation is a Digital Equipment Corporation VT 102, which is an enhanced VT 100 terminal. The current terminal type is show in the ''mode'' line \Kermit displays at the bottom of the screen when it is running in terminal emulation mode.

MODIFYING THE MSKERMIT.INI FILE

1. ***Entering the correct telephone numbers.*** The MSKERMIT.INI (.INI) file can be used to assign frequently needed character ''strings'' to otherwise unused keys and to tailor the keyboard to a user's most common functions. Storing dialing instructions is one common need for users who use an auto-dialing modem to connect to a remote host. Redefining certain features of Kermit such as communications settings is also often desirable. The distributed .INI file, for example, removes the standard definition from the Home and End keys (which move to the beginning and end of the display buffer respectively), since on many PC's it is distracting to press them accidentally.

   Function keys F1 and F2, when simultaneously struck with the Alt key, have been set to dial fictitious telephone numbers for UNIX and CompuServe computers, respectively. These numbers will have to be changed to meet your needs. Additional lines can be added for other computers which you may wish to access. The dial up command string ''ATD'' preceding the telephone number is specific to Hayes compatible modems and should be changed for other modems.
2. ***Configuring Kermit to access a UNIX host.*** For UNIX users, the default options provided with this version of Kermit are generally acceptable. Items to note are: the baud rate (the default is 1200) and the definition of the Backspace or back-arrow key. By default, Kermit sets the Backspace key to send a DEL character. For many users this key should be defined to send a Backspace character for line editing.
3. ***Removing lines.*** It may be necessary to delete some lines as well to modify some. For instance, if you are using an acoustic modem, you may have to dial the telephone yourself, so the automatic dialing commands assigned to function keys will have to be removed.
4. ***Altering the .INI file.*** The file MSKERMIT.INI file can be modified to fit your communications needs. In order to change the file you can use WordPerfect in the following manner.

F5	List files key. Locate the file by moving to the correct directory with the change directories option (7). When you have found the file, highlight it.
5	The option to retrieve a text file that does not contain embedded codes. Alter the file as needed.
Ctrl-F5	Text out key
1	Save the file
MSKERMIT.INI	The name of the file to be saved

POTENTIAL PROBLEMS AND THEIR SOLUTIONS

1. *There is no indication that the microcomputer is sending data.* If there is no sign of anything happening make sure your modem (or the direct to computer connection) is plugged into the communication port (COM1 or COM2) Kermit is using. This information is shown on the mode line when Kermit is in terminal emulation mode. The Kermit command "set port" is used to change it. Also, external modems must be turned on.
2. *The host computer does not send a present signal or no login message is received.* You may have dialed the wrong number or the host computer may not be running. Try dialing again later.
3. *A login message is given and responded to, but entry is denied.* You may have forgotten your password or the account that you are using may have been disabled. Contact your user services/system administration office for assistance.
4. *Data that is transmitted is garbled.* This is caused by communication protocol errors. The baud rate, parity, stop bit, or other settings may not be set correctly for the host to communicate effectively. If you can recognize some of the characters as what you are typing, you may have the parity set incorrectly. If each character you type causes many characters to be echoed, and they are the same ones, the speed is probably set to the wrong value. Remember, most modems operate at 300–1200–2400 baud but most direct connections are at 4800–9600 baud.
5. *Data that you have typed does not appear on your screen.* If the remote host is responding to what you type you are probably connected to a half-duplex system. The Kermit command "set local-echo on" will cause Kermit to echo the characters you type so you can see them.
6. *Data that you have typed appears twice on your screen.* This is the opposite of the problem described above. If the remote computer is responding, both it and Kermit are echoing your characters to the screen. The Kermit command "set local-echo off" will keep Kermit from echoing the characters that you are typing.

Getting Assistance

Intercomputer communications is a complex process given the diversity of computers available. Not all of the problems that can occur can be discussed here. Neither are all of the solutions immediately obvious. If the procedures discussed here do not function as they are described, contact the system administrator or user support personnel for the host computer you are trying to work with for assistance.

USING KERMIT INTERACTIVELY WITH A UNIX HOST

Why UNIX?

There are many host computers available on college campuses. It has been estimated that 90% of the colleges that teach computer science have a UNIX system available to them. UNIX is an operating system with many features that have begun to appear in MS-DOS. Microcomputer to UNIX communications can be used to access many UNIX programs of interest to the college student: electronic mail, text processing, national computer networks and bulletin boards, and text analysis programs.

Starting Kermit-MS

The MSKERMIT.INI file has been preconfigured to communicate with most UNIX hosts. In order to access a UNIX computer you will also need an account name and a password. Without these you will not be able to log on to the computer. You will also need a computer with a modem that allows the PC to communicate correctly. The MSKERMIT.INI file distributed with this book does not have the correct telephone number to call your UNIX computer, so this will have to be changed. The communications process is started by turning the modem on, if it is an external modem, placing the Kermit disk in drive A, obtaining the DOS prompt "A>," and typing the command

Kermit

The Kermit program will begin to execute. As it is loaded into memory, Kermit locates the MSKERMIT.INI file and modifies itself to conform to the desired environment.

do unix The command for setting the PC to interact effectively with a UNIX host. "do UNIX" executes the appropriate macros in the MSKERMIT.INI file. You will receive the prompt "Kermit-MS>."

c Connect with the modem

Logging On

If you have an automatic dial modem and if you have entered the correct telephone number in the MSKERMIT.INI file, enter

Alt-F1 Alternate key with function key F1, to dial the UNIX computer. The command contained in the MSKERMIT.INI file is set to dial a Hayes-compatible modem.

If you have configured this file for a dialup modem, you should hear the number being dialed and then the high pitch whine of the host computer acknowledging your call. If you are using an acoustic modem, you may have to do the dialing yourself. When the host's whine is heard, place the telephone receiver in the modem's sockets making sure that the cord is in the correct socket. At the completion of the connection with the host computer you should see a login message something like

```
login:
```

Enter your assigned login name **in lowercase.** UNIX is sensitive to case and almost always expects to receive commands and entries that use lowercase characters. After entering the login name, you will receive the prompt

```
password:
```

When passwords are entered, the host will not echo them back to the screen for reasons of security. Enter your assigned password. If both the login and the password have been entered correctly, you will obtain a prompt such as

```
Welcome to the goodcollege system (4.3 BSD)
% TERM (dialup)
```

The welcoming message and the "%" prompt may be different from system to system. Some additional lines may be printed. The "%" prompt is the request of the host computer for you to enter valid commands. It is the same type of prompt that the microcomputer provides when it displays "A>" or "B>."

The cursor is flashing behind the "TERM (dialup)," or similar command. The UNIX computer needs to know what type of terminal you are using. In lowercase, enter

vt102 The type of terminal emulated by your PC

↵ Enter key

Running a Program or UNIX Command

At the next receipt of the "%" prompt you can type UNIX commands. Try entering the following commands in lowercase, waiting until the "%" prompt returns before entering each command

who	Who is on the system? A list of login names will appear.
↵	Enter key
ls	List the names of files available
↵	Enter key. The response may be the names of files or it may be the simple return of the prompt if there are no files to list. This command is similar to the DOS dir command.
date	Confirm the system date
↵	Enter key

These three commands will suffice to demonstrate that you are able to execute UNIX host computer commands just as though you had logged on as a user from a dumb terminal.

Returning to the Prompt "KERMIT-MS"

As you experiment with the remaining Kermit commands, it will be necessary for you to switch control back and forth between the UNIX host and the DOS microcomputer. At any point you can return control to the DOS computer by entering

ctrl-]	Control simultaneous with the closing bracket
c	The letter "c." After this key sequence has been entered you will again see the prompt "Kermit-MS>," which confirms that you returned control to the MS-DOS computer. At this point you can enter Kermit commands such as **send** and **receive.** Commands can be edited before being executed. Editing can be made with the commands listed in Figure 20–2.

Backspace	Delete the character to the left of the cursor
Ctrl-W	Delete the word to the left of the cursor
Ctrl-U	Delete the entire command
?	Type a brief message describing what you are expected to type in the current field
Esc	Escape key. If enough characters have been typed in the current field or keyword to uniquely identify it, Kermit will supply the remainder of the word.
=	A wildcard character matching single characters in filenames, equivalent to the "?" in MS-DOS

Figure 20–2. Kermit Command Line Editing Characters.

Kermit COMMANDS

Kermit has a large number of commands and options, many of which cannot be covered here. Use the documentation for Kermit to explore these choices. The key commands available in MS-DOS are those seen in Figure 20–3.

The **dir** Command

One example of a Kermit command is **dir.** It is essentially the same as the DOS command and uses wild cards in the same way DOS does to specify which filenames are to be listed. The filenames listed are for the files on the default drive. Try the command to see which filenames are listed.

The **set drive to** Command

If you wish to change the default drive, you can do so with the **set drive to** command. For instance, change the default drive to B by entering

set drive to A:	The change drive command
↵	Enter key

BYE	Log off remote host computer
CLEAR	Clear key definitions
CLOSE	Close log files and stop logging remote session
CONNECT	Connect to host system
CWD path	Change working directory
DEFINE	Define a Kermit-MS macro
DELETE file	Delete a local file
DIR [file]	List the filenames in the local directory. Wildcards and named files are permitted.
DO macro	Execute a macro expansion
EXIT	
FINISH	Shut down host computer's server functions
GET file	Retrieve files from host computer operating in server mode
HELP	Obtain help messages from host computer services available
HOST command	Send host computer the command specified
LOCAL	Prefix for local file management commands
LOG SESSION filename	Capture terminal session in file or on printer
LOGOUT	Notify host computer your session is to be ended
PUSH	Temporarily exit from Kermit-MS
QUIT	Exit from Kermit-MS
RECEIVE	Open a file that will receive data from remote computer
REMOTE	Prefix for remote file management commands
RUN command-file	Execute an MS-DOS command or program
SEND file	Transmit a file to remote computer
SERVER	Set computer to respond to the directives of the remote computer
SET parameter	Give parameters new values
SHOW parameter	Display the values of parameters
SPACE directory	Inquire of disk space available
STATUS	Inquire of all parameter values
TAKE	Execute Kermit commands in a named file
TYPE file	Display the contents of a local file
VERSION	Display the program version number of the Kermit in use

Figure 20–3. Kermit Commands.

You will not see a difference in the Kermit prompt to indicate that the default drive has been changed.

The **connect** Command

Return to the host computer by entering

c Connect. The entire command can be entered, or it can be abbreviated to "c"

↵ Enter key. Control is returned to the host computer precisely to the point where control was left. The cursor is still visible at the same location as when you returned control to the microcomputer.

RUNNING C-KERMIT ON THE UNIX HOST

Unlike many software packages, Kermit on the microcomputer works best when the host computer also runs its own version of Kermit. At the UNIX prompt, "%," enter the command

`Kermit`	Execute the Kermit program on UNIX
↵	Enter key. After a short wait the prompt will change from "%" to **"C-Kermit>"** indicating that Kermit on UNIX has been successfully executed. Figure 20–4 displays the situation that has been set up.

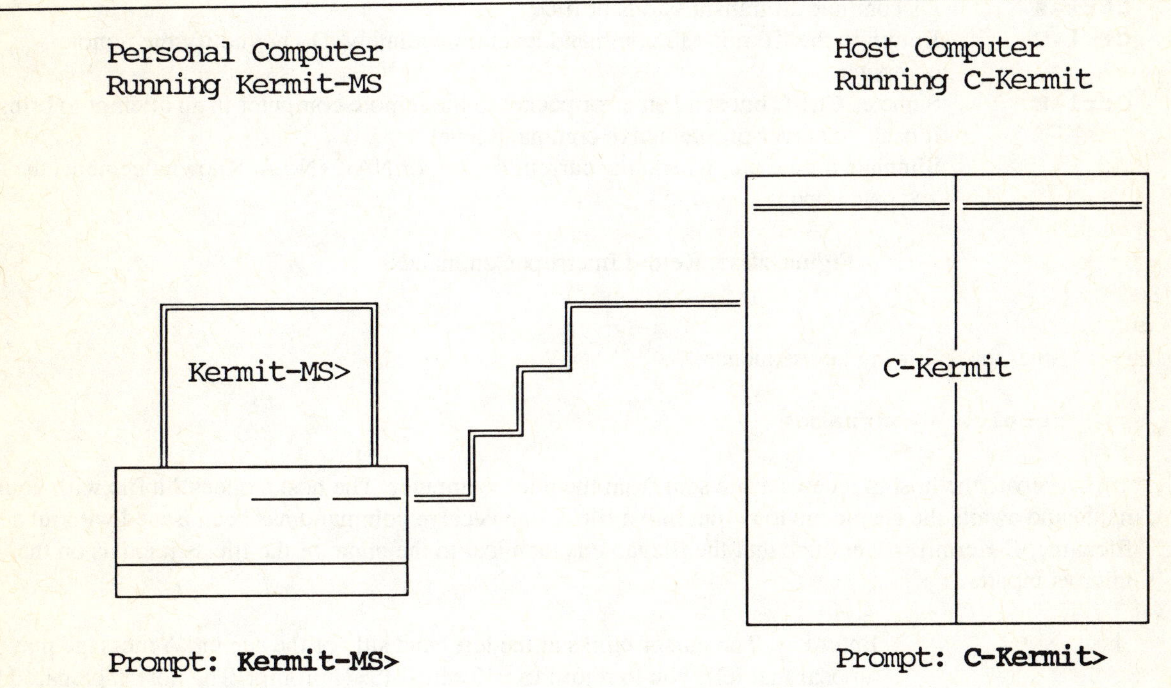

Figure 20–4.

Two versions of Kermit are now running on the two computers. Kermit-MS is running on the PC and C-Kermit is running on the host. The two Kermits are designed to communicate with one another easily. Their commands are known to each other and when they exchange data, they do so by exchanging packets of data that are surrounded by envelopes of additional information that allow the computers to determine whether their exchanges have been conducted correctly. Many other communications software packages do not set up this symmetry. They run on the PC, but the host computer has no well developed capacity to relate to the personal computer.

Uploading Files

The passing of files from the microcomputer to the host computer is called uploading. In attempting to upload files, MS-KERMIT must be able to:

1. Locate the file by disk drive and, perhaps, by directory. Kermit is quite capable at finding files if they are given correct pathnames, filenames, and extensions.
2. Send an ASCII or text file if no special options are used. Files to be transmitted must only contain the standard printable characters. They should not contain control characters, escape key sequences or embedded word processor commands for centering, tabbing, or bolding, for instance.

Kermit is able to transmit binary files, which are files treated as strings of 0s and 1s with no special significance, but this option will not be discussed here.

3. Communicate directly with C-KERMIT.

The process of uploading files begins by obtaining the C-KERMIT prompt on the host computer. If you have the prompt "Kermit-MS>," type the letter "C" and press Enter to return to the host. You will transmit the file MSKERMIT.INI, a readily available text file. In issuing the **receive** command, substitute your last name for "<yourname>." Should it become necessary to interrupt the transmission, you can choose from the commands described in Figure 20–5.

`Ctrl-X`	Stop sending the current file but continue attempting to send other files, if any
`Ctrl-Z`	Discontinue all transmissions of files
`Ctrl-C`	Return to the Kermit-MS command level immediately. Do not notify the remote computer
`Ctrl-E`	Same as Ctrl-C but send an error packet to the remote computer in an attempt to bring it back to server or interactive command level
↵	Simulate a time out, resend the current packet, or NAK (No AcKnowledgement) the expected one

Figure 20–5. Kermit Interrupt Commands.

Enter the following key sequence:

`receive <yourname>`

Prepare the host to receive a file sent from the microcomputer. The host "opens" a file with your name and awaits the characters to be put into a file. If the **receive** command has been issued without a filename, C-Kermit will assume that the filename is identical to the name of the file as it exists on the microcomputer.

↵	Enter key. The cursor blinks at the left hand side of the screen. A message may appear that tells you to return to "Kermit-MS>" prompt. The host is prepared to receive data.
`Ctrl-]`	
`c`	Return control to the microcomputer, the prompt "Kermit-MS" appears
`send`	
`mskermit.Ini`	For this exercise, the file to be transmitted is MSKERMIT.INI, the file that contains the commands for configuring Kermit to its host computers. Be aware that a replica of the file is being sent to the host, not the original file.
↵	Enter key. The screen shown in Figure 20–6 appears.

```
        Kermit-MS: V2.30 8 Jan 1989

        File name: <filename>

Kbytes transferred: 0
           Sending: In progress
 Number of packets: 1_
     Packet length: 17
 Number of retries: 0
        Last error: None
      Last warning: None
```

Figure 20–6. The Kermit Transfer Screen.

Information on the screen changes rapidly if the transfer is carried out without an error. Since the file is a small one, the transfer is carried out quickly. Larger files will take correspondingly longer. Throughout the transfer, brief as it is, Kermit keeps you informed about the amount of the file that remains to be transmitted, about the number of packets that have been transmitted, and about any retries that must be made. A retry is made when a packet is not received in correct condition. The microcomputer does not send the next packet until it has received an acknowledgement from the host that the prior packet has been received correctly by the host. Should you detect an abnormality, the commands in Figure 20–5 can be issued to interrupt the transfer. Upon completion of the transfer, the prompt "Kermit-MS>" is returned

c Connect to the host computer. The prompt, "C-Kermit>" returns when you press the Enter key

Before proceeding, notice that the sequence of up loading requires you to open the file on the host before sending the file to the host.

Downloading Files

The process of sending a file that is on the host computer to the microcomputer is called downloading. The sequence involved is as follows:

send <yourname>

Prepare the host to send the file with your last name to the microcomputer. The host attempts to transmit packets which are not acknowledged by the PC since the microcomputer has not yet been prepared to receive a file. In this command the file must be named in order for the host to know which file to send.

↵ Enter key. The cursor blinks at the left hand side of the screen. The host is prepared to send data.

Ctrl-]
c Return control to the microcomputer; the prompt "Kermit-MS" appears. Place a disk that has space for a new file in drive A.

receive eraseme For this exercise, the file to be opened on the microcomputer will be called ERASEME, a name that suggests that it is to be destroyed without significant effect.

↵ Enter key. The Kermit transfer screen reappears. Upon completion of the transfer, the prompt, "Kermit-MS>" is returned.

Confirm that the file has been received on the microcomputer with the **dir** command. Enter

dir The directory command
↵ Enter key. A list of filenames is displayed, one of which should be ERASEME.
c Connect to the host computer. The prompt "C-Kermit>" returns when you press the
↵ Enter key

Notice that the sequence of downloading is not the reverse of uploading. When downloading, you initiate the sending operation from the host before returning control to the microcomputer. Once the receive command is issued, the microcomputer opens a file and awaits packets from the host. If the receive command on the PC was issued first, the PC would wait for the host to send a file. There would be no way that you could return to the host to issue the send command.

The preceding sequences showed how files could be passed between the two computers. At the end of the completed commands, identical copies of the files, albeit with different names, reside on both computers. The error checking routines guarantee that the files have been transmitted correctly.

Quitting C-Kermit

Exit C-Kermit by entering

q Quit Kermit
↵ Enter key. The "%" prompt appears

Capturing the Host's Output on the PC's Disk

One of the reasons for transmitting a file to the host computer is to manipulate the data it contains with a program on the host that is not available on the microcomputer. When the program that manipulates the file runs, it produces output that is sent to the screen of the microcomputer in the same way that it would send output to a terminal. A simple example of a running program will suffice to show how a program's output will appear. Enter the UNIX command

cat<yourname>cat is a command that is comparable to the MS-DOS command
type. cat lists the contents of the file named <yourname>.
↵ Enter key. The lines of the file are listed on the screen of the microcomputer. Once the file has been listed, the UNIX prompt reappears. The text of the file is not available for further manipulation.

Suppose that the program was more complex and produced pages of data. As the data scrolled off the top of the screen, you would have lost the ability to see it, interpret it, and use it for any other purpose. You might wish to capture the output in a file on your microcomputer. For instance, if the output was from a program that listed the monthly sales for 10 sales people over the last 3 years, you might wish to transfer the data into your word processor for inclusion in an annual report. To capture the output from the UNIX-located command or program, execute the following commands:

cat <yourname>
cat. Do not press the Enter key. Leave the cursor at the right of the filename.
Ctrl-]
c Return control to the microcomputer. The prompt "Kermit-MS" appears
log session output The log session command opens a file called OUTPUT on the microcomputer. This filename was arbitrarily chosen and has no special meaning. It could have been named OPUT, MYDATA, or any other name of use to you.

↲ Enter key, to complete the connection
↲ Enter key, to complete the command
`c` Connect to the host computer again. The cursor is still at the right of the UNIX command. Before issuing the next command, be prepared to watch the red light on drive A go on and then off.
↲ Enter key, to complete the **cat** command. The lines of the file are again listed on the screen of the microcomputer. As the file is listed, the red light goes on. The light goes out when the transmission is complete. The UNIX prompt reappears. Although the red light went out, all of the data may not have been entered into the file with your last name. Some of this data is in a temporary holding area in RAM called a buffer.
`Ctrl-]c` Return control to the microcomputer. The prompt ''Kermit-MS'' appears.
`close` **Close** the file. Before closing the file, Kermit-MS will ''flush'' the data from the buffer, placing it in the file and then closing the file. The prompt ''Kermit-MS>'' reappears.
`c` Connect
↲ Enter key, to return to the host

Capturing the Host's Output on the PC's Printer

It may be desirable to capture the output of a UNIX program or command on your printer. The **log session** command used above was followed by the filename which was to hold the data. Output can be directed to the printer with the same command except that the reserved word PRN (either lowercase or uppercase) is substituted for the filename. PRN is the special file, the printer. The rest of the command sequence is identical to that described for capturing data on the disk. Repeat the sequence, substituting PRN for the filename and watch the data print out. The close sequence must be included.

LOGGING OFF OF THE UNIX HOST

You should still have the ''%'' prompt from the UNIX host. Enter

`logout` The logout command. This command may be different for the system you are using. If logout does not produce the login message, find the correct logout command (possibly ''exit'' or Control-D).
↲ Enter key
`Ctrl-]`
`c` Return control to the microcomputer. The prompt ''Kermit-MS'' appears.
`q` Quit Kermit-MS
↲ Enter key. You exit Kermit and the DOS prompt returns.

OTHER KERMIT SET COMMAND OPTIONS

The options shown in Figure 20–7 are available. The default values are generally satisfactory for most users. Key options are described earlier in the chapter. More complete information on how the options are used can be found in the Kermit Reference Manual.

AUTOWRAP	Sets line wrap during terminal emulation
BAUD	Sets transfer rate of the communications port
BELL	Sets the bell on/off at the end of a transmission
BLOCK-CHECK-TYPE	Sets the level of error checking for file transfer
DEBUG	Displays packet contents during file transfer
DEFAULT-DISK	Sets the default disk drive for file operations
DESTINATION	Sets the default destination device for incoming files
END-OF-LINE	Sets the packet terminator
EOF	Sets the method for determining or marking the end of the file
ESCAPE	Escape character for the connect command
FLOW-CONTROL	Enables or disables XON\XOFF
HANDSHAKE	Sets half-duplex on/off
HEATH19	Sets the computer to emulate a Heath/Zenith 19 terminal
INCOMPLETE	Sets the ability of Kermit-MS to accept incomplete files
KEY	Specifies key redefinitions and keyboard macros
LOCAL-ECHO	Specifies which host does the echoing during connect
MODE-LINE	Sets a mode line on/off during terminal emulation
PARITY	Specifies the parity type to be used
PORT	Selects a communications port
PROMPT	Redefines the prompt to something other than ''Kermit-MS>''
RECEIVE	Requests remote Kermit to use specified parameters
REMOTE	Allows interactive use of Kermit-MS from back port
SEND	Use the parameters given during file transfer
TAKE-ECHO	Controls the echoing of commands from TAKE files
TIMER	Terminates file transfer if problems are encountered
WARNING	Specifies how to handle filename collisions

Figure 20–7. Set Command Options.

EXERCISES

A. Communicate with the UNIX computer again. Try commands at the ''%'' prompt such as:

% calendar 1988	Displays the calendar for 1988
% look equi	Displays words that start with ''equi''
% who	Displays login names of people on the system
% finger <login name>	By substituting a login name, finger will tell you more about the person logged in

Practice uploading and downloading other text files that are saved with the WordPerfect Text Out key (Ctrl-F5).

B. Obtain a reference book on UNIX computers. Try out other commands and operations.

C. Users of this book have an introductory package of information available to them from an on-line information service called CompuServe. The package is available to you through the instructor who will receive it from Wm. C. Brown Publishers. Fifteen dollars worth of computer connect time is available to find out about CompuServe. CompuServe offers access to databases for business information, news services, electronic shopping, money matters, reference services, and travel. It provides electronic mail and electronic bulletin boards.

The MSKERMIT.INI file has been preconfigured to access CompuServe. You will have to change the telephone number to the correct one for your state as shown in the information package. The correct settings can be used by loading Kermit and pressing

`do comp` To execute the macros that sets the baud rate to 300 (or to the speed you designate in the MSKERMIT.INI file), stop bits to 1, parity to even and duplex to full.

`c` Connect with the modem

If you have an automatic dial modem, enter

`Alt-F2` Alternate and function key 2, to dial Telenet

Other instructions you need for logging on and accessing CompuServe resources are available in the introductory package. Once you have logged on, explore parts of the system that interest you. Find out about CompuServer.